D0326045

The Trust Frequency is a brilliant perspective which links our ancient global native spirit with conscious contemporary science. We are the novo shamans creating and celebrating the emerging world culture with moral responsibility for all living creation. Yahete!"
SONNE REYNA. Yaqui-Carrizo peace chief.

The Trust Frequency is a real gem for anyone wanting to see the world transformed. 'Ten Assumptions for a New Paradigm' is a brilliant formula for making it happen."
JOHN RENESCH. Futurist, author: *The Great Growing Up: Being Responsible for Humanity's Future.* www.Renesch.com, www. TheGreatGrowingUp.com

The Trust Frequency opens the MIND to connect directly to the HEART of the Source of Creation. When reading this amazing book, you begin your journey into TRUST. The book moves at such a pace that I could not put it down!"
AMOR LUZ. Indigenous Wisdom Keeper, Healing & Transformation Facilitator

"We are at a point in time in which the default paradigm of science is having great difficulty explaining all the scientific findings. We are in need of good, grounded discussions that bridge the worlds of science and spirituality; that suggest a paradigm that is more inclusive. *The Trust Frequency* does this, and is thus a powerful contribution to the question of life's underlying paradigm."
STEPHEN SIDEROFF, PhD. Clinical Psychologist, Department of Psychiatry & Biobehavioral Sciences, UCLA. www.ThirdWind.org

"A wonderfully lucid guide to living more fully and deeply on this Sacred Earth, by two loving and highly evolved conscious guides. *The Trust Frequency* is good medicine for all those seeking more fully human lifestyles and a global culture of peace, generosity and sustainability for our common future on this wondrous planet."
HAZEL HENDERSON, PhD. Futurist, president of Ethical Markets Media LLC., author: *Building a Win-Win World*; co-author with Daisaku Ikeda: *Planetary Citizenship.* www.HazelHenderson.com, www.EthicalMarkets.com

"What impressed me most about the *The Trust Frequency* is that it is written from a higher dimensional awareness and clarity that energetically transfers to the reader. It explains the shift in consciousness unfolding on our planet and how everything is frequency and vibration, and how by releasing assumptions we can choose to vibrate at the higher frequency of love and trust and move into the heart of Oneness. It leaves us with the inspiration and recognition that this is our destiny."
DEBORAH ROZMAN, PhD. CEO HeartMath Inc. www.HeartMath.com, www.HeartMastery.com

"Neuroscience informs us that changing our minds actually changes our brains. It also is unlocking the brain's keys to happiness and compassion. The information in this book is urgently needed to move us into the next great human adventure. We stand at the threshold of a paradigmatic shift of consciousness. Learning to live in *The Trust Frequency* in resonance with the Universe is the way to achieve an upward planetary evolution."
JUAN ACOSTA-URQUIDI, PhD. Cellular Neurophysiologist. Working with Energy Healers at the Interface of Science and Spirituality. www.EnergyMedResearch.com

"*The Trust Frequency* reminds us to listen and pay attention to the emerging evolution in human consciousness, and to question and explore our collective agreement regarding the story we tell ourselves about the purpose and meaning of being human. *The Trust Frequency* is truly a great textbook for the cross-examination of a new and ancient model of mind and being, that first must be given context and firm footing in shared reality."
LEIGH J. McCLOSKEY. Artist, author, actor, visual philosopher. Founder of Olandar Foundation for Emerging Renaissance. www.leighmccloskey.com

"*The Trust Frequency* is one of the most brilliant, consciousness-transforming, perhaps even life-changing books I have ever read. It is clear when reading this masterpiece that the two writers are extraordinarily great souls with a cosmic and divine view of this world."

BARBARA GLUCK. Photographer, co-founder: The Light Institute of Galisteo, The Global Light Network, The Soul Matrix Clearing, Healing and Empowerment System. www.BarbaraGluck.com

"Is there is a magical frequency of love that exists for all of humanity 24 hours a day no matter where we are and what we are doing? The authors describe just such a state in *The Trust Frequency*. They liken it to the place the Buddhists call Nirvana. But how do we get there from here? According to Bailey and Marlow, it's all about consciousness and where we choose to focus the one thing we actually have the ability to control: our minds."

SHAERI RICHARDS. Author: *Dancing with your Dragon: The Art of Loving your Unlovable Self.* www.DancingWithYourDragon.com

"For those who are awakening to the call of the new energies that are emerging on the planet as the potential to transform our consciousness and the way we live our lives, *The Trust Frequency* is for you. For those who have not yet started to awaken, please read this book."

PENNY SLINGER. Author, visionary, artist. www.64dakinioracle.org

"Open *The Trust Frequency*, and welcome yourself into a poetic, philosophical, scientific, artful, and ultimately very personal exploration into who you are, what is real, and how you can participate in the next phase of our evolution."

CASSANDRA VIETEN, PhD, Executive Director of Research, Institute of Noetic Sciences, co-author: *Living Deeply: The Art and Science of Transformation in Everyday Life.*

"Some books are good, some are great. Others are filled with such wisdom, you carry them with you, dog-eared and book-marked, to remember the extraordinary lessons tucked amidst the pages. This book is one of the latter - a 'work of heart' which has inspired me to activate *The Trust Frequency* in my own life, and to bring these powerful insights and actions to the leadership development programs we are creating in the world."
TARA M. SHEAHAN. Founder, Conscious Global Leadership.
www.ConsciousGlobalLeadership.com

"This book brings a wonderful gift to the human race. Thank you for bringing the spirit of the truth at the heart of the indigenous way of knowing in such a loving manner."
MARILYN YOUNGBIRD. Arikara/Hidatsa Tribal Elder, International Holistic Health Teacher.

"...*The Trust Frequency* takes on the great evolutionary, visionary and practical task the authors refer to as the 'radical re-invention of our species.' Weaving together ancient indigenous wisdom, the wisdom of our own Western traditions, and modern scientific understanding, this book is a key tool in the evolutionary 'upwising' we are experiencing today."
STEVE BHAERMAN, aka Swami Beyondananda, co-author with Bruce Lipton: *Spontaneous Evolution: Our Positive Future and A Way to Get There From Here.* www.WakeUpLaughing.com

"Thank you so much for your enthusiasm and brilliance. I love *The Trust Frequency!* Great work!"
BARBARA MARX HUBBARD, PhD. Futurist, author: *Conscious Evolution: Awakening Our Social Potential.*

T_{HE} TRUST
FREQUENCY

Ten Assumptions For A New Paradigm

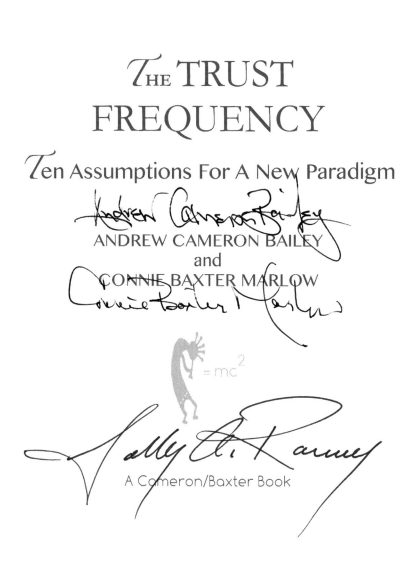

ANDREW CAMERON BAILEY
and
CONNIE BAXTER MARLOW

$= mc^2$

A Cameron/Baxter Book

A WORD OF EXPLANATION

A stylized image of Kokopelli is used throughout this book to symbolize the wisdom of the native peoples of the world. The *Trust Frequency* vision is, in its essence, a synthesis of indigenous wisdom, Eastern mysticism, and quantum science. We also use the wonderful science fiction term "grok" to describe the nature of the profound understanding this book calls for. Finally, we do not use the word "frequency" in the reductionist scientific sense of cycles/second or Hertz, but more in the metaphysical 1960s sense of "vibrations."

KOKOPELLI

Kokopelli is a sower of seeds, a fertility deity, usually depicted as a humpbacked flute player (often with feathers or antenna-like protrusions on his head), who is venerated by Native cultures in the American Southwest. Like most fertility deities, Kokopelli presides over both childbirth and agriculture. He is also a trickster, and represents the spirit of music. Kokopelli is one of the most easily recognized figures found in the petroglyphs and pictographs of the Southwest.

GROK

"To understand so thoroughly that the observer becomes a part of the observed - to merge, blend, intermarry, lose identity in group experience. It means almost everything that we mean by religion, philosophy, and science - and it means as little to us (because of our Earthly assumptions) as color means to a blind man."

Robert Heinlein. *Stranger in a Strange Land,* (1960)

Dedication

We dedicate this book and these ideas to our children Lila, Java, Alison, Bruce, Daniel, Consi, Chela, and Jonny, and to our grandchildren, Eliah Dune, Logan Mae and Juniper Bess, and to the children and grand-children of each and every one of our readers.

This book describes the world they will inherit; a world of love, joy, peace, and abundance.

THE TRUST FREQUENCY

Preview Edition: Aspen, Colorado, October 15, 2012

First Edition: Aspen, Colorado, December 21, 2012

www.TheTrustFrequency.net
e-mail: TRUST@thetrustfrequency.net

ISBN 978-0-9887547-1-3
Cover by Andrew Cameron Bailey
Design by Andrew Cameron Bailey & Conor Johnson

$\mathcal{T}$ABLE OF CONTENTS

Acknowledgements   xiv

Preface   xvi

Prologue   xxiv

Foreword   xxvi

Introduction   xxxv

PART I: THE TEN ASSUMPTIONS

INTRODUCING THE ASSUMPTIONS   1

DEFINITIONS   19

THE FIRST ASSUMPTION   23

We live in a conscious, loving Universe

THE SECOND ASSUMPTION   37

The Universe loves us unconditionally

THE THIRD ASSUMPTION   55

We create Reality by the power of our Consciousness

THE FOURTH ASSUMPTION   71

The Seven "A"s are our requests to the Universe

CONSCIOUSNESS & THE SEVEN "A"s:

Awareness, Assumption, Attitude,

Attention, Alignment, Action and Allowing   77

THE FIFTH ASSUMPTION   101

Free Will is an Absolute Law of the Universe

THE SIXTH ASSUMPTION   113

Circumstance guides us on our Journey to Wholeness

THE SEVENTH ASSUMPTION   129

Humanity is on an evolutionary upward spiral

THE EIGHTH ASSUMPTION   153
    There is only NOW, this precious present moment
THE NINTH ASSUMPTION   177
    All of Creation is One
THE TENTH ASSUMPTION   189
    The Trust Frequency is real
A NOTE ON CONSCIOUSNESS   213
The Time Before Time   217
CONCLUSION   227
STANDING ON THE SHOULDERS (a meditation)   229
PART II: FOOD FOR THOUGHT   231
    A MEDITATION ON PRAYER   232
    EINSTEIN AND HUBBLE   241
    PAN-INDIGENOUSNESS   247
    HOW MANY WILL IT TAKE?   252
    PRESCRIPTION FOR PEACE   257
PART III: APPENDIX   259
    STORY TIME   261
        I Am Indigenous (a poem)   262
        A Land Within A Land   263
        The Big Baseball Game   267
        Larry's Choice   272
        True Trust Tales   284
        Vows Of Love   297
    CONNECTION EXERCISE   298
    RECOMMENDED READING   299
    ADDITIONAL RESOURCES   306
    ABOUT THE AUTHORS   307

THE TRUST FREQUENCY

An elevated state of being where the soul's destiny awaits, with more abundance, balance, freedom and joy than we can imagine. It is where the true nature of the Universe is experienced. It is available to anyone, anywhere, anytime.

ACKNOWLEDGEMENTS

We honor the brilliant minds and open hearts - the masters, saints and prophets, throughout the ages - who opened the doors to an expanded reality for those of us who have the urge to go within and beyond. We quote many of you in this book.

We honor the friends and family who have stood beside us and behind us, quietly supporting us as we walked the dusty trail to freedom – freedom from old thinking, freedom from cellular conditioning. It's been a wild and wonderful ride.

We thank the major Wall Street banks for providing us with a roof over our heads and financial freedom for the several years it took to pull these ideas together and shape them into this book. We honor them for then pulling the rug out from under us and thereby cleansing us of the last vestiges of fear - fear that our rational, trust-embracing minds could not access.

We honor the good friends who have hosted us on our peripatetic journey over the years, as we wrote the book: Al and Sun Lundell for welcoming us at Future Peak as artists-in-residence for six glorious months as the book came to fruition. Marcia and Tony Fusaro, Patti and George Stranahan, Pam Moore, Merinya Hucks and Terry End for providing inspirational retreats and solid friendship in the Roaring Fork Valley, Colorado. Kenny Mann for lovingly sharing her charming abodes in the Hamptons. Cousins Rupert and Ruth White for always welcoming the TrustMobile in their driveway in Brunswick, Maine. Jane and Don

Woodruff for their open-door policy in Pittsfield, Maine. Cousin Julia French for maintaining our health when the times got tough.

Many people helped with the evolution of the book: Melanie Krasnay read and re-read the evolving manuscript through the years, always with a brilliant, informed mind and a critical eye. Ingrid Hardy provided unerring support on all fronts. Suzy Collins, Teresa Johansing and Daniel Saenz contributed to the upward spiral of these ideas as they moved toward final expression in this book. Rita Marsh, Jean Owen, Barry Chapman, Karen Connington, Jordan Thompson, Bud Wilson, and Lisa Tully supported our unfolding vision with dedication and enthusiasm. Sally Ranney carried the vision in her own work and provided courage to fly beyond the *status quo* over the past two decades, culminating in the inspiring foreword to this book. Jack Baxter provided loving (albeit puzzled) support every step of the way.

Conor Johnson, a graduate of our very first Monday Night Class series in Aspen, selflessly dedicated many hours to formatting the book in the InDesign program.

And finally, for their personal support and encouragement, we honor these luminaries in the human potential movement: Jean Houston, Ralph Abraham, Hazel Henderson, Marilyn Mandala Schlitz, Matthew Gilbert, Lynn Andrews, Leigh J. McCloskey, Dean Radin, Barbara Marx Hubbard and Steve Bhaerman.

To one and all, thank you, thank you, thank you! We could not have done it without you!

Andrew and Connie

PREFACE

How do we, the authors, know the stuff that we know? This book, which is intended to trigger the reader's own inner knowing, presents a radical and unique world-view distilled from indigenous cosmology, quantum science and the world's spiritual traditions, as well as our combined personal life experience and intuition. Where did this synthesis come from? What were our greatest influences?

ANDREW'S STORY

Who am I? What is "real", and what is man-made illusion? Why is it vital to know the answers to these questions? For me it began in South Africa at the age of fourteen, when I discovered the writings of Lobsang Rampa and Jack Kerouac. I was as fascinated by the tales of flying Tibetan Buddhist monks as I was by the beatnik American "Dharma Bums." At the same time I was doing my best to be a good Anglican, and pondering the nature of the mysterious all-knowing, omnipresent entity called "God." Some years later, in a university anthropology course on comparative religion, I found part of the answer I was looking for, in the cosmology of the Australian aborigines. By that time I was a college lecturer in organic chemistry, and, thanks to my science training, had a vestigial idea of what quantum physics was about. Up until that moment, nothing in the mainstream religions had made much rational sense to me. They were obviously man-made constructs, all of them. The aborigines, however, were different.

They spoke pure, poetic quantum science. Their take on the nature of the Universe resonated in me in ways that neither Western science nor world religion had done.

Arriving in California in late 1969, after delivering a 90ft. sailboat across the Atlantic and arriving in the New World during a meteor shower on my 26th birthday, I was befriended by an American I had serendipitously met on my last night in London, a bearded Jerry Garcia look-alike named Ralph Abraham. Other than that brief encounter, I knew not a single person anywhere in the Americas. I was truly a stranger in a strange land. Ralph was one of the world's great mathematicians, soon-to-be father of Chaos Theory, and a frequent presenter at the Esalen Institute in Big Sur. He lived in Santa Cruz, at the very heart of the northern California consciousness-expansion movement. I knew nothing about any of this at the time, but my inspiration for traveling to California included two words I had encountered in a 1968 Life magazine article: "cosmic consciousness."

Hitchhiking north on Highway 101 from Los Angeles for the very first time, I had a powerful experience of synchronicity. I was picked up in Santa Barbara by a man who introduced himself as Jeffrey Love. He was heading for Santa Cruz, but needed to make a stop along the way, if I didn't mind. I had all the time in the world, I told him. The stop turned out to be the Esalen Institute on the cliffs of Big Sur. It was a glorious January day. On the winding curves of Highway One, high above the blue Pacific, Jeff asked me what I was planning to do in Santa Cruz. I mentioned my London encounter with Ralph Abraham. "Aha!"

he exclaimed. Ralph and Jeff, it turned out, were partners with an Indian master musician in an educational venture called the Pataal Foundation. *Pataal* means "navel" in Sanskrit, Jeff explained. Planet Earth has two spiritual navels, or poles, one near Rishikesh in the foothills of the Himalayas, and the other in Santa Cruz, California, our destination later that same day. I had definitely entered another dimension.

A lot was going on in Santa Cruz at the time. For example, a certain Richard Alpert, PhD, the controversial Harvard psychologist and LSD proponent, had parked his '67 Volvo in Ralph's California Street driveway and gone off to India in search of a guru, as many spiritual seekers were doing at the time. Dr. Alpert returned with a new name: Baba Ram Dass. The nascent guru settled in Santa Cruz, the surfing capital of the world, and the rest is history. In another instance of synchronicity, Ram Dass set up shop in the rented house in the little village of Soquel that was my first home in America, shortly after I moved out and up into the Santa Cruz Mountains, and his Harvard psychedelic research colleague, Ralph Metzner, initiated me into the mysteries of an ancient meditation practice called *agni yoga*.

I arrived in Northern California a few years too late for the Summer of Love, but my timing could not have been better. Looking back, I can see that I had landed right in the center of things at the perfect moment. I was a competent athlete and an intellectual graduate student at that time, but my spiritual ignorance was almost complete when I arrived in Santa Cruz. Ralph Abraham, [unbeknownst to him] helped launch me on a path which led to decades of inner work with the likes of Ralph Metzner, Stanislav Grof, Pir Vilayat Inayat Khan, and Persian mystic and sufi poet Javad Nurbhaksh.

Further information and inspiration came from the wise ones: Paramahansa Yogananda, Aldous Huxley, Hazrat Inayat Khan, Teilhard de Chardin, Sri Aurobindo, Jalaluddin Rumi, Ervin Laszlo, Bruce Lipton, Rupert Sheldrake, Jean Houston, Brian Swimme, Barbara Marx Hubbard, the Kalahari Bushmen, the Toltec elder Tlakaelel, Victor Vernon Woolf, and others too numerous to mention. One and all, I bow to the divine in you, and humbly thank you for all you have given the world. Finally, I honor my beloved partner, Connie Baxter Marlow, whose extraordinary vision provided the inspiration and the backbone of this book.

CONNIE'S STORY

Growing up in Maine in a family of visionary philanthropists - governors, mayors, legislators and community leaders - I noticed that not everyone in the world lived according to the principles of generosity and love. As a teenager, I read about Florence Nightingale and knew in that moment that humanity has an astounding capacity for love. I realized that something was missing in our understanding, something that led us to create a world-out-of-balance. I set out to find the missing pieces of the paradigm. I went to Europe in 1968, after graduating from U.C. Berkeley with an honors degree in Economics, and disappointingly, found only the roots of the very mind-set that had created my own culture. In 1976, in a bookstore in Santa Fe, New Mexico, I picked up a book of poetry from a Native American perspective. I knew at that moment that I had discovered some important missing pieces. Five hundred Indian nations knew the pathway to the heart. They had a resonance to, and a reverence for, all of life and the unseen forces of the universe – a trust-based paradigm.

As a mother in the 1980s I knew I had to expose my children to this way of being in order to bring balanced humans to the playground of humanity's evolution. I began to take my children to hear Native American storytelling, and to witness Native American dances and ceremonies in Santa Fe and the nearby pueblos. The cosmology we experienced aligned with the ideas I had been resonating to.

Take the *Sermon on the Mount,* combine it with John Lennon's *Imagine,* add *Star Wars, The Holographic Universe,* Thoreau's *Civil Disobedience,* and *The Field of Dreams,* throw in a bit of *Black Elk Speaks* and a little quantum science, and one glimpses the world-view Andrew and I share. When he and I met at the Omega Institute in 2003 it was immediately evident that we resonated to the same knowing. It has been an inspiration to fly with a fellow eagle, high into the realms of Spirit, from whence we "report back all that we see."

My journey to understanding the Trust Frequency began in 1988 with something I called "The Malaise." My body said: "Stop the world, go inside." I thought I had the world by the tail, and suddenly I couldn't function. I had three young children and it seemed I was dying.

Allopathic medicine couldn't discover what was wrong. The

doctors prescribed a drug and wished me well. The drug made my brain fuzzy. This was unacceptable to me, and a friend suggested I see an acupuncturist. Acupuncture was not well accepted at the time but there was a Chinese woman practicing it, so I became a regular with her. This led to further explorations into alternative medicine and triggered an inner journey of awareness. A friend in Santa Fe suggested I see a shamanic healer there. The shaman told me to write him with my experiences over the next three months. Astounding things began to happen, synchronicities beyond the explicable. My watch would stop at significant moments, and start again days later, on time. Eventually, after months of reporting these events to the shaman, he wrote to me and said: "You have made contact with the divine energies and they are communicating with you through your experiences. You are an old soul that awakens to the mystical very easily."

Then it began. It became apparent that it was not my children's education that led me to the Native Americans, it was my own destiny path. Visionary elders started coming into my life and became my friends. I created forums for them to share their extraordinary world-view through the 1990s in Aspen, Colorado, and I subsequently journeyed to the Hopi, the Maya, the Lakota, the Wabanaki, the Tarahumara, and the Ute with my children, and finally, after meeting Andrew, to the Kalahari Bushmen in Africa.

This close association with these open-hearted elders, as well as personal experiences that brought me new information, lead to my deducing that there exists a frequency realm where the true nature of the Universe lives. I could tell intuitively when

I was being shown a piece of Truth by the energies, and I would add the new piece to my evolving world-view. I have spent over two decades disseminating the understanding of the conscious loving Universe I had discovered: books, films, photography exhibits, ceremonies, lectures, performances. I was proposing ideas that even the visionary elders didn't fully understand. It's an evolutionary upward spiral. My insights were bringing and expanded articulation of the nature of the Universe.

I thank Lakota Grandfather Wallace Black Elk for being my seeing-eye-dog into another reality, and for being a good friend for over fifteen years. I thank Ute elder Grandmother Bertha Grove and her son Alden Naranjo, for sharing wisdom and being my friends, Grandmother Kitty, Gram Twylah Nitsch, Marilyn Youngbird, Spiritwalker, and Larry Littlebird for giving me important clues and friendship, and beloved Penobscot elder Arnie Neptune, who shared his heart-felt understanding of the love that drives all things; my Hopi friends, Ernestine, Catherine, Ramona, Marcella and the others, and the Maya in the jungles of Chiapas, Mexico, Chan K'in Cuatro and family, Joseph Campbell for paving the way into indigenous cosmology, Henry David Thoreau for being a key bridge between the mystical and the practical.

My children. Alison, Consi and Jonny joined me on the journey, often taking my hand and leading me into the unknown. Thank you! My ancestors, Mayflower Pilgrims William and Alice Mullins, Priscilla Mullins Alden and John Alden, and James Phinney Baxter and Percival P. Baxter for putting their lives and political careers on the line for the higher good of humanity.

Finally I thank my parents Jack and Alice Baxter, who respected my divine autonomous sovereign being-ness from the outset and gave me the personal power and self-trust to TRUST THE LOVING UNIVERSE!

$\mathcal{P}$ROLOGUE

A NEW PARADIGM

Most of us are familiar with the term "paradigm shift." Many of us feel that a paradigm shift is long overdue, but what exactly is a paradigm? How do we shift it? Why would we want to? A paradigm, whether scientific, spiritual, or social, is simply an individual or collective belief system, a set of agreed-upon assumptions about a particular subject. The paradigm we address in this book is nothing less than the consensus reality that determines the world we experience, our collective world-view. Let's ask ourselves: are we 100% satisfied with our existing reality, or could our lives (and our world) use a little improvement? Have we been running on an outdated operating system? Is it time for an upgrade? Is an upgrade possible? The authors think so.

THE HIGH ROAD TO HAPPINESS

We'd all like to be happier, more connected, more successful, more loved and more loving. Where do we begin? Here is the key. We can choose to shift our current paradigm by replacing some of our most fundamental assumptions about the nature of reality, by examining and modifying our core beliefs, and thus updating the world-view that drives our individual and collective existence. This may not be easy, and it may not happen overnight, but it *is* possible. In fact it is already happening. This book offers powerful keys to the "shift" many predicted for the year 2012, the initial phase of conscious evolution, in which *homo sapiens* chooses, at last, to exercise its free will and awaken into a vastly higher, more peaceful, more loving, more abundant, more joyful existence, a world beyond dualism. What lies beyond the shift? *Homo sapiens sapiens? Homo intelligentsia?* The true human? *Humanity 2.0?* Happiness?

To find out, all each of us has to do is to change the one thing over which we have complete control ... our own minds.

ACCESSING THE TRUST FREQUENCY

Welcome to the Trust Frequency, the vibratory realm where the soul's destiny awaits, with more abundance, joy, beauty and peace than we can imagine.

As you read this book, you will:

* Gain a new perspective on the nature of the Universe.
* Uncover and replace core beliefs that stand in the way of the evolutionary upward spiral to higher consciousness.
* Align with your own inner knowing.
* Discover that the laws that apply to you differ depending on your frequency, i.e. your state of consciousness..
* Learn about the role of free will, and your ability to choose your frequency and thereby your reality.
* Embark on your "hero's journey" to wholeness, and find yourself living in a conscious, loving Universe.

ENJOY!

*F*OREWORD

*"Climate change has, unambiguously, put humanity on notice
that we are on the cusp of great change, of making a critical choice
about ourselves. Only collaboration at the global level will solve climate
change, because it affects all human and natural systems. Nothing
and no one will escape. This high level of collaboration can only
take place if we let go of the tenets of the existing paradigm."*

For more than three decades, while Connie Baxter Marlow has been on her unfolding journey to the Center of Reality, I have been toiling in the fields of environmentalism to save the genetic archives, and the last best places on Earth, and most recently to avert climate change. Our paths crossed often in the early years, but less so as we each became more earnest in our endeavors, found partners, and our work took us around the world. But always, when we reached out to each other, it was as if we had had a cup of coffee just the day before. We discovered two old friends coming together in common cause – to understand the true nature of things and the evolution of human consciousness.

Ten years ago in a gathering of indigenous wisdom keepers at the Omega Institute in New York, Connie met her life-partner, Andrew Cameron Bailey. It was a match made in heaven, as is obvious once you begin reading *The Trust Frequency*. To Connie's visionary Native American-oriented articulations, Andrew brought quantum science, a worldwide comparative religion perspective, and many decades of spiritual practice, not to mention the cosmology of the Bushmen of the Kalahari, the world's oldest living people. This book is the result of that fortuitous meeting in

2003, as is their inspiring documentary film *IN SEARCH OF THE FUTURE: What Do The Wise Ones Know?*

As these ideas were evolving, it was essential for me to apply to 'real life' what might appear to many to be an esoteric exercise. I asked Connie, then Andrew, the same question year after year: "Where does the rubber hit the road? What are the practical applications of understanding the true nature of things, and how, really, does this make a difference in a person's every day life?"

It became obvious to me as the years passed, that, even with all the progress conservationists and environmentalists had made, overall we were losing ground. Then, to vastly complicate matters, the accumulation of human-caused carbon dioxide and other greenhouse gases in the atmosphere now has us on a trajectory to a 4 degrees Celsius (7.6 degrees F) increase in the planet's temperature. This is total anathema to most of life as we know it. We still have time to avert the worst impacts, if... and this is a big IF. An even more formidable question is: Why are we continuing to do this to ourselves and our children, now that we know what we are doing and understand the consequences of our actions?

The capital IF means doing all the things we are now striving towards: limit emissions, get international treaties in place, push for aggressive political and economic solutions, and much more. But that is not enough, and at the end of the day, these measures will not accomplish what is needed, which is essentially saving ourselves from ourselves, and keeping our one and only home planet livable.

The answer to the capital IF, and to the questions, is the same - we must change our existing belief system, and the resulting behavior, which has hypnotized us for centuries upon centuries. Those beliefs are underscored with core assumptions that have created a paradigm rooted in fear, doubt, guilt, scarcity, blame, competition and suffering. The products of this paradigm are war, violence, poverty, suppression of women and minorities, terrorism and radical religious fundamentalism, depletion and destruction of nature, nuclear weapons, pollution and the most daunting of all challenges in human history - climate change!

We have all heard about paradigm shifts, but where have you seen a guidebook that charts a path for how to actually shift a paradigm? This is the brilliance of *The Trust Frequency*. It is a courageous and tenacious navigation through the erroneous assumptions that created the existing planetary situation. It tells us step-by-step how to advance the process of conscious evolution by changing those assumptions and thus manifesting a different reality. We can create a world that each of us in our heart of hearts dearly wants to experience. The tenets of the new paradigm are: love, gratitude, trust, peace, collaboration, dignity, kindness, sharing, sustainability and abundance; restoring, respecting and replenishing nature.

Climate change has, unambiguously, put humanity on notice that we are on the cusp of great change, of making a critical choice about ourselves. A problem, as Einstein said, cannot be solved in the same consciousness in which it was created. In the case of climate change, one country, one community, or one technology cannot solve it. Only collaboration at the global level will solve climate change, because it affects all human and natural systems. Nothing and no one will escape. This high level of collaboration can only take place if we let go of the tenets of the existing paradigm. To do so, we have to dig deep into the root cause of humanity's suffering and our unconscious, harmful actions against one another and Mother Earth. We are being called to explore and upgrade our current assumptions and belief systems, to understand ourselves and to awaken to the reality of the evolution of human consciousness; to find the "high road" to knowing our true nature, the true nature of the Universe, to heal our planet and ourselves.

In view of the above, the timing of this book is profound. The authors bring forth a deep understanding of the genesis of the consensus reality we humans have created in the world. And because change is inevitable, they make the case that a new way of being is inevitable. With free will, we have a choice to design the future. We can usher in an evolutionary leap in human consciousness - for which we have been preparing over the centuries, often by experiencing *what doesn't work*!

Marlow and Bailey gently open the door to universal truths and awakened consciousness, introducing us carefully and methodically to our defective assumptions; the beliefs that have imprisoned us, limiting our experience of life, our full human potential, and our understanding of the true nature of things. Through deep subterranean inquiry and a synthesis of quantum physics, 'original knowledge' of the ancients, and the living wisdom of the indigenous peoples, they demonstrate that quantum physics is now confirming that consciousness is in all things, animate and inanimate, and that everything is connected in the Oneness, the undifferentiated consciousness. Everything. And, that separateness, differentiated consciousness, is merely one of the assumptions we have collectively agreed upon.

The Oneness Consciousness of Being is unconditional, unimpeachable, un-corruptible. It is the omnipresent creative Force and Source of the Universe, experiencing itself through trillions upon trillions upon trillions of manifest forms and the potentiality of the yet un-manifested. We are, like everything else, One with the creative Force and Source. We have the power to create our individual reality, and to co-create and participate in collective realities. We can create our experience of life deliberately or by default. The Universe doesn't have a preference. It is up to me. It is up to you. It is up to us. After all, we humans developed both the nuclear bomb and the Mona Lisa, as a friend likes to remind me.

So, as conscious manifestations of the Oneness, what we choose individually or collectively, whether it is a thought about our partner, a good deed for a friend, or to go to war with a neighboring country, it is the level and refinement of our consciousness that matters. If the assumptions upon which we base our actions are erroneous, riddled with misbeliefs, fear and doubt, then that is exactly what will manifest in our world. The tricky part of all this is that our reality mirrors our assumptions. As the authors tell us, we have the power to create a catastrophe or a paradise, depending upon how refined our awareness is of the assumptions that hold us in place.

The Trust Frequency identifies the faulty, fear-based assumptions to which we have collectively subscribed, beliefs which fly in the face of the True Nature of the Universe, and which obscure the view of our own true nature. Connie and Andrew have shot a straight arrow directly into the heart of those false beliefs. Further, they have put forth a coherent new set of assumptions for creating the new world. They remind us that collective realities have more power than individual thought-forms, and a new collective reality, a new consensus, is called for at this critical time. Rich with explorations, explanations and history, *The Trust Frequency* is a must-read for anyone who wants to expand their understanding of human consciousness and potential - anyone who wants to shift their own life from fear to trust and to merge their "separate" ego with the Divine self.

I have come to the conclusion that a shift in the consensus reality is absolutely essential if we are going to really heal climate change. Climate change is a mirror of our present collective interior reality. If the authors' new assumptions were embraced by the collective free will of society, the vibration of such positive thought forms would change the course of human history. This is a huge undertaking, but it is the only enduring solution. Buckminster Fuller, whom both Connie and I had the privilege of experiencing, said the best way to change a paradigm is to make the old one obsolete. It is not easy, as this book points out. But think about it like this: it wasn't hard to leave behind telephone booths when cell phones became available, or typewriters when computers came on the market.

"Wisdom comes from the feet," the Hopi say, referring to direct experience. The reality we experience depends upon our energetic field and our attitude, our world-view. We do have the choice to up-date our assumptions, to upgrade our operational software to the highest, most refined consciousness; to re-calibrate our personal frequencies, expand our understanding, and help create the emerging new way of being, at home, in business, and in the world.

And that is the clarion call of our time, the "Call to Arms," arms that embrace the Earth with love, gratitude and respect; hearts that are open to the Oneness of all that exists, and each other, in trust, peace, harmony and abundance. With the guidance in this book, we can deliberately and consciously design the future we have always dreamed was possible. We don't have to run on the fuel of fear any more. We can decide, through our free will, where we want to direct our attention. We humans created the world we live in, and we can re-create it.

Remember, all of the exciting changes and discoveries throughout history were at one time just beyond the edge of our awareness. What we discovered or created was already there! All we need to do is be persistent in our quest for discovery.

Sally A. Ranney
Aspen, Colorado

Sally A. Ranney is a true Renaissance woman: published author, public speaker, television anchor, gifted artist, pianist, composer, horsewoman, mother, wilderness guide, environmental activist, and green business strategist. She has dedicated her life to protecting the genetic archives of the planet, securing conservation custody for millions of acres of wild places in the United States, Alaska, Chile, Argentina, Africa, and Canada. She worked closely with U.S. Presidents Carter and Clinton, and was appointed by President Reagan to serve on the Presidential Commission on Americans Outdoors.

Her experience spans thirty years in the areas of land, water and energy policy, biodiversity, wildlife protection, and climate change. A resource policy analyst for the Wilderness Society, she co-founded American Wildlands, serving as its President for twenty years.

Her accomplishments and honors are far too numerous to mention all of them here. For more on Sally Ranney, please visit her web site: http://www.sallyranney.com.

FOREWORD

*O*PENING PRAYER

Grandfather, Creator of all that exists,
With this Sacred Pipe, hear my prayer:
As the new day dawns,
Let all people begin anew
To walk the Good Red Road of Life.

May we forget our differences,
May we remember our likenesses,
Let us hear what we have not heard,
Let us see what we have not seen,
It is the spark of the Universe,
The Oneness of all Life.

In such a way may we be blessed,
Blessed, in a sacred manner.
Wayne Eagleboy

*I*NTRODUCTION

Our senses enable us to perceive only a minute portion of the outside world. If you want to find the secrets of the universe, think in terms of energy, frequency and vibration.
Nikola Tesla

The Universe is wider than our views of it.
Henry David Thoreau

To conquer fear is the beginning of wisdom.
Bertrand Russell

Just as every drop of the ocean carries the taste of the ocean, so does every moment carry the taste of eternity.
Nisargadatta

The upwising has begun!
Swami Beyondananda, comedian

*T*he Trust Frequency paradigm is a readily-accessible scientific and spiritual construct built upon a visionary, original understanding of the nature of the Universe. Drawing from quantum science, indigenous cosmology, Eastern mysticism and the authors' own intuition, this book presents a world-view that, once adopted and acted upon, leads inevitably to happy, peaceful and successful individuals and communities.

The synthesis underlying this vision is well-supported

by the leading thinkers of the human species, from as far back
in time as the Vedic philosophers of ancient India, Emerson,
Thoreau and the American Transcendentalists, Goethe, Einstein,
David Bohm, Teilhard de Chardin, and in our own time, Ervin
Laszlo, Jean Houston, Fritjof Capra, Alan Watts, Barbara Marx
Hubbard, Stanislav Grof, Rupert Sheldrake, Bruce Lipton, Dean
Radin, Gregg Braden, Brian Swimme, Ken Wilber and many
others. In addition to these well-known cutting-edge scholars,
spiritual teachers and philosophers who are profoundly influencing
humanity's emerging planetary world-view, this book, perhaps
uniquely, acknowledges and integrates the cosmology of the
indigenous peoples of the world, the Bushmen of the Kalahari,
the Australian Aborigines, and the Native Americans - the Hopi,
Lakota, Maya, Toltec and others. Brief quotes from many of these
visionary way-showers are woven into the text of this book.

> *In all affairs it's a healthy thing now and then to hang*
> *a question mark on the things you have long taken for granted.*
> Bertrand Russell, PhD, philosopher

AN EVOLUTIONARY TOOLKIT
This book presents a radical, non-dualistic way of seeing the
world, and a way to integrate the experience of undivided Unity
into the "real" world. In other words, here is a practical strategy
for the reader to implement a fundamental upward shift in his or
her own consciousness, by intentionally choosing to vibrate at a
higher frequency. A good metaphor for the latter action would
be the elevation of one's frequency from the lowest or root

chakra (corresponding color: red) to the highest or crown *chakra* (corresponding color: violet) by the focused application of one's conscious attention and intention.

What emerges is a vision for the imminent appearance of the "true human," or *Humanity 2.0*, a vision distilled from the collective wisdom of our entire species. This wisdom is then broken down into a realistic method of applying these ideas to the vibratory state of the individual, and ultimately, to that of society as a whole: the Ten Assumptions. A profound upward shift in the collective consciousness can be initiated by examining and replacing certain outdated, erroneous assumptions about the nature of reality. The result is nothing less than a major upgrade to the human operating system.

> *Information, when combined with experience, becomes knowledge. When this knowledge becomes the frequency upon which we base our thoughts, words and deeds, then we are entering the resonance called wisdom.*
> Michael Brown, *The Presence Process*

A TIME OF CONVERGENCE

We are approaching the end of the Age of Reason, the Age of Analysis, a rather grim 400-year era of logical, left-brain-dominated, reason-based mechanistic thinking which developed in the 17th Century courtesy of Isaac Newton and René Descartes, and triggered the Industrial Revolution, the last great paradigm shift.

In the past hundred years, science has undergone a

profound expansion, and partly as a result of that expansion, humanity as a whole is now entering an age of synthesis, a time of convergence of opposites, of holistic thinking, and resolution of the paradoxes and contradictions which have puzzled, depressed, and divided us forever. With the few exceptions mentioned above, our most brilliant thinkers, our greatest scientists, religious leaders and philosophers, those most of us entrusted with the task of doing our thinking for us, have painted a picture of a bleak reality that has us imagining that we are separate from the rest of the Universe, that the Universe is a gigantic, lifeless, unconscious machine which somehow also contains (or is contained by) a separate super-conscious something called "God" or "Jahweh" or "Allah," that there are two invisible (but real) destinations called Heaven and Hell, that we have to die to get to either of those places, and that each of us is split into a "higher" and a "lower" self. Over the centuries, these somewhat irrational concepts have developed into a set of unquestioned fundamental assumptions, a paradigm, a consensus reality, that governs the lives of the vast majority of individuals in the "developed" world. As a direct result, *homo sapiens* has become the most schizophrenic species in the history of the Universe, and few, if any, of us has any idea of what to do about the situation.

That is about to change. Humanity possesses a vast untapped potential. We are entering into a time of awakening, of spiritual healing, where our "divine selves" and our "egos" re-combine at a higher point on the evolutionary upward spiral, and the confusions of the past are resolved once and for all. We will no longer be psychologically divided beings, with "higher" and "lower" selves, but will be mature, fully-integrated individuals simultaneously experiencing our unlimited, universal selves and our connection to the Unified Field, All-That-Is, while at the same time living our everyday existence from a higher vibratory place, a place of trust and love. The world we will then experience will be very different from the current one, which is built on a foundation of erroneous, fear-based beliefs. It is the most amazing time to be alive!

> *You are not your present structures of understanding.*
> *You inhabit a multi-dimensional reality far beyond*
> *any structure of thought that could ever be created*
> *by your human mind. Know that you are not your*
> *thoughts, you are not your ideas, you are not your*
> *descriptions of the world around you. You are a being*
> *of pure consciousness who has chosen to manifest on*
> *the physical plane. You have incarnated to bring out,*
> *develop and enjoy the beauty of the created realms.*
> Ken Carey, *Return of the Bird Tribes*

THE TRUE NATURE OF THE UNIVERSE

The human species, in the opening decades of the 21st Century, is presented with an unprecedented challenge and an extraordinary opportunity – the possibility of a radical re-visioning and re-invention of ourselves, the possibility of conscious evolution.

Our old, distorted assumptions, the beliefs that we inherited from our predecessors, have inevitably given rise to the world we see around us, with all of its absurdities and contradictions. As we shall see, humanity's prevailing paradigm, its consensus reality, is based on flawed, limited, fundamentally erroneous assumptions about the universal laws that govern our existence. These universal laws will be referred to in this book as the "true nature of the Universe" and will be described in detail in the forthcoming chapters.

The rational-mechanistic model of the universe, while highly effective in terms of technological progress, has resulted in the loss of some of humanity's most precious abilities.

Our erroneous belief systems stem partly from the reductionist scientific materialism of the past several centuries, but the roots of the human predicament go much deeper, to the very beginnings of our social systems and the origins of the doubt, fear and separation that have plagued mankind from the start.

> *Man has doubted the Creator since the*
> *beginning, and that doubt has plagued him.*
> Wallace Black Elk, Lakota Elder

METAMORPHOSIS

We are at a critical moment in the development of our species, a turning point. Our most brilliant, courageous and visionary thinkers are discovering and unveiling our true nature, our purpose, our destiny, and our intimate, connected relationship with the rest of existence. Recent advances in astrophysics, quantum science, anthropology, cosmology, psychobiology, the contemplative practices and communications technology have engendered a vast expansion of our understanding. For the first time in its several hundred thousand year history, humankind has the information and the perspective it needs to stop, step back, gaze up at the stars, go inside, and ponder the big picture: where did we come from, what we have become, where are we going, and why?

If we don't like what we see, what can we do to change the situation? Who says the current consensus reality is the only possible option, the only game in town? We have, a small percentage of us at this point in time, become aware that we humans, as a species, are still evolving. We are also beginning to realize that we can (and indeed must) get involved in our own evolution. While there are some who are still struggling with the very idea that our species is a work in progress, evolving physically, mentally and spiritually over time, others are in the process of a great awakening. Conscious evolution is now a real possibility. In fact, it is inevitable. Like the caterpillar transforming into the butterfly, the metamorphosis is already underway. It is written into our DNA. Our imaginal cells have been activated. The process is unstoppable. Having begun to awaken, we will not readily fall back to sleep.

THE TEN COMMANDMENTS

Let's go back in time a few thousand years. Moses had a mission. Jesus had a mission. This book has a mission, so let's get right to the point. Moses came down from the mountain with a freshly-inscribed stone tablet carrying the Ten Commandments, a list of proscriptions, of "thou shalt nots," designed primarily to impose control on the Israelites of his time, an unruly, semi-wild, warlike tribe of shepherds, artisans and philosophers with deep and ancient roots in the libertarian goddess-worshiping religions of the region. The only "thou shalts" in the list were the two enjoining the Israelites to love their god Jahweh and to love their parents. Both deity and parent were stern and forbidding authoritarians, and therefore not easy to love, so the first two commandments were even more difficult to obey than the other eight.

A couple of millennia later, at the peak of the Holy Roman Empire, a latter-day Israelite named Jeshua ben Yusuf, these days known as Jesus of Nazareth, proposed a kinder, gentler set of commandments, featuring a much greater emphasis on loving, not only god and parent, but also one's neighbor. One's neighbor was to be loved "as oneself," perhaps the first time in the world's literature that we find mention of self-esteem, the self-acceptance or love of self that we now know to be essential to spiritual and psychological health. Love thyself. Love thy neighbor. Love everyone. Good advice if ever we heard it.

The messages of both these prophets, along with those of countless others, taken in their pure form, have had an enormous and positive civilizing influence on human society, no question. And yet our world remains mired in poverty, disease, greed, inequity, war and violence. Why did humanity not simply adopt the tenets of its Wise Ones, who to this day maintain that all we have to do is to love, honor and respect one another, and all the bad things will go away? That would have been a no-brainer, but for some reason it seems that we had some learning to do.

Why, one might ask? Why all the suffering, all the struggle, all the pain? The answer, as we are now realizing, is this: we had to undergo, as part of our evolutionary learning curve, every event in our personal and collective histories in order to bring us to this very point in time, ready for the next step in our unfoldment. It has taken us a lot of hard work and a lot of suffering to get to this point. We have been distracted, trapped in complacency, paralyzed by uncertainty. Are we ready, at last, to wake up and to move into a higher reality? Do we have any alternative, if we are to survive and to thrive?

OUR HIGHEST ASPIRATIONS

The shift requires, firstly, that we awaken to the fact that our individual and collective assumptions, the core beliefs upon which we base our reality, the distorted ideas which we as a supposedly intelligent species have not questioned or examined for millennia, no longer serve us, if they ever did.

Secondly, we must make a conscious choice to do something about it. That is where the information in this book comes in. By assimilating the ideas in Part One, and by deploying our innate intelligence, our intuition and our free will, by choosing to change a few of our most fundamental assumptions, we can individually and collectively change our world, permanently, painlessly, and in a few short years. As we come into alignment with the true nature of the Universe, free of the fearful illusions of the past, we are enabled, each of us, to discover and actualize our highest aspirations. We find ourselves in an unimaginably more beautiful world, the world of the Trust Frequency, the world the Buddhists call Nirvana.

OUR DOMINANT WORLD-VIEW

Moses, Jesus and the leaders of 21st Century Earth, despite the millennia that have gone by, share a world divided by incompatible, competing cosmoligies - a confusing plethora of rival sects, whether religious or secular. One fundamental disagreement dividing today's world is that between what Harvard economist David Korten calls the "Distant Patriarch" theory (primarily Judaism, Christianity, and Islam) and the "Grand Machine" theory, aka the Newtonian scientific paradigm. Directly or indirectly, these incomplete and limiting belief systems are responsible for much of the fear many of us experience on a daily basis. We are afraid of everything; scarcity, drought, famine, wild animals, the neighbors, lack of money, losing the money we have, bacteria, old age, Al Qaeda, disease, comets, storms, other religions, the Devil, God, computer viruses, the CIA, a nuclear holocaust, mice, communists, Americans, cat hair, religious zealots, terrorists, the police, you name it. The list goes on and on and on. There is almost nothing that someone, somewhere, isn't terrified of.

LIVE IN FEAR, OR LIVE IN TRUST

Our dominant world-view is based on fundamental assumptions of scarcity, competition and separation. Is it any wonder that we have created the conflicted world we see today? We had to work with what we were given, with the consensus reality that has been handed down to us, generation after generation. What alternative have we had? Now however, as unlikely, as challenging, as the idea may seem, now that we live in a radically inter-connected quantum world where new ideas can go viral and spread like wildfire and change everything, we face an unprecedented opportunity: we can change our world simply by changing our beliefs, the contents of our minds. It's up to us. We can continue to live in fear, or we can wake up, exercise our free will, and choose to live in trust.

PARADISE WHEN?

Who would disagree that there has to be a better way to manifest as humans? We all know that the world as it exists today, with its wars, poverty, disease and distress, is lacking something critical. It is simply not right, in some fundamental way. We all agree that a world based on love and trust would be infinitely preferable to the one we are living in. But how can we bring about such a profound change? The answer, to drive the point home again, is this: we humans need to change our assumptions. In order to change our assumptions, we need to examine our existing ones. If necessary, we need to root them out and replace them with more accurate ones.

We need to be willing to remodel the very foundation of our reality. If we find our existing beliefs inadequate or outdated, we must come up with a set of alternative assumptions to take their place. That is the goal of this book: to discover and propose ten basic assumptions to replace some of the existing beliefs that have dominated and distorted our world for thousands of years.

Wild, utopian thinking, you say? Absolutely! It's the only way. Anything less will not do the job. Virtually every society has a myth or folk-story about a long-ago time when we all lived in harmony, in a paradise of balance and abundance. What if that paradise, that Garden of Eden, lies in the future, not the past? What if we've had it all backwards? What if it has been here all along? What if it's right here, right now? What if we can get "there", simply by changing our minds, our beliefs, the way we think about things? It's worth a shot, don't you think?

> *In a holographic universe there are no limits to the*
> *extent to which we can alter the fabric of reality.*
> *What we perceive as reality is only a canvas waiting*
> *for us to draw on it any picture we want.*
> Michael Talbot, *The Holographic Universe*

So, dear friends, unless you're completely satisfied with the *status quo*, why not join us in the greatest adventure ever undertaken, a conscious paradigm shift for the whole of humanity? The key to the shift lies here, in the following Ten Assumptions, in the Trust Frequency. It's basically a matter of choosing the vibratory frequency in which we exist, and as we shall see, it's all in our thoughts, the only things over which we have truly independent control, once we wake up and get beyond the limitations of our conditioned minds.

> *Love vibrates rapidly. Fear has a slower rate of vibration.*
> *Those who channel fearful energies find that as time passes,*

the fear vibration grows heavy, depressing. Eventually it brings
sleep, gloominess, discouragement, despair.
The love vibration brings enthusiasm, energy, interest, perception.
Ken Carey, *Return of the Bird Tribes*

We may not be able to change our outer circumstances immediately, but our inner landscape is ours to re-design and re-decorate as and when we choose. With a more positive world-view, we see our circumstances in a more positive light. We realize that, far from being victims of circumstance, circumstance is in fact our best friend. It is our unerring guide. Once we accept the ideas in this book, and integrate them into our beings, we can create a future beyond our wildest dreams. The only question is: do we dare? Do we have the courage?

Turn the page, read on, and find out whether these ideas resonate with your own inner knowing. At first, we suggest that you try them on as an exercise, an experiment. Apply them to your life as absolutes and see what happens. Be forewarned: this process triggers a deep cellular cleansing of old habitual thinking. It is not going to feel good sometimes. It's going to be a wild ride. It's going to take all the courage, all the trust you can muster, and that's not always easy. But, here's a secret. The process is extremely liberating - emotionally, psychologically and spiritually liberating. Your fears, your worries, your anxieties, your stress, melt away like the illusions they are, and you find yourself with a brand-new and much more positive perspective on life. That alone is worth the effort. Is it not?

A SUCCESS UNEXPECTED IN COMMON HOURS

Henry David Thoreau, the nineteenth-century Transcendentalist author, visionary and activist, had an important realization during his famous stay at Walden Pond, one which summarizes our vision eloquently, one that can set us all free once we *grok* it.

> *I learned this, at least, by my experiment:*
> *that if one advances confidently in the*
> *direction of his dreams, and endeavors to*
> *live the life which he has imagined, he will*
> *meet with a success unexpected in common hours.*
>
> *He will put some things behind, will pass an*
> *invisible boundary; new, universal, and more*
> *liberal laws will begin to establish themselves*
> *around and within him; or the old laws will*
> *be expanded, and interpreted in his favor in*
> *a more liberal sense, and he will live with the*
> *license of a higher order of beings.*
> Henry David Thoreau, *Walden*

This book is about to take you on a journey of deep, personal discovery, during which you can apply Thoreau's visionary insights to your own life – and you can begin to "live with the license of a higher order of beings," starting right now, this very moment.

The spiritual power I wear is much more beautiful and much greater. We call it wisdom, knowledge, power and gift, or love. There are these four parts to that spiritual power. So I wear those. When you wear that power it will beautify your mind and spirit. You become beautiful. Everything that Tunkashila creates is beautiful.

Wallace Black Elk, Lakota Elder

Part I

The Ten Assumptions

*I*NTRODUCING THE ASSUMPTIONS

We are all visitors to this time, this place.
We are just passing through. Our purpose
here is to observe, to learn, to grow, to love...
and then we return home.

Australian aborigine proverb

The Ten Assumptions offered in this book, along with the
accompanying Definitions, when adopted whole-heartedly,
without doubt or compromise, elevate one into a higher vibratory
reality, a state free of fear and anxiety. You may not find it easy
to accept some or all of the propositions offered, and that's OK.
You have two choices. Either make a sincere decision to accept
these assumptions as absolutes, as they are presented, or adopt
those that you feel good about and develop your own set of
assumptions. For instance, not everyone is comfortable with the
concept of reincarnation, or the idea of a spirit world. Trust your
own intuition, and proceed accordingly. The important thing is to
be sure that the assumptions that form the foundation for your
life are your *own* beliefs, chosen by you, not un-examined ones
imposed on you by others.

Either way, the process will not work for long if we merely
try to add the new assumptions as an overlay over the old ones.
Our old, subconscious beliefs will continue to exercise enormous

sabotage power over us. We have deep and sometimes difficult work to do, in order to replace our deep-seated and often poisonous core beliefs with a higher understanding. As we must do periodically when our tired old computer grows sluggish and finicky, we have to implement a major upgrade to our operating system. But, having done that successfully, everything changes.

We find ourselves in a magical, abundant world, a world of grace and ease. We may or may not choose to have much in the way of money or material stuff, but everything we need is always there, right when we need it. It's not that we no longer have to work, *per se*, it's that our work and our play become indistinguishable, in the same way that, in the indigenous world, the secular and the spiritual are indistinguishable.

Choose a job you love, and you will never
have to work another day in your life.
Attributed to Confucius, philosopher (551–479 BCE)

NOTE: The phenomenon this book calls the "conscious, loving Universe" is emphatically not a mere mental construct, an abstract intellectual fantasy. It is a profound biological reality. In fact, it is the *only* Reality. It is nothing less than Life Itself, ever-evolving, ever-unfolding Life. It is not separate from us. Each of us is inextricably entangled with It. It *is* us! We *are* It!

In some strange sense, the universe is a participatory universe.
John Wheeler, PhD. quantum physicist

*Physicists have speculated that entanglement extends
to everything in the universe, because as far as we know,
all energy and all matter emerged out of a primordial Big
Bang. And thus everything came out of the chute already
entangled. Some further speculate that empty space,
the quantum vacuum itself, may be filled with
entangled particles. Such proposals suggest that
despite everyday appearances, we might be living
within a holistic, deeply interconnected reality.*
Dean Radin, PhD, physicist

*There is no reality except the one contained within us.
That is why so many people live such an unreal life.
They take images outside them for reality, and never
allow the world within to assert itself.*

Hermann Hesse, novelist

WHAT YOU SEE IS WHAT YOU GET

As quantum science teaches us, we create what we put our
attention on. The phenomenon is called the "observer effect,"
and is the subject of the "Einstein's Mouse" conundrum. A little-
recognized consequence of the phenomenon is that when we
spend our evenings agonizing over the latest tragedies on TV or
watching YouTube rants about the Great Conspiracy, Goldman
Sachs, the Trilateral Commission and the dreaded Illuminati, we
align ourselves vibrationally and participate in the same frequency
with the fear-based consensus reality, an insidious collective mental
construct that holds enormous, hypnotic power over our entire
society. Furthermore, by our participation, we help to co-create,

perpetuate, and consolidate the *status quo*, even if we think we are doing the opposite.

Many liberal Americans, for instance, listen religiously to National Public Radio, in the belief that it is important to stay informed. By doing so, we unknowingly reinforce the consensus reality. We become unconscious collaborators in a scenario that none of us would intentionally design, were it up to us, but we go along with the herd, unaware that there is any alternative. So compelling is this "reality," that we can barely conceive of anything else. It's a figure-ground situation, like the famous painting of the young girl and the old woman. When your conscious awareness is focused on the old crone, it's impossible to see the young girl, and *vice versa*. Unconsciously, without knowing it, we empower everything we place our attention on, whether for "better" or for "worse." What can we do about this relatively unknown but vitally important power of the human mind?

It's a little like this: you and your sweetheart are sitting in the theatre. The orchestra strikes up, the audience erupts into applause, the cast bursts out onto the stage, and the show begins. The problem is, you can't see a thing. There is a wonderful replica of a hand-carved Etruscan column six inches in front of your face, and all you can think about is why you spent $100 for the worst seat in the house. What can you do? You shuffle in your seat, move your head a few inches to the left, and presto! You too can watch the show. All it took was a change in perspective, a shift of focus. You had a choice. And, as a bonus, you find yourself closer to your beloved. All you had to do was to change your point of view.

So it is in our daily lives. If we shut off the TV, ignore the headlines, knowing that they are nothing but illusory and depressing distractions, and focus instead on what is good in the world, on the boundless beauty and inspiration that surrounds us, we not only improve our own lives, we become a source of positive energy and inspiration for those close to us.

AN OUTDATED WORLD-VIEW

Here is a fundamental fact. No matter what culture we belong to, our current societal paradigm, our consensus reality, is determined entirely by our collective basic assumptions about the nature of the Universe. These assumptions are our community's deepest core beliefs, the unquestioned axioms upon which most of us base our lives. The problem is that these foundational assumptions are not necessarily either accurate or permanently fixed in time. This is not common knowledge. Assumptions are by definition something we take for granted. We rarely, if ever, examine or question them. And yet, these assumptions, these core beliefs, determine every thought we think, every feeling we experience, every attitude we adopt, every decision we make, and every action we take, individually and collectively. We don't take a breath without assuming there's air to breathe. We don't sit down without assuming the chair will support our weight.

Our most fundamental assumptions were inherited from our predecessors, were culturally imposed on us from birth, and reflect, unless we have undertaken some powerful inner work, the outdated world-view and cosmology of our antecedents, our caregivers, our teachers, our priests, our culture heroes. Most of these assumptions were developed a long time ago, to serve a very different world from the one we inhabit today. They were developed by people who lived in a great deal of fear and ignorance. Being subconscious, our collective belief system holds enormous power over us, and keeps us trapped in a hypnotic trance from which it is not easy to awaken.

> *I think we ought always to entertain our opinions*
> *with some measure of doubt. I shouldn't wish people*
> *dogmatically to believe any philosophy, not even mine.*
> Bertrand Russell, PhD, philosopher

The outer forms these assumptions take vary enormously depending on where and when we live, what culture we were born into, what religion or philosophy we ascribe to, what historical period we are talking about, and so on. Consider a San bushman hunter-gatherer in the year 10,000 BC, a Harvard law professor at the turn of the 19th century, an Islamic fundamentalist in present-day Afghanistan, a Hindu guru in Vedic times, a contemporary New York heroin addict, a 17th Century Zulu warrior, a medieval farmer in Italy, and the 21st Century Czechoslovakian mistress of a London stockbroker. These folks are all, undeniably, members of our species *homo sapiens*, and yet the cosmology, the world-view of each, might well be unrecognizable and incoherent to each of the others. They might as well be from different species, living on different planets in different universes, in different vibratory realities. In fact, that is a pretty good description of the situation.

Furthermore, each of these disparate cultures attempts to understand and describe those realities via unique languages that have their cultural assumptions built into them at the root level.

WE CAN TURN THE PAGE

However, as we reveal in this book, we can change our entire reality simply by changing our world-view, our belief-system. We are not talking about "just another" belief system here, or a "religious conversion," but about a carefully-considered and consciously-chosen new set of assumptions upon which to base our existence. This is something that has rarely (if ever) been attempted before, at least voluntarily. If our world-view, our cosmology, is indeed so mutable, what is to prevent us as individuals and groups from making up our own reality, from re-thinking and re-creating our world from the ground on up? Indeed, looking around, it is obvious that, even in our own culture at this particular moment in history, there are numerous co-existing realities. We are by no means all on the same page.

The important thing to realize is - we can turn that page at will. There are plenty of precedents for exactly that. To cite a few current examples; since the 1960s, numerous children of Irish Catholic parents have chosen to become agnostic intellectuals; many of the past few decades' converts to Eastern mysticism are from Jewish backgrounds; intellectual American novelists have become Zen Buddhist monks; and the offspring of atheist communists have become devout born-again Christians.

We are, of course, not talking about merely adopting a pre-existing mystical, spiritual or philosophical path, as most of the above converts have done, without examining or changing our deepest assumptions. We are talking about going way deeper, all the way down to the very foundations of our beings. By doing so, we each have the potential to become something that has never existed before.

The point? Everything about our inner life is mutable, flexible. Nothing is set in stone. We have the right, the freedom and the ability to change our minds, using our innate power of discernment to shift our perceptions, and to re-think reality based on the newest and most inspiring information available to our consciousness. This is not just an intellectual process. It also calls for the activation of, and trust in, our intuition, our feelings. Once we learn to resonate to our deepest inner knowing and to act from that place, we can consciously choose to change our vibratory rate, to elevate our frequency, to move into the Trust Frequency.

Or not. It's our choice. The result, if change is what we choose? Everything shifts as our inner perceptions shift, and our outer world is never the same. The newspapers may, for the moment, still be reporting the latest versions of the same old stuff, but our attitude, our perspective, our world-view, our vision of reality, has changed, and we experience things very differently. The inescapable fact is, we create our own reality, individually as well as collectively. The nature of that reality is up to us.

As challenging as it might be to accept, we are *personally* responsible for everything that unfolds in our lives. Everything,

without exception, even the actions of others. We each write the
script for our own life's movie, whether we know it or not, and
the characters in our movie are our own creations, like it or not.
The movie can be a romantic comedy, a Greek tragedy, or a horror
story. It can have a happy ending. Once we decide to make the
"shift," we have become part of the "solution," and the "problem"
is on its way out. We can re-write our movie, any time we like. If
we choose not to, the past stays present and we remain stuck in
our old ways of being. Again, it's our choice.

IT'S ENTIRELY UP TO US

Not everybody realizes that each and every one of us has a
world-view, and that our world-view depends entirely on our
assumptions. *"What? I have a world-view? You know, I never thought
of that!"* a brilliant scientist friend exclaimed recently. This is not
something we are taught in grade school, or even in graduate
school, but things are changing as we humans become more
aware of who and what we are, as we begin to understand our
relationship to the Universe, and as we realize that it is entirely up
to each of us to choose the reality we wish to live in.

WE CO-CREATE THE FUTURE

That being the case, why not take the job seriously and create a
reality, and by extension, a future, that is a direct outgrowth of
conscious intention and intelligent choice? Rather than the future
being something that just happens to us, something beyond our
control, something imposed on us from the outside, what if the

future, like our individual reality, is in fact something that we came to this planet to create, to co-create, with our fellow humans?

NIRVANA IN THE HERE-AND-NOW

Can we learn to relax, listen deeply, and act on our inner promptings in a state of trust, with full confidence that everything is unfolding to a perfection beyond our wildest imaginings? Can we learn to trust that our task is to choose to allow pure Love to manifest in the physical realm? Do we have any idea what that might mean? All of these questions will be discussed in the forthcoming chapters, as we present and describe a coherent new paradigm which, with a little practice, will move the reader into a state of being called the Trust Frequency, a state that is nothing less than Heaven-on-Earth, Nirvana in the here-and-now.

The nature of the phenomenon we call the future, very simply, depends on our assumptions about it, and how we act upon those assumptions. Consequently, the future we are creating depends in equal measure on our fundamental assumptions about the world, about ourselves, about our species, and about the mechanics of the Universe we inhabit.

THE OMEGA POINT IS RIGHT ON TIME

Now that *homo sapiens* has had a few hundred thousand years to sit around the campfire and ponder the big picture, now that self-reflection, indigenous wisdom, quantum science, technology, spirituality and philosophy have come together to give us a picture of the Universe as profoundly mutable, ever-evolving, inter-connected and conscious, now that the Internet has united our species in ways previously unimaginable, the time has at last arrived when we can take personal responsibility for our lives and the future of our planet and our species. Teilhard de Chardin's prophetic vision of an evolutionary quantum leap in human consciousness, a move to a higher vibratory frequency, which he called the Omega Point, is right on time, and the time is now!

IT BEGINS WITH ME

The process of upgrading the operating system of our entire species may look like a daunting if not impossible task, but as the new science of chaos theory teaches us, in this radically-connected post-Newtonian world, a very small cause can have a very large effect. I *can* make a difference. You *can* make a difference. Together *we can* make a difference. A book like this *will* make a difference. All we have to do is do it. The journey of a thousand miles begins with a single step. It begins with me, with you, with each of us, as we wake up and rub the sleep from our eyes.

What we think is fundamentally important. We are in the process of thinking up the future. If we have a bad fantasy, we'll have a bad future. Therefore it really, really matters what we do, what we think, what philosophy we hold and how we support other people sharing in the same philosophy, because the interconnection of all people into a collective will, could really create a paradise of the future. If that is possible, then we have to do it.
Ralph Abraham, PhD. mathematician, philosopher
(from the authors' film *In Search Of The Future*)

A NEW WAY OF SEEING

The essential point, one that few of us recognize at this point in history, is that we each have the right, the freedom and the innate ability to consciously choose and modify our own reality and to alter the underlying beliefs which define and create that reality. As we ponder each of the "new" assumptions in the forthcoming chapters, we will also look at the corresponding "old" assumption on which current consensus reality is based, a reality that has conditioned our minds to believe that the limited and limiting world most of us experience is the only game in town.

More often than not, the "new" assumptions are quite literally the polar opposites of the old ones. If we have the courage to invert much of what we have been taught, to flip many of our basic, unconscious beliefs one hundred and eighty degrees, we find ourselves approaching a "truth" that aligns with the timeless wisdom of the indigenous elders, visionary scientists, mystics, shamans, poets, spiritual masters, saints and prophets of all ages and cultures. We begin to trust that truth and to change our behavior, and the world begins to change with us.

> *The greater part of what my neighbors call good*
> *I believe in my soul to be bad, and if I repent of*
> *anything, it is very likely to be my good behavior.*
> *What demon possessed me that I behaved so well?*
> Henry David Thoreau

This wisdom, this way of seeing the world, is not new. On the contrary, it is ancient. It was brilliantly articulated by Vedic scholars, the *"rishis,"* over five thousand years ago. It is pretty much universal among indigenous societies. It has been available since the dawn of time, but has awaited the advent of quantum science and a growing understanding of the indigenous world-view to find an articulation that the "developed" world can accept, assimilate, and act upon.

Other than a few extraordinary way-showers, a few masters, saints or prophets, known and unknown, no individual or society has yet lived a trust-based reality in its pure form. The frequency of fear has been the dominant energy on the planet for a very long time. That fear has influenced everyone's behavior, including those with an outwardly trust-based cosmology, such as the indigenous peoples of the world. Indigenous people, with few exceptions, have displayed fear-based behavior as out-of-balance as anything the so-called developed world has displayed, fantasies of the "noble savage" notwithstanding. The twin demons of fear and doubt have infected our entire species for so long, we can scarcely imagine a trust-based world.

However, all is not lost. Far from it. *Homo sapiens* stands at the brink of a true quantum shift, an evolutionary leap, which will elevate our species from the long-established fear-based paradigm into a love-and-trust-based reality. Our hearts are opening, one by one. The Earth herself is evolving towards a higher frequency.

Open your heart to others.
When you do so, you will feel our spirit.
It will make you dance
And it will make you happy.

And then you, too, will be a Bushman.

From *Kalahari Bushman Healers*: Edited by Bradford Keeney, PhD

THE LIZARD BRAIN

Ask yourself a few questions, questions you have probably never been asked before. What are your ten most basic core beliefs about the nature of reality? Can you name them? If so, would you write them down for future reference? They will come in handy later, as a reference point, as you embark on your process of inner change. Now, ask yourself this: when did you first adopt these beliefs, these assumptions, these ideas that define the way you live your life, the way your life feels to you? Where did they come from? Would you agree that most of your deepest-held beliefs about the world, about the nature of reality, were already firmly in place by the time you were three or five or seven years old? Would you agree that you did not consciously analyze or choose any of these ideas, attitudes, opinions and concepts before integrating them into your world-view and burying them deep in your unconscious? Did you have any idea who developed these beliefs, what their concept of reality was, and where their ideas originally came from? How could you have? You were a little child.

We think you see the situation. Our collective consensus reality was crafted, consciously or otherwise, and locked into place many generations ago, by people who lived in a great deal of fear and ignorance, and who lacked much of the information that we take for granted today. It is not hard to see that the world-view upon which the world currently operates is seriously out of date, if not just plain wrong. Much of it seems to have originated in the ancient reptilian "fight or flight" brain, the so-called "lizard brain," and it no longer serves us. On the contrary, it is dangerous in the extreme.

There are powerful forces in place, of course, to keep things just the way they are, including the fundamentalist religions and the totalitarian political systems of the world, as well as multi-national corporate interests and the corporate-owned news media. On a more subtle level, even the most liberal traditions and social systems, based as they inevitably are upon erroneous assumptions, serve to keep humanity trapped in an outdated web of illusory misbelief. It's nobody's fault. It's just the way it is.

THE ONLY WAY OUT IS UP

It is going to take a profound shift on the part of intelligent and open-minded individuals, people such as ourselves, to make a deep commitment to ourselves and our communities, and to help trigger the change and the growth called for in this book. There is going to be resistance, both inner and outer. Old habits die hard. On the other hand, the "new" assumptions presented in this book make so much sense, and they are so much more attractive than most of our existing beliefs, that adopting them is an active pleasure, a thrilling liberation from bondage. What a relief it is to wake up into a conscious, loving, abundant, interconnected Universe, and to let go of the cold, dead, mechanical illusion brought to us by Newton, Descartes and Darwin, those great but limited genii of the past who based their realities on the same fear-based assumptions as everyone else. They thought that reason alone would save us.

Please be assured that not everyone suffers from a completely negative, fear-based world-view. That is not what we are suggesting. Most of us are not cowering under the bed-sheets, afraid to face the world. Each of us is a mix of the positive and the negative, a balance of trust and fear. In fact, it is remarkable how much trust each of us does manifest in our daily lives. How otherwise would any of us get up and face the challenges of each new day? Humans are innately trusting beings, or we would not have survived this long, but we have put our trust in the wrong place. For the past four centuries, we have trusted our left-brain, reason-based view of the world and ignored everything else. That was the logical thing to do.

Given our unbalanced history, and the current state of affairs, it is astounding how much we continue to trust our institutions, our governments, our parents, our religions, and our societies. Will we ever grow up and learn to think for ourselves? Sadly, many intelligent people think not, and have essentially given up on our species.

This book, we think you will agree, offers a practical solution to the human dilemma, a viable way out of the convoluted and unhappy mess we have created. It's a question of consciousness, of the evolution of consciousness. And that can only be accomplished by changing some of our ideas. The only way out is up! Read on, have faith in your own intuition, and welcome to the Trust Frequency. This is an exciting journey. It is nothing less than the high road to happiness, individually, and to a transformed society, collectively!

$\mathcal{D}$EFINITIONS: A GLOSSARY OF TERMS

$\mathcal{T}$o ensure that we are sharing the same terminology, that we are speaking the same language, we must pause briefly and define a number of key terms and concepts. Without a clear understanding of how these basic terms are used, it will be impossible to get the full benefit of this book. Most of these definitions will be obvious, but others may seem unfamiliar, a far-fetched stretch of the imagination. However, each of them is scientifically, intellectually and/or spiritually well-established.

NOTE: To be effective, it is essential that you take these definitions and the Ten Assumptions that follow as absolutes, for the purpose of this evolutionary exercise.

ASSUMPTION
A fundamental core belief, which we take to be true without question.

PARADIGM
A set of agreed-upon assumptions which, taken together, create our consensus reality, our world-view.

FREQUENCY
The vibrational rate that determines the characteristics of a particular reality. There is a broad spectrum of frequencies, each with its own reality and with its own distinct laws.

HUMANITY
A collection of divine, autonomous, sovereign beings who have

chosen to incarnate on Earth to learn, grow and flourish on
their soul's journey to wholeness, each with an individual
purpose and a unique gift.

SOUL
An individualized spark of consciousness embodied in form.

WHOLENESS
The state of Oneness or Unity with All-That-Is.

FREE WILL
The inalienable right to choose and modify one's frequency,
and hence one's reality.

CIRCUMSTANCE
The seemingly uncontrollable outward events that determine
and influence our decisions and direction in life.

LOVE
The fundamental unifying and creative force of the Universe.

THE UNIVERSE
All-That-Is, both manifest and un-manifest. Also known as
God, Creator, Atman, Brahman, Jahweh, Allah, Great Spirit,
the Great Mystery, the Force, the Quantum Field and so on.

CONSCIOUSNESS
i. Universal consciousness: the primordial life energy of the
Universe.
ii. Human consciousness: The active and passive phenomena
of Awareness, Assumption, Attitude, Attention, Alignment
(or Attunement,) Action and Allowing.

THE FIRST ASSUMPTION

We Live In A Conscious, Loving Universe.
There Is ONLY Love.

Current Assumption

The universe is mechanical, lifeless, and utterly unaware of our existence. It contains life, on this planet at least, but the universe is not in and of itself alive. It is not conscious.

*So, boldly traveling in the opposite direction,
if the founders of all the great world religions are
correct in their assertion that "God is Love," and
if "God" is in fact identical with the Quantum
Field as understood by science, and if the Quantum
Field is in fact All-That-Is, namely the Universe,
then the logical, analytical mind can only come to one
conclusion: the Universe is Love. Ergo, the Universe
loves us! How could It do anything else?
There is no rational alternative.*

THE BEE AND THE INDIAN

Western science has made enormous progress over the past few hundred years in terms of understanding the material universe and the mechanics of how things work on a physical level. Nevertheless, there still remain vast areas of mystery. We still don't know, for instance, how the humble bee can perform its busy, apparently random activities from flower to flower to flower, and then, satisfied, make a dead-straight "beeline" back to the hive with unerring accuracy. How does it distinguish its own hive from the hundreds of others in the vicinity? How does the bee's navigational system work?

Is it related to the navigational system used by the Native Americans and the other aboriginal peoples in their original state, as observed by Henry David Thoreau in the Maine woods in the mid-1800s? Thoreau marveled at his native guide's ability to travel through apparently featureless woodland for days on end, always unerringly confident in the knowledge of exactly where he was. A Penobscot Indian from Maine, Joe Polis could take to the woods with nothing more than a blanket and a pipe, an axe and a gun, and not only navigate, but survive (and thrive) for days and weeks without apparent effort.

THE UNIVERSE IS ALIVE

Are the bee and the Indian in the above examples tapping into the Quantum Field, the invisible connective matrix containing all information, where navigational co-ordinates, and all other needs, are routinely available for the asking? If so, we must ask the question: what else don't we know? What have we forgotten? What other great secrets remain to astonish us, as human knowledge and understanding unfold? The greatest scientific revelation about the nature of the Universe, as postulated locally for planet Earth in James Lovelock's *Gaia Hypothesis*, will be this: It's alive! It's conscious! It's intelligent!

> *The mystical truth that there is nothing but consciousness*
> *must be experienced in order to be truly understood, just as*
> *a banana, in the sensory domain, must be seen and tasted*
> *before a person really knows what a banana is.*
> Amit Goswami, PhD, physicist

As far as we can tell, *homo sapiens* has more potential than any other species for knowledge, understanding, co-operation, creativity, wisdom and love. The human species might just be the crown jewel of creation. If that is the case, why are we not more conscious? Why have we, so far, failed to create a world of peace, love and abundance? What went wrong? Is there any such thing as "wrong?" Have we learned our lessons yet? Well yes, in fact. We have learned our lessons well. Having done so at last, we are about to choose to align with our true loving nature, our higher destiny.

All of Creation is awaiting the opening of the human heart and the release of the love contained therein. That's why all aspects of this conscious universe are cooperating with us to make it look like we are destroying everything, when in fact everything is fine outside of the bubble of illusion that we have created with our erroneous assumptions. Remember – we create and manifest what we believe to be true.

Each form of created life is energy manifesting in matter, ever-changing, ever-flowing into something always capable of more expression, more unfoldment, more revelation of spirit world potential. The true human is designed to aid the development of all life forms, drawing out their ever-expanding capacities to provide always fuller revelations of that which lies in the heart of God.
Ken Carey, *Return Of The Bird Tribes*

WHEN YOU COME TO A FORK IN THE ROAD, TAKE IT

Roughly four hundred years ago, the Western mind-set came
to a fork in the road. It bifurcated and split into two, with the
emergence of the rational-materialist "Grand Machine" paradigm
pioneered by Isaac Newton, René Descartes, Charles Darwin
and others: the Age of Reason, a.k.a the Enlightenment. It was
a massive paradigm shift. It changed everything. Prior to that
time, Western cosmology, the way we perceived the Universe,
was largely determined and controlled by the Church and its
"Distant Patriarch" cosmology*. The faithful were told what to
believe, what to think, when and how to pray, and how to act, and
should you come up with something different, well, there were
consequences, as Galileo, Copernicus, Bruno, Joan of Arc, and
many other "heretics" were to discover to their chagrin. Original
thinking was discouraged, to say the least. Then the Age of
Reason dawned, bringing logic, analytical thinking, mathematics,
technology, the printing press, modern medicine, the Volkswagen,
the hula-hoop, the hydrogen bomb, space travel, and ultimately a

social experiment called democracy, to the world.

ZEN CAME EINSTEIN

Many enormous benefits accompanied the new scientific paradigm, undeniably, and yet, something vital was lost along the way. In the Old World, everything was inter-connected, everything was created and sustained by the omnipresent, omnipotent divine force known as "God," "Jahweh," "Allah," "Brahma," "Atman" and by a thousand thousand other names. Thanks to dualism and reductionist science, modern technological man, cut off from his spiritual roots, now finds himself disconnected, alienated, living a meaningless life in a fundamentally meaningless world. The universe itself is seen as merely an enormous, lifeless machine, and "God," to the educated intellectual, is at best a concept, a tradition, a superstition, an old-fashioned intellectual construct, to be rolled out on Sundays and major holidays, if at all. The idea that the Universe could be conscious, alive, and aware of us in any way, is regarded as absurd, the domain of primitive belief-systems and outdated, delusional thinking. Earth's biosphere is the only known place where life exists, and aside from extraterrestrial speculations and sci-fi fantasies, that is the end of the story, according to the rational-materialist world-view.

Unexpectedly, in 1905, the scientific paradigm shifted once again. Along came Einstein and the quantum physicists, and suddenly, it was no longer possible to know everything, to predict outcomes with precision, to do what science had always promised: to make us the eternal masters of physical reality.

A strange, unpredictable mystery entered the scientific domain, with the strange, unpredictable result that science began to affirm some of the "weird" and "spooky" concepts previously relegated to the spiritual domain. The crisp boundary between physics and metaphysics began to blur. The ongoing attempt to understand the true nature of the universe began to reveal this: the Universe is more like a thought than a thing! And if the Universe is an inconceivably enormous thought-form, we have to ask ourselves the obvious question: who or what is doing the thinking? And if someone or something is doing the thinking, how can that be, unless...? That someone or something must be conscious. It must be alive. There is no other possibility.

AN OMNIPRESENT, INVISIBLE MATRIX

Which brings us full-circle to the earliest religio-spiritual concepts of so-called primitive man. In the terminology of the relatively new science of anthropology, the world's oldest "religion," the cosmology of the ancient hunter-gatherers, presumably the most "primitive and ignorant" people on earth, is *animism*. Animists experience an *anima mundi*, a living Universe in which everything is alive, everything is conscious, the rocks, the trees, the earth, the sun, sky, moon and stars, the very air we breathe. They know that everything is inter-connected, by an omnipresent, invisible matrix, and that every thing influences every other thing, in real time, no matter where it is located in the physical Universe. Sound familiar? Is this not precisely what the most advanced speculative physicists are telling us today, in their hotly-debated treatises on the subject of quantum entanglement and non-locality?

RANDOM MUTATION

To return to the subject of assumptions, then, what is the prevailing assumption about the nature of the Universe in current planetary culture? At least in the mainstream of the so-called developed world? What is our current model of the universe? Unquestionably, the universe is seen as mechanical, lifeless, and utterly unaware of our very existence. It contains life, on this planet at least, but the universe is not in and of itself alive. It is not conscious. Contemporary science acknowledges the existence of consciousness, obviously, but has little to say on the subject. That is left to the philosophers, the psychologists, the metaphysicians and the theologists.

The universe, to the scientist, consists of an enormous collection of waves and particles, ranging from macro to micro, randomly bouncing about and colliding with one another, all carefully obeying Newton's and Einstein's often contradictory laws, and somehow, along the way, producing a primordial quantum soup, a rock stew, out of which emerges us, *homo sapiens*, you and me! No coherent explanation is offered for this mysterious process, other than that it involves random mutation and natural selection. Quite a remarkable hypothesis, come to think of it. What science-fiction author would dare to base a novel on such an outlandish scenario? How many readers would buy such a book, unless its intention was purely satirical?

We are all descended from Irish stew!
Spike Milligan, comedian

Is the reductionist rational-mechanistic model true? Almost certainly not, at least not in the way it is currently taught. Is it taught as ultimate truth? Oh yes. Does it determine our reality, individually and collectively? Again, yes. Very much so. And if we live in an unconscious, uncaring, lifeless universe, why should we care about anything? What do we matter, what does anything matter? Who cares? It's every man for himself, neo-Darwinian natural selection reigns supreme, and may the Devil take the hindmost.

WE ARE PROFOUNDLY INTER-CONNECTED

At the other end of the cosmological spectrum lies the proposition put forward in this book: the Universe is anything but an inert, lifeless machine. It is conscious. It is super-conscious. It is Consciousness itself. It is not only alive, It is Life itself. It is not only loving, It is Love itself. Now, we do understand that this is suspiciously close to what the animists, the Hindu *rishis*, the gurus, and the founders of the world's great religions have said from the start. We confess. This is not an original concept, but that's OK with us. In fact we feel validated, re-assured, to have the support, not only of the world's most intrepid scientific thinkers, but also of the world's wisest spiritual visionaries and of the world's most ancient people.

Philosophers and psychologists have had great difficulty understanding how inert, dead matter can lead to living consciousness. But that's not how it happens.
In our quantum view of the universe, consciousness

is ubiquitous. Intelligence is everywhere. And the deeper
you go beneath the surface, the more intelligence, the
more dynamism, the more awareness, until at the
foundation of the universe there is a field of pure,
abstract universal intelligence – universal Consciousness.
John Hagelin, PhD, physicist, brain researcher

Both quantum science and shamanic spirituality, as well as the world's mystical traditions, not to mention ancient "primitive" animism, say that we are deeply inter-connected, that some invisible matrix (the word means "mother," incidentally) exists throughout the universe, that our every thought contributes to the All-That-Is, and that we matter. We are important. Without us, nothing happens. Every part is essential to the whole. In a holographic universe, such as the one we inhabit, every part *is* the whole. There is no such thing as separation. Separation is a man-made, doubt-based concept. It is completely imaginary, although it appears very real in the lower frequencies.

I am he as you are he as you are
me and we are all together.
John Lennon, songwriter

Crazy, no? Taking the discussion to its logical conclusion, we see that this all-connecting, all-inclusive matrix, which has been known intuitively since the dawn of time, is precisely equivalent to what science calls the *Unified Field*, (or better yet, the *Quantum Vacuum* - don't you love that term?) which is precisely equivalent to what the Hindus call *Akasha, Brahma* or *Atman*, which is precisely equivalent to what the Native Americans call the *Great Spirit*, which is precisely equivalent to what the Jews, Christians and Muslims call *Jahweh, God* or *Allah*, which is precisely equivalent to what the Zulus call *Nkulunkulu* and Yoda calls *The Force*. We choose to call "It" the *Conscious Loving Universe*, a term that is not burdened by the baggage accumulated by centuries of organized religion, and thus free of divisive exclusivism and dogma.

MAY THE FORCE BE WITH YOU

Science and religion are not really separate, except in the fragmented, compartmentalized, left-brain-dominated mind of post-modern industrialized homo sapiens. So, boldly traveling in the opposite direction, let us ask ourselves: if the founders of the great world religions are correct in their assertion that "God is Love," and if "God" is in fact identical with the Quantum Field as understood by science, and if the Quantum Field is in fact All-That-Is, namely the Universe, then the logical, analytical mind can only come to one conclusion: the Universe is Love. Ergo, the Universe loves us! How could It do anything else? There is no rational alternative.

From the highest perspective, there is nothing but Love. Consequently, we are Love! We are loved. We are Love, Lover and Beloved, undivided, inseparable, indistinguishable. This understanding is the single most healing revelation available to us. It changes everything.

> *God is the sacred name for Reality.*
> *Reality is the secular name for God.*
> Michael Dowd, Christian minister

LOVE IS ALL YOU NEED

What is Love, love with a capital "L"? What does it do? What is its function in the Universe? The "Love" we are talking about is known by many names. For example, it was called *Akasha*** by the ancient Hindus. In the Abrahamic religions, Judaism, Christianity and Islam, it is universally agreed that "God is Love." The Love we are talking about is the primordial energy that creates and sustains the physical and the non-physical Universe, and may therefore be related to the subatomic gluon*** described by contemporary quantum scientists, and even to the recently discovered Higgs boson.

"Love" is perhaps the most misunderstood concept in the history of the human species. What we need to understand is the nature of the Love we are referring to. Clearly, we are not referring to everyday, romantic love, or to sex, or to friendship, or in fact to anything related to a human emotion. In human terms, the word "love" is closely aligned with the word "acceptance," but neither is that what we are talking about. We are talking about Love with a capital "L," the boundless power referred to in the *Star Wars* films as "The Force," the invisible but all-powerful energy field that pervades all of Creation. The space between the stars is not empty. It is filled with Love. As we said in the Definitions above, Love is the fundamental unifying and creative force of the Universe, and the critical thing to *grok* is that that Love is unconditional, absolutely unconditional. The Universe loves us more than we can possibly understand, as we shall see in the next chapter.

*Harvard economist David Korten uses the terms "Grand Machine" and "Distant Patrirch" to describe the competing dominant coamologies that make up current consensus reality. Dr. Korten proposes an all-encompassing "Integral Spirit" world-view as the "new story" that will at last awaken and unite humanity. This world-view is identical to the Trust Frequency paradigm.

**Akasha: the basis and essence of all things in the material world; the first material element created from the astral world (Air, Fire, Water, Earth are the other four in sequence.)

*** Gluon: a subatomic particle of a class that is thought to bind quarks together.

 THE SECOND ASSUMPTION

The Universe Loves Us Unconditionally.
It Gives Us Everything We Ask For.

Current Assumption

The universe does not know we exist.
How could it love us?
It's a great big machine, nothing more.
It would be absurd to say it loves us.

The entire process is literally mechanical, so much so that we can speak in terms of the mechanics of the Universe. That means we can figure out how it works and come to a rational, coherent understanding of the forces that govern our lives. Then we are in a position to decide how to get our thoughts in order, and how to adjust our vibratory state so that we actually live a life beyond our wildest dreams.

You're wearing scientific blinders that keep you from understanding.
Underneath, you have a belief that consciousness can be understood
by science, that consciousness emerges in the brain, that it is an
epiphenomenon. Comprehend what the mystics are saying!
Consciousness is prior and unconditioned. It is all there is.
There is nothing but God!

Joel Morwood* in conversation with Amit Goswami, physicist

$\mathcal{N}$ow we're in trouble, and we're only at the Second Assumption.
No longer can we hide, in blissful (or more likely, painful)
ignorance, behind the apron-strings of those who came before us.
It is time for *homo sapiens* to grow up, and to step into the "sapient"
aspect of our beings. As author J.K. Rowling (*Harry Potter*) said
in her 2008 commencement address at Harvard, there is an
expiration date on blaming our parents for our troubles. It is time
for each of us to take responsibility for what unfolds in our lives.
Absolute responsibility. With the new understanding of the nature
of reality that this book presents, our perceived "troubles" rapidly
fade away, and we cease to see ourselves as the "victims" of an
uncaring universe.

The cat is out of the bag, the bag has evaporated into the
quantum mists of time, and the cat is everywhere. *Meow!*
Let's see where this takes us. There is an immediate and obvious
paradox. If there is indeed nothing but Love, then how do we
account for the countless unpleasant things we read about in the
daily news? If God, or the Universe, whatever you want to call It,
is all-powerful, all-loving, and if nothing exists but Love, why then
do we see poverty, nationalism, war, violence, disease, and so on?

How can that be? It makes no sense at all from the rational point of view, unless we take another look at the definitions above, the ones we asked you to accept as absolutes. Let's start with Love:

Love is the fundamental unifying and
creative force of the Universe.

That is hardly your grandmother's concept of love, is it? It has very little to do with holding hands, St. Valentine's Day, champagne and roses, or making babies. Love with a capital "L" is a universal, all-pervading force, an inconceivably vast, infinitely powerful, limitlessly creative energy. Like the human love that holds two people together, and keeps the family together as the children grow up, the Love we are describing holds the entire Universe together as It unfolds. Love creates and sustains everything, from subatomic particles to mega-galaxies. It's the glue! It's the gluon! It's the Higgs Field. It's everything.

In terms of quantum physics, the phenomenon we are calling Love sounds a lot like the universal, omnipresent subatomic *gluon* which binds everything to everything else, at the most fundamental level. It has power, unlimited power, and in a less conscious, less loving universe, (yes, we know this sounds like a contradiction, but hang in there) that power could certainly have seen to it that all was in perfect, predictable, abundant, eternal harmony on this beautiful Earth.

Perhaps it was that way in the Garden of Eden, when everything was in perfect balance and nobody had to work, make decisions, or think for themselves. However, nothing in the definition above implies that the Universe will impose anything on us, including perfection. Think about that. In fact, the situation is precisely the opposite. We are free, completely free. The Universe is so hands-off in the day-to-day operation of our lives, and we are collectively so ignorant of the nature of the unconditional Love of the Universe, that on the surface it looks as though we have been given too much freedom, and have made a serious mess of things. However, that is exactly as it should be.

The current situation, challenging as it seems, is exactly as it was meant to be. It is what it is, and could not be anything else. It is the inevitable result of the countless trillions of free-will decisions that humanity has made from the very beginning. The trouble with all of those decisions, of course, is that they were made in the context of a defective set of assumptions. Fortunately for the future of our species, the stage is now set for the next evolutionary step in human development, one approach to which begins with understanding and adopting the ideas in this book.

THE NATURE OF UNCONDITIONAL LOVE

The greatest difference between the Love of the Universe, and the kind of love we humans are accustomed to, is that the Love of the Universe is absolutely unconditional. It is critical to understand this. Unconditional means unconditional – absolutely no conditions are imposed on us. The Universe created us, put us on the Earth, and set us loose. Here we are! Expressed another way, we humans chose to come to planet Earth, to incarnate into the physical, with the inalienable right of free will. Either way, here we are, living in a lovely but conflicted world entirely of our own making.

Difficult as it might be to accept, considering the mental bondage most of us endure, we humans are free, absolutely free, free to make of our lives what we will, with the unconditional, non-judgmental, loving support of the invisible forces of the Universe. Now that's Love with a capital "L!"

We are prisoners of our own minds.
Wallace Black Elk, Lakota elder

Free yourself from mental slavery.
None but ourselves can free our minds.
Bob Marley, musician

This realization has profound consequences. The Universe, or "God" (whatever you perceive that to be) is not running the show! You are! I am! We are! Of course, that is not really accurate. Separation is an illusion, a compelling holographic projection that originates in our minds. Since there is no such thing as separation, there can be no real difference between us and the omnipresent energy field we call God. As the Sufis say, God is closer than your own jugular vein. It's our planet, our life, and it is our choices that determine the nature of that life. And yet, we are not alone. We are not abandoned. Far from it. God is not busy seventeen eternal universes down the way, having completely forgotten about this little experiment here. He, She, or It is right here, right now, always has been, always will be, ready willing and able to fulfill our every desire and need.

As Connie is fond of saying, *"the Universe is standing at attention, awaiting our every request. It is chasing us around with a silver platter to offer us every experience we need to become the gift we promised to bring to the party."*

In fact, this is such an absolute that we can think of it in terms of a familiar mechanical metaphor, computer programming. The Universe, and the invisible powers that create and sustain all life, are programmed to give us everything we ask for. Everything. They must. They have no alternative. They love us unconditionally. This is a given, one of the immutable laws of the Universe. It is Its nature. It is absolute. *Ask and ye shall receive.* What could be more wonderful? Would a loving Universe do anything less?

> *Once you make a decision, the Universe conspires to make it happen.*
> Ralph Waldo Emerson, philosopher

CAREFUL WHAT YOU ASK FOR

So what's the problem? Why are we not living in a pristine paradise, with all the abundance, peace and harmony we could possibly imagine? Well folks, there's a catch. Freedom's not just another word for nothing left to lose. Along with the freedom, the free will, and the unconditional support, comes this startling and unavoidable fact: we get exactly what we ask for. No more, no less.

But wait! We didn't ask for this mess. We didn't ask for war, for poverty, for AIDS! Or did we? Let's dig a little deeper. Do we understand *how* our requests are sent to the Universe? Are we certain we know *what* we're asking for? Do we understand how we are doing the asking, intentionally or otherwise? Is it a matter of getting down on our knees and praying? Is it about becoming absolutely clear as to what we want, and verbalizing that specific desire?

> *Oh Lord, won't you buy me a Mercedes-Benz?*
> Janis Joplin, singer/songwriter

That's not quite it, although that approach might work, if you're in the right vibratory state, if you're in the Trust Frequency, if you are aligned with your soul's highest purpose. Were you one of the millions who bought and watched the DVD *The Secret* and tried to implement the "Abraham/Hicks" information in a quest for material wealth and the happiness you hoped that would bring? If so, you took a giant step forward in the evolution of consciousness: you discovered and learned to use an aspect of the power inherent in human thought and intention. You discovered that you can manipulate the unified field to manifest what you desire. Now, that's power! We are extraordinary, powerful beings who are so loved that we are given everything we ask for. That is an absolute. What most of us don't understand, however, is the complexity of what makes up our request. It is a multi-dimensional, many-faceted process. Nor do we understand the responsibility that comes with this power.

Perhaps you watched *The Secret* and, a week later, that shiny, brand-new, black Mercedes sports car really did manifest in your driveway. Perhaps a wonderful new partner really did walk into your life. Perhaps you really are the new CEO of Google. Stranger things have happened, although for the vast majority of those who tried so hard to manifest their dreams and desires, nothing much happened at all. Why? What critical element was missing?

OUR THOUGHTS ARE OUR REQUESTS

You know the answer already, in your inner being. It is this: we send our requests to the Universe via our thoughts, our consciousness. It's a frequency thing, a vibration thing. We know that, if we've got this far in this book. Furthermore, we now know that the nature, the frequency, of our thoughts is determined by our underlying assumptions. The question is, however, do we realize that our thoughts, manifested through our awareness, attention, attitudes and actions, are in fact *our requests* to the Universe? Do we realize that our thoughts and our resulting behaviors are the mechanism whereby we create our lives? It is critical that we understand this. The Universe is, in its deepest essence, a thought-form, a gigantic inter-connected inter-active web of thought. It follows that each thought we think is a part of that web. Every thought, without exception. There can be no alternative, can there?

So let's, just for a moment, think about the vibrational differences between fear and love. Let's think about the consequences of entertaining fearful thoughts. Let's think about worry, about anxiety, about negativity. Worry can be looked at as a form of "negative prayer." Our thoughts, whether positive or negative, are our requests to the unconditionally loving Universe, which goes ahead and fulfills our requests without judgment, so we inevitably create what we worry about. If I think an anxious, fear-based thought, let's say "I can't pay my rent this month" then guess what? I enter the scarcity frequency and bingo! I can't pay my rent this month, exactly as I requested. I un-intentionally created the situation, using the power of my consciousness. Next month may be a different story, fortunately, because, once we change the vibratory nature of our thoughts, our frequency changes, our consciousness expands, our requests to the Universe change, and so, eventually, do the outer circumstances of our lives.

As our frequency shifts to a higher state, we change both our inner attitudes and our outer behavior. We literally enter another reality, and the external circumstances of our lives change as and when appropriate, to reflect our new vision of the world. In the meantime, we are no longer attached to the outcome of our desires. This is extremely liberating.   The entire process is literally mechanical, so much so that we can speak in terms of the *mechanics* of the Universe. That means we can figure out how it works and come to a rational, coherent understanding of the forces that govern our lives. Then we are in a position to decide how to get our thoughts in order, and how to adjust our vibratory state so that we actually live a life beyond our wildest dreams.

To reiterate, the Love of the Universe is absolutely unconditional. Therefore all requests, without exception, are responded to and fulfilled without judgment. This is a fundamental, immutable, universal law.

*It is time to use your powers wisely and create realities
that are worthy of who you are. You can do this by
changing what you communicate to be real to the Universe
through your focus, and the identity you project by way of
that identity's behavior. If you do not make this fundamental
shift, you will continue to transmit the same old tired
requests to a Universe that will dispassionately and lovingly
respond with the same old tired and often toxic answers.*
Diana Luppi, *ET 101*

Fear-based negative thoughts and actions lower our vibration
and put us firmly in the fear frequency and generate undesired,
negative results just as surely as love- or trust-based positive
thoughts and actions raise our vibration, put us in the Trust
Frequency, and generate positive, desirable results. Collectively-
held beliefs and assumptions are exponentially more powerful than
individual thought-forms, so the vibratory state of our collective
belief system is critically important. Ultimately, each of us is in
charge of our own frequency, but be warned, walking in trust in
a fear-based consensus reality is not always easy. The generations-
deep conditioning of fear imbedded in our cellular memory has
created an almost insurmountable challenge. Although, having said
that, it's a lot easier to live in trust than to live in fear, period.

Do you see the scope of the situation our species faces?
This is not going to be a stroll in the park. It might feel more
like a stagger through the primeval swamp at times, as we
cleanse ourselves of old beliefs and habits, but we have to start
somewhere, and the awakening begins within each of us. We

have to learn to make the right requests, which becomes easy to the point of being automatic, once we have updated our belief system. The process is closely related to what the Buddhists call "right thinking." Right thinking is simply not possible if we base our thinking on false premises. Do you see how critical it is that we understand the vibrational consequences of our beliefs, thoughts and resulting behaviors?

> *The electron is made of the same stuff thoughts are made of. We're living in a wholly conceptual universe!*
> John Hagelin, PhD, physicist

Again, every thought and its underlying set of assumptions carries a particular vibration, which determines the frequency realm we inhabit at any particular moment, and the laws that apply to us in that realm. Consider the well-known saying "God will move mountains for those who trust in His loving power." It's not actually "God" who moves the "mountain." When we are in a state of trust, it is we who have ascended into the Trust Frequency, where there are no mountains in our way. The insurmountable obstacles that confront us in the lower frequencies simply do not exist in the higher planes. Such obstacles are a creation of our lower consciousness, of our conditioned mind, with the Universe dutifully fulfilling our every request. Fortunately, each obstacle we encounter in our lives is in fact an opportunity in disguise, a lesson waiting to be learned.

> *There are no problems, only opportunities.*
> Paramahansa Yogananda, yogi

AN ACCURATE REFLECTION

Returning to the subject of assumptions, then, it is clear that our core beliefs condition and determine our thoughts, and that our thoughts, as direct manifestations of our consciousness, have the power to determine what we create in our lives. If we carry negative core beliefs, such as "I am unlovable" for instance, or "I am unworthy," or "there is no such thing as God." "I am all alone in the world," or "there is not enough," the loving energies on the planet must organize themselves to present a reality based on what we believe to be true. That is how it works. That is how connected we are. That is how loved we are. That is how unconditional the Love of the Universe is. That is how involved we are in the day-to-day creation of our own reality, how responsible we are, each and every one of us, for whatever unfolds in our lives, no matter what form it may take. The outer circumstances of our lives accurately reflect the inner state of our beings, even to the extent that our souls will magnetize and influence other people's behavior towards us. We humans are far more profoundly inter-connected than we realize.

Once we understand that our assumptions are our requests to the Universe, and looking around us, we observe that the fundamental assumptions of the vast majority in our current society are based largely on fear, scarcity and doubt, and thus lie pretty low on the vibratory scale, we see the genesis of the conflicted world we see today. It is a mirror of our current consciousness, an accurate reflection of our collective inner state. We humans have created the world as it exists today, through our thoughts, decisions and actions over the centuries. Fortunately, that being the case, we can choose to re-create the world, once we have awakened and adopted a more accurate and positive vision of reality. That will be quite an undertaking, but what could be more important?

EACH FREQUENCY HAS ITS OWN LAWS

Consciously or otherwise, we choose the laws that govern our lives, moment by moment. Every thought has a specific frequency determined by the emotions and the feelings associated with that thought. We all know how it feels to be in love, and how, in that elevated vibrational state, the entire world seems magical. The laws that apply to us are somehow different, of a higher order. We also know how it feels to be afraid, or worried, or abandoned, or disappointed, and how, in that lowered vibrational state, the entire world seems bleak. If we believe in scarcity, if we place our attention on lack, our low vibratory state corresponds to the fear frequency. There is scarcity in the fear frequency. The illusion of scarcity creates poverty, famine, greed and hoarding, just as surely as the illusion of separation creates mistrust and national boundaries and barbed-wire fences and war.

We place ourselves in a particular frequency by the thoughts we choose, and by the actions we take related to those thoughts. Each frequency has its own laws and absolutes. We each choose the frequency we inhabit, whether consciously or not, and consequently, we actively choose the laws that govern our lives.

Of course, the vibratory situation is not completely cut-

and-dried. It is not a case of black or white. At any given time, each of us as individuals, and our society as a whole, expresses a mix of the positive and the negative, the fearful and the trusting, the competitive and the nurturing. The conditions we experience in our lives are the way the loving Universe mirrors to us what we believe to be true on the unconscious as well as the conscious level. Our outer lives are a perfect reflection of our inner reality, and constantly, moment by moment, show us the pathway to our own hearts, to our soul's purpose, if we pay attention. Once we understand that, we can use these indicators to go inside, examine our core beliefs and change them when and if we choose to do so.

So, for example, the next time someone shows up in our lives and treats us "just like Dad," we might want to thank that person for showing us our unconscious feelings about Dad, and giving us the chance to grow, instead of choosing to react in anger and denial and thereby endlessly perpetuate our unconscious behavior.**

IT STARTS WITHIN EACH OF US

How can we change the circumstances of our individual lives, and, more importantly, improve the way our lives feel? By changing our assumptions, obviously. It's really as basic as that. It's one of the few things we can do, without needing permission from anyone else. We don't have to go down to City Hall or the county building and stand in line for a New Assumption Permit. We can change our minds any time we like. Every woman takes that for granted, or at least so it seems to the men in their lives. How can we change the collective mind-set? By changing our own. It starts within each of us as individuals, as tiny sparks of light in the darkness. We are not powerless pawns swept along by the overwhelming tides of history. We are incredibly powerful spiritual beings with the inalienable right and ability, each of us, to re-invent ourselves and to change our world, and to influence, to awaken, those around us by our loving example, by the positive vibratory frequency that we emanate. As we come to understand the conscious loving nature of the Universe, and the fact that we are inseparable from It, we become an unstoppable force for positive change in the world. We stop seeing ourselves as victims. We stop playing the blame/shame/guilt game. We stop projecting our self-guilt onto others.

We humans created the "civilized" world we live in today, every aspect of it. Accordingly, we can re-create it. All we need is the vision, some version of the information in this book, and the desire, courage, will and patience to apply it. We will inevitably have to overcome some resistance emanating from our own conditioned minds, and from our friends and family in the consensus reality, who will inevitably think we have gone crazy, but with practice, operating from the Trust Frequency becomes second nature. Once these new assumptions settle deep into our beings, we learn to live and breathe them the way we did the old ones.

> Each individual's thoughts, attitudes and emotions emit
> energetic fields. These individual field environments not
> only affect you, your health and perspective on life, they
> also can influence your relationships and experiences in

your social field environments as you interact with people,
or even if you are merely in the same room with other people.
Can we change our individual, social, and even planetary field
environments and create the ones in which we choose to live? Yes!

Institute of HeartMath Newsletter Fall 2009. Vol 8 No. 4

* *Joel Morwood, author and mystic: In the early 1980's Morwood left a*
successful film career in Hollywood to pursue a mystical path. He is the
director of the Center for Sacred Sciences in Eugene, Oregon.

** See *Vows of Love,* on page 301.

THE THIRD ASSUMPTION

We Create Reality By The Power Of Our Consciousness.

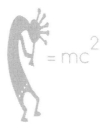

Current Assumption

Consciousness has nothing to do with reality.

Reality is something external, something that happens to us.

It was fixed in place long ago by forces beyond our control.

Life is pretty much a roll of the dice. Luck of the draw!

*The boundless diversity of existence
is the ever-unfolding Universe coming
to understand and experience itself
and its unlimited potential for creative
expression. One of the ways the Universe
explores its own potential is to imagine
and then create powerful, visionary creatures
such as ourselves, and then set them free.
We are cosmic thought-forms made manifest.
We are roving sensory organs of the divine.*

THE THIRD ASSUMPTION   57

*Because you have the power to create absolutely anything
you want, your natural state is one of infinite abundance.
In your natural state you don't "lack" anything. Nothing
is missing. No desire ever goes unfulfilled. As an Infinite Being,
you're also in a constant state of joyfulness and peace.*
Robert Scheinfeld, author

*No problem can be solved from the same level
of consciousness that created it.*
Albert Einstein

There is nothing either good or bad, but thinking makes it so.
William Shakespeare

What exactly is consciousness? That is a question that
has challenged scientists and philosophers since the day we
discovered fire, if not a million years earlier. We will go into the
subject in great detail in the next chapter, and again later in the
book. (See "A Note on Consciousness," page 217.) For now, it
is sufficient to understand that there are two fundamental types
of consciousness that concern us here, Universal consciousness,
and human consciousness. The former can be thought of as the
underlying, all-pervading primordial life-energy of the Universe,
while human consciousness is that aspect of the aliveness of the
Universe which each of us can access and experience through
our individual bodies, brains and minds. At the highest level, of
course, there is only one undifferentiated consciousness, but we
humans nevertheless experience our individual realities through
the filters of our own minds and the contents thereof, namely our

assumptions, beliefs and opinions, our world-view.

The boundless diversity of existence is the ever-unfolding Universe coming to understand and experience itself and its unlimited potential for creative expression. One of the ways the Universe explores its own potential is to imagine and then create powerful, visionary creatures such as ourselves, and then set them free. We are cosmic thought-forms made manifest. We are roving sensory organs of the Divine. Our part is to engage joyfully with the great adventure of life, and thereby share our every experience with the ever-unfolding Source from whence we came.

It is helpful, as well as scientifically legitimate, to think of the Universe and all of its component parts in terms of frequency, wavelength and the interactions among those parts and frequencies. It all comes down to vibrations. Depending on how one defines consciousness, any advanced contemporary physicist would have to agree that we humans are highly conscious electromagnetic beings living in a highly conscious, interactive, radically inter-connected electromagnetic quantum Universe, a Universe that we do not yet fully understand. Scientific phenomena such as quantum entanglement, the observer effect and bi-locality are now well established. Our cosmology, our understanding of the nature of the Universe, is rapidly evolving. We are just beginning to glimpse the possibilities.

Let us consider a fairly well-understood phenomenon: light. The characteristics of light are determined by its frequency, by its vibratory rate. Invisible infra-red vibrations, which we experience as heat, occur beneath the visible range, and then at ever-higher frequencies, the colors of the visible spectrum from red through violet are experienced, and then higher still, we move into the invisible ultra-violet range, once again beyond the reach of the human sense of sight. And there are countless higher and lower harmonic frequencies of radiation, each one of them with its own unique characteristics, such as radio waves, X-rays and cosmic rays. The segment of the electromagnetic spectrum visible to the human eye is merely a tiny segment of All-That-Is.

INFINITE POSSIBILITIES

So it is with the Universe, which consists of, and manifests as, an unlimited number of possible vibratory realities or universes, each with its own distinct laws, each vibrating within its own distinct frequency spectrum. The inhabitants of one reality may be quite unaware of the inhabitants of another, in the same way that the conscious, living microorganisms that make up our bodies may be quite unaware that the year 2012 was an election year in America. It is a matter of scale, in many cases.

Countless "alternative universes" co-exist with this one, in much the same way that the vast array of telephone, television, microwave and radio channels co-exist in different frequencies in the airwaves all around us. With the appropriate "tuner," we can decide whether to watch the evening news, answer a cell phone call, or listen to Beethoven's Fifth Symphony. Or we can shut everything off and go to sleep. The different vibratory realities are still there, all around and inside of us, but we are completely unaware of them.

The appearance that all (or most) of us seem to share a pretty consistent world is because everyone sharing the "human reality show" is attuned to the same fundamental set of frequencies. At some level, we, or the subatomic information we are composed of, have made an agreement to appear in this form. At least for the time being.

> *You create your world by your thoughts.*
> *You create your own world. Once you*
> *speak it out there, that's the way it's going*
> *to be, that's where it started. That's the way*
> *the world was created, with a thought and*
> *a word, and then everything came into action.*
> Bertha Grove, Ute tribal elder
> (from the authors' film *In Search Of The Future*)

Each of our fundamental assumptions and its accompanying emotional, vibrational frequency is associated with a particular segment of the frequency spectrum of the Universe. Our relationship to that frequency is determined by our thoughts, which are outgrowths of our consciousness – our assumptions, and the attitudes and actions that go along with them. We are all familiar with the 1960s concept of "bad vibrations" and "good vibrations."

> *I'm pickin' up good vibrations.*
> The Beach Boys

These terms can be taken quite literally. A negative, fearful thought carries a lower "vibe," a lower vibratory energy, than a higher loving or trusting thought. It is not too difficult to rank our assumptions according to the scale of frequency, and from this ranking, we can get a pretty good idea of the consequences of using negative and erroneous assumptions to determine our reality. And yet that is exactly what humanity has done, unconsciously, for hundreds of generations. We would never do such an absurd thing if we were consciously aware of what we were doing. Would we?

THERE ARE NO MISTAKES

As we saw in the previous chapter, the Universe is completely neutral as it fulfills our requests. Put another way, its love is unconditional. The Universe simply reads the emotional/vibratory message we send it, and responds accordingly. It is rather like the printer attached to my laptop, which prints out precisely what I tell it to, once I hit the "print" button. The printer makes no judgment as to content. It simply follows my instructions.

> *The reality that you live is nothing more than an*
> *audio-visual demonstration of where your attention is.*
> *The universe presumes that your attention is on what*
> *you want and graciously provides you with more of the same.*
> Diana Luppi, *ET 101*

Consciously or not, we choose our frequency each moment of each day. We send the vibratory message, act accordingly, and BAM! Here we are in the reality of our choosing. If our assumptions are based primarily on scarcity, fear, and separation, we create precisely those things in our lives, whether intentionally or not. Very often, as we consciously attempt to create something we desire, the opposite occurs, because our fundamental negative beliefs, with their accompanying emotional fields, override the positive outcome we are trying to imagine and create. Deep down in our subconscious, the saboteur is at work, signaling to us that we have work to do. Which, it turns out, is a blessing in disguise. Remember, there is only Love! The more we begin to understand what is going on, the more we become grateful for the messages we receive from our "higher selves," from circumstance.

AN UNCOMPROMISING COMMITMENT

The challenge of this transformative inner work is to go deep, deep enough to root out our old, unconscious, outdated core beliefs, and to replace them permanently with new assumptions of our own conscious choosing. This is not easy work, and it is easy to fool ourselves into believing we have made the shift. The process will not be effective if we merely attempt to overlay the new ideas on the foundation of a pre-existing belief system that we have seen to be hopelessly flawed. We will simply be building a new house of cards. In order to gain long-term access to the Trust Frequency, one must make a deep personal commitment. It is not sufficient to read this book, to say: "Oh yes, I know that," to assume that the job is done, and move on to the next "self-help" book on the shelf without ever actually doing the real work. It takes an uncompromising commitment to one's own inner growth, and the willingness to put these ideas into practice, no matter what. The challenge is to act (translate thoughts into action) from a place of trust in the conscious loving Universe!

THE LAW OF ATTRACTION

A great deal of attention has been given lately to the so-called Law of Attraction, also known as the Law of Manifestation. These "laws" are, in fact, alternative ways of looking at the Third Assumption. In a nutshell, as 2005's *The Secret* and *What the #$*! Do We (K)now!?* pointed out, the reality we create directly depends on where we choose to put our attention. If we place our attention on the negative, on things we don't like or want, we attract, and thereby empower and reinforce the negative, which is one of the reasons the "do-gooders" of the world are not as effective as they might wish. Think about it. By focusing one's attention on environmental "problems," for instance, we may just be worsening and perpetuating those very problems. We place ourselves firmly in a stressful lower frequency realm where unpleasant things happen, and we thereby add our emotional energy to the negative. We amplify the frequency where the "problems" are very real and unsolvable. The good news is that, by so doing, we will create circumstances that, if we are alert, will act as guideposts on our journey.

A RADICAL UPWARD SHIFT

Buckminster Fuller recommended that, instead of attempting to fix the existing paradigm, a much more effective course of action is simply to create a new one. The outdated paradigm then simply fades away. That is exactly what we are proposing. It is much easier to change ourselves, than to try to compel change in others. It is better to focus on creating what we want, rather than on fighting against what we don't want, to put our energy towards waking up and co-creating a green world of peace and harmony, rather than on angry blog posts and demonstrations against polluters, because, once the changes we are talking about in this book take effect, there will be no need for an "environmental movement."

Pollution will have become a long-forgotten aberration. Greed, hoarding and the attendant social inequities will vanish, and war will be an absurdity. We honor and respect all those brave, well-meaning souls out there in the political world and the anti-war, civil rights, environmental and social justice movements, but only in a radical upward shift in human consciousness do we see real hope for permanent change. Everything else is the equivalent of putting a Band-Aid on a hemorrhage. It's hopeless. It's a solution-less dilemma, much like allopathic medicine trying to fix the symptoms while ignoring the underlying cause of the illness. It doesn't work. The only way out is UP!

LISTEN, ALIGN, ALLOW

Thanks to the valuable information brought to the world by programs like *The Secret*, it is now widely established that it is possible to manipulate the universal consciousness to get what we want. The enormously popular film and book offered tools and ideas for implementing the Law of Attraction, and spawned an entire industry based on the Abraham-Hicks "manifestation" principles. *The Secret* made millions for the person who made the film, made stars of the people interviewed, and may well have helped a lot of other people to achieve their material and other goals. For many, however, it simply did not work in the long run. It gave a tantalizing glimpse of the possibilities, but it also laid some important groundwork for those of us who are ready to wake up to a higher reality.

Why did *The Secret* not work? Most of us, unfortunately, are still operating from a fear-based paradigm, in which we have been trained and conditioned to seek security and love through achievement and material possessions in a scarce universe where we must compete to survive. The acquisition of more stuff is not going to help us, in the long term, no matter how good that new Mercedes, that new job, or that new relationship makes us feel at first. The information in this book goes well beyond *The Secret*. In fact, it provides vital information that *The Secret* was missing. We need deep, permanent inner change if we are to find true fulfillment, and that is not going to happen if we continue to base our reality on a set of erroneous assumptions, including the idea that material success will make us happy, or that there's a quick fix that does not require any effort on our part.

On the other hand, once we realize that we are unconditionally loved, in a conscious, loving, abundant Universe that is waiting for the gift we promised we'd bring to the world, then we automatically become happy. Rather than trying to manipulate the Universe to fulfill our desires, we seek instead to discover what the Universe wants for us, and we listen to our inner guidance, align with what we hear, and then allow the Universe to do its part. We remember our unique gift, and become our unique purpose. We have moved into the Trust Frequency, and it no longer matters how much material stuff we do or do not accumulate. At the same time, there is no limit to the abundance that may come our way.

IT'S NOT WORKING

Most of us are constantly engaged in a sincere and ongoing attempt to improve the world we live in, whether in the limited sense of "selfishly" improving our own lot, or for the larger good of humanity. We study the news, we listen to NPR, we do everything in our power to be well-informed, a certain percentage of us even go to the polls and elect a new "leader" every four years. We put our faith in the messy social experiment called democracy. Against all odds, we hope that the next round of politicians will be better than the last. We see the inadequacies of the world, and we set out to change things. We view ourselves as responsible co-creators of a better world for our children's children. The problem is, we, our elected leaders, and everyone else are still operating under the same old set of fear-based assumptions, the very ones that got us into this intractable mess in the first place. It's not working, and it never will, for obvious reasons.

IT'S THE LAW

On the other hand, if our deepest assumptions about ourselves,

about the world, about our bodies, about our species, about
the Universe, come from a higher vibratory frequency, if we
take for granted the fact that we are fundamentally good, that
we are loving, that we are loved, and that the Universe is a safe,
supportive, abundant place, we effortlessly, with ease and grace,
create and attract to ourselves prosperity, security, and love, and
contribute to the creation of a peaceful, joyful, abundant world
for those around us. It is our thoughts that do the creating. Put
another way, it is our state of consciousness (as manifested
through our thoughts) that does the creating, by determining our
frequency, and by delivering our creative requests to a receptive
and unconditionally loving Universe. A positive mind-set creates
positive outcomes and abundant health, and the opposite is equally
true. That is the way it works. It's the law. The loving Universe
simply reflects back to us the hidden contents of our minds.

THE PICTURE IS ALREADY PAINTED

There is another, even higher, way of looking at this. Let's step
back for a moment and ask ourselves: Is it really a matter of
working to co-create a better world, or of simply awakening to a
paradise that already exists? What if everything is already perfect?
What if the picture is already painted? What if the "sustainable"
world we are working so hard to create is already here? What if
the entire concept of sustainability is merely a pale shadow of
an abundant reality that already exists, that has always existed?
What if it has been here all along just waiting for us to wake up,
recognize it, and align with it? What if there's a party going on and

we're all invited, but we've mislaid the directions which would tell us how to get there?

> *The picture is already painted, it is perfect. Let it be.*
> O'Dell, Lucille & Arnold, Robin: *Endless Song of Infinite Balance*

The Secret tells us we can use the Law of Attraction to manipulate the infinitely abundant Universe to get what we want, or more accurately to get what we think we want at any given moment. This may well be true, but why would we do that if the Universe wants more for us than we can imagine from the perspective of our limited conditioning in the lower frequencies? Is the Law of Attraction really the answer? Perhaps not, unless it is combined with the kind of inner work suggested by this book.

Our challenge is to develop so much trust in the guidance and support of the loving Universe that we feel confident walking into the unknown, moving in the direction of a reality that we are unable to see clearly from our current perspective, but knowing from a very deep place that we are on the right track, that we are aligned with our higher purpose.

THE FOURTH ASSUMPTION

Our Awareness, Assumptions, Attitudes, Attention, Alignment, Actions and Allowing Determine Our Frequency. They Are Our Requests To The Universe.

Current Assumption

What do these things have to do with my life?
In any case I do not make assumptions.
Assumptions make an ass out of you and me.

There is a very big difference, vibrationally, between mentally visualizing something and hoping and praying that it will manifest, on the one hand, and deeply knowing that it is so, and taking committed action accordingly, on the other. The emotional and mental state, and therefore the frequency, of the latter, is completely different from the former, and this is what distinguishes the two.

So far in this book, we have examined the way in which the state of our consciousness, namely the vibratory rate of our subconscious and conscious thoughts, feelings, beliefs, opinions and attitudes, determines the frequency at which we are vibrating. We have learned that what we think and believe actively creates our individual and collective experience as human beings. Our vibratory state is what dictates the nature of our reality. Quantum science says that, as the observer, we are the indispensable agent which brings the material world into being. Nothing exists until it is observed, at which point the reality experienced by the observer emerges from the *implicate* or hidden order and manifests in the *explicate order*, to use the terminology of physicist David Bohm.

Breaking it down, it is our consciousness, which consists of our awareness, our assumptions, our attitudes, the free-will choice as to where we place our attention, our degree of alignment with our inner guidance or higher purpose, and, most importantly, the committed actions we take, that determines the frequency we inhabit, which in turn, brings into being the reality we experience. Every aspect of it, without exception. There is one more indispensable factor. Lastly, we must let go, surrendering any attempt at control. We must step back, trust the unknown, and allow the loving Universe to do its part. The picture is already painted, remember? This is where we can gauge the quality of our trust, our sincerity, our willingness and ability to let go of the fear-based need for control, without holding back. Are we capable of an unconditional commitment to a new, trust-based way of being in the world? Ultimately, it's not about sincerity or willingness, it's about a full-blown, no-holds-barred immersion into a higher trust-based vibratory reality where such terms are meaningless. Please know that this is not always easy. It takes practice!

BEINGS OF POWER AND BEAUTY

As a species, we do not have a very positive self-image. Most people, in the developed world at least, assume that we are insignificant, meaningless and powerless specks, lost in the vastness of an incomprehensible and unconscious universe. There are those who sincerely believe that the world would be better off without us. This attitude towards *homo sapiens* is understandable. It is an inevitable outcome of the fundamentally negative assumptions about ourselves, and feelings about our consequent behavior, that have dominated our social belief systems for thousands of years, no matter what culture we come from. And yet...

> *Although you appear in earthly form*
> *Your essence is pure Consciousness.*
> *You are the fearless guardian of Divine Light.*
> *So come, return to the root of the root*
> *Of your own soul.*
> Jalaluddin Rumi, 13th Century Persian sufi poet

There is another side to the story, one vastly more inspiring. How many of us know, truly know, that we are beings of boundless power and beauty? Of the millions of species on this planet, we are the only ones with the potential to elevate ourselves, should we choose to do so, to a higher state of consciousness. We have already been shown some of the possibilities by visionary forerunners like Jesus and Buddha, Mozart, Gandhi, Leonardo and Einstein. The dolphins and the whales are already there, perhaps, highly conscious, social beings that they obviously are. But the dolphins and the whales, wise, peaceful and harmonious as they might be, do not seem to possess our potential for art, for music, for invention, for community, for celebration, for conscious evolution, for space travel, for manifestation on an unimaginable level. Or at least we are unable to see their true nature from this frequency. We appear to be unique.

> *What a piece of work is a man, how noble in reason,*
> *how infinite in faculties, in form and moving how*
> *express and admirable, in action how like an angel,*
> *in apprehension how like a god! The beauty of the*
> *world, the paragon of animals - and yet, to me,*
> *what is this quintessence of dust?*
> William Shakespeare, *Hamlet*

THE SEVEN A's

What exactly is consciousness? Scientists and philosophers alike have a hard time defining the phenomenon. A few years back, we participated in a sold-out conference in Santa Monica concerning the issues raised in the film *What the #$*! Do We (K)now!?* This highly popular film looked at quantum science and human consciousness and interviewed a dozen or more leading thinkers, philosophers, academics and researchers. During the final panel discussion featuring many of the authorities in the film, which was specifically about the subject, someone from the audience asked the question: "how do you define consciousness?" Interestingly, the panel was flummoxed. Nothing resembling a consensus was reached.

Is it possible to define consciousness as experienced from the human perspective? We are not talking about esoteric brain science here, but about how consciousness works from the inside, from the operator's standpoint. The inner workings of our individual and collective consciousness can readily be understood if we break the phenomenon down into seven elements, seven words co-incidentally beginning with the letter "A": Awareness, Assumption, Attitude, Attention, Alignment (or Attunement,) Action and Allowing. We call them the Seven A's.

Once we understand the workings of our own consciousness, and put that understanding to work in the context of our newly upgraded assumptions about the nature of the Universe, in other words, once we have installed our new, improved operating system, there is no stopping us. We have become exponentially more intelligent. We are using more of our innate abilities. We have effortlessly and consciously evolved into a higher state of being.

CONSCIOUSNESS & THE SEVEN A's

The fact is, consciousness is vastly more than physics or psychology have yet dared to imagine. Consciousness lies at the deepest root level of the universe, predating everything in creation. Consciousness was, before anything came into being. If there really was such an event as the Big Bang, it can best be described as the un-manifest becoming manifest, the implicate becoming explicate, the unborn-but-living Universe awakening into self-awareness, with each and every sentient being throughout all of time and space contributing, through the phenomenon science calls quantum entanglement, to that ever-unfolding awareness.

Once more, we need to take a break. Let's make sure we understand the meanings of these eight vital terms. The dictionary that came with our trusty old Mac laptop computer offers the following definitions:

CONSCIOUSNESS

<u>noun</u>: *the fact of awareness by the mind of itself and the world.*
On the superficial level addressed by this dictionary definition, consciousness is defined as merely "the fact of awareness by the mind." Clearly however, consciousness is more than a mere "fact." There is a vast spectrum of states of human consciousness, ranging from total anaesthesia to deep sleep to the various levels of awake-ness, all the way up to the highest levels of super-conscious "enlightenment." There are levels of consciousness far beyond that encompassed by the human mind. Consciousness is in fact the primordial manifestation of the energy of the Universe. It is literally beyond human comprehension.

THE SEVEN A'S

For practical purposes, on the level of human experience, we can break the phenomenon of consciousness down into its seven interwoven aspects, the Seven A's:

AWARENESS

<u>noun</u>: *having knowledge or perception of a situation or fact.*
The most fundamental and obvious aspect of consciousness is the phenomenon of awareness. An unconscious entity is, simply,

one which has no awareness. An unconscious person has no idea of his or her surroundings, whereas a conscious person perceives his or her inner and outer environment, on a level corresponding to his or her degree of awake-ness. Pure awareness is the super-conscious unconditioned state that is the goal of meditation, Nirvana. The meditator is simultaneously aware of everything and of nothing, dissolved into the All-That-Is.

ASSUMPTION

<u>noun</u>: *a thing that is accepted as true or as certain to happen, without proof.*
Our awareness is profoundly conditioned by our assumptions, by our core beliefs concerning the nature of reality. The nature of our assumptions and their vibratory rate or frequency has a huge effect on the state of our consciousness, creating a filter through which all of our perceptions and experiences are channeled. Anything excluded by the filter is removed from our perception, or it is distorted beyond recognition, with profound implications for the human experience.

ATTITUDE

<u>noun</u>: *a settled way of thinking or feeling about someone or something, typically one that is reflected in a person's behavior.*
Our attitude, the stance we adopt toward any given subject, is almost entirely determined by our assumptions about that subject. It is virtually impossible to have a positive attitude concerning someone or something we hold negative assumptions about and vice versa.

ATTENTION

noun: *notice taken of someone or something; the regarding of someone or something as interesting or important.*

By attention we mean the conscious focusing of our awareness on a particular object or subject. As humans, we have a great deal of control over the nature, focus and intensity of our attention. Depending on where and how we choose to focus our attention, we place ourselves in vibratory alignment with the subject of our attention, for better or for worse.

ALIGNMENT

noun: *arrangement in a straight line, or in correct or appropriate relative positions; a position of agreement or alliance.*

The foregoing aspects of our consciousness work together to place us in "a position of agreement or alliance" with whatever it is that we have chosen to place our attention on. We have the freedom to choose to align ourselves with the highest vision of which we are capable. Or not.

> *When we align ourselves with the purposes of heaven and act in common accord, we have all of the natural forces working with us, supporting us, helping us.*
> Ken Carey, *Return of the Bird Tribes*

ACTION

noun: *a thing done; an act; the fact or process of doing something, typically to achieve an aim.*

Our actions, when taken in the context of conscious choice and decision, in alignment with our inner guidance and intuition, constitute the most active aspect of our consciousness. They serve to activate the mechanisms of creation. Our actions are our consciousness made manifest in the material world.

ALLOWING

<u>verb</u>: *to give (someone) permission to do something; to give the necessary time or opportunity for.*

The final aspect of our individual consciousness is possibly the most important. It is the one where we step back in a state of trust, surrender, and let go of our individuality, melting into the oneness, and allowing the Universe to play its part. We act and then release. The power is in the release.

WE PLAY A VITAL ROLE

The Seven A's each relate to free-will choices we can make, which in turn determine our frequency, which in turn determines our reality. Do you see how free we are, once we understand the power of our own consciousness, and learn to use these wonderful tools?

THE HIGHEST FREQUENCY

What is an assumption? Without question it's an idea, an opinion, a belief, a thought-form, but it's more than just a cerebral or intellectual concept. It also has certain feelings or emotional connotations associated with it. There is a close relationship to another word: attitude. Taken together, we can say that our assumptions are some combination of thought, understanding, feeling and attitude, each of which, in turn, corresponds to a particular vibratory frequency. Based on the nature of these thoughts, feelings, and attitudes, we can say that every assumption carries a particular frequency. As we become more sensitive, we can clearly feel or sense the difference between a higher vibration and a lower one. We easily distinguish between the frequency associated with fear and doubt, and the frequency associated with love and trust. As we become more spiritually attuned, we become increasingly aware of everything in between. There exists an unlimited number of these vibratory states, each with its own distinct reality, and its own distinct laws.

The highest spiritual frequency is the Trust Frequency, which is identical to the state the Buddhists call Nirvana. We could think of it as "Heaven." It is the portal to a world of unfathomable peace, abundance, and harmony. For most of us, this higher world is beyond our ability to conceive, since we are conditioned to accept the laws in our current frequency as real, and as the only reality available to us. Is there something higher, a vibratory state beyond the Trust Frequency? There's no way to know, from our current perspective, but there may well be. Why not? If the Universe is infinite, why should there be any limitation on consciousness?

At the lower end of the vibratory spectrum we find, predictably, the fear frequency, with all of its unpleasant phenomena, like doubt, suspicion, aggression, violence, disease, greed, hoarding, poverty and so on. We could think of it as "Hell." Between the two extremes, there is a vibratory continuum wherein each of us spends most of our time, somewhere on the undulating scale of our ever-unfolding life. We are all capable of experiencing the full spectrum, and most of us already have, to some extent. We have all been in love. We have all been in fear. The question is, can we consciously choose our place on the continuum, and if so, how? Is this something we can learn? The answer is: yes!

VISUALIZE THIS

Beginning in the late 1960s there was born a movement that became known as the "New Age," a worldwide societal awakening which spawned a number of bestselling books by Louise Hay, Lynn Andrews, Deepak Chopra, Wayne Dyer and numerous other visionaries. The movement coincided with, or rather, emerged from, the widespread introduction of Eastern mysticism, Native American thought, psychotropic substances, psychotherapy, organic gardening, and the peace, consciousness, feminist and environmental movements to an unsuspecting Western society. Personal spirituality began to replace organized religion, which had become increasingly antiquated and irrelevant in the post-industrial world. A major upgrade in the collective consciousness had begun.

One of more popular New Age techniques had to do with affirmations, simple positive statements that proliferated as bumper stickers and refrigerator magnets. All one has to do, according to the proponents of this method, is to repeatedly visualize, meditate upon, or think about the outcome we desire. This is a good step in the right direction, a practice closely related to the techniques offered in *The Secret*, where students of the "Law of Attraction" are taught to place their mental focus on the things they want to manifest, and not on the things they do not want. Think "I want to be rich," as opposed to "I do not want to be poor."

COMMITTED ACTION

Unfortunately, as discussed in the previous chapters, it's not quite that simple. There are still major missing pieces to the puzzle. There is work to do, inner work. First and foremost, our flawed assumptions are deeply involved in the manifestation process, and they very often sabotage us. One cannot overlay trust on a fear-based paradigm. Mere positive thinking will not transform our lives permanently, Norman Vincent Peale notwithstanding.

We have to go deeper. And there is another critical element: we have to "walk it," not just "talk it." It's not enough merely to visualize the life we desire, although that certainly helps. Our *committed actions* are also a vital part of the process. It is our actions, and the degree of trust in which we take those actions, that determine the frequency we are operating from, and "lock in" the desired outcome from the undifferentiated quantum field of all possibility. It's a little like hitting the "return" key or the "save" command on your computer, once you are satisfied with what you have entered.

It is clear from the previous chapters that we create our own reality, individually and collectively, and that the outer circumstances in our lives are the result of the thoughts, decisions and actions we have taken throughout our lives. But why do so many of the things we want most, our most treasured dreams, seem unobtainable, out of reach? As we now know, this is the result of unconscious basic assumptions. What can we do about the situation?

DISCERNMENT

Visualization techniques, positive thinking, and *The Secret* were important steps in showing us an unsuspected potential of the human mind. The knowledge that we have the power to manifest our desires has been an important revelation in the unfolding awareness of humanity, and in our understanding of the mechanics of the Universe, but this book takes it to a higher level. In this next stage of our development, we must ask ourselves, what *do* we want, really, and *why*? Where *do* our desires come from? Do they originate in our trusting/connected/aligned higher selves or in our lower, fear-driven separate egos? It can be quite challenging to tell the difference, sometimes.

The fact is, we can manifest anything we desire, if we choose to, but there is a more exciting and inspiring alternative. Now that we understand the vibratory consequences of a fear-based paradigm, it is easy to see that blindly manifesting desires which come from a lower frequency, from fear of poverty, or from greed, insecurity or competitiveness, has a serious downside to it. We need to ask ourselves: why would we continue to enmesh ourselves in a world-out-of-balance and remain engaged in a fear-driven reality where the human heart and spirit are negated and bottom-line economics robs us and everyone around us of our birthright of health, beauty, joy, balance and abundance?

To lift ourselves out of the *status quo*, to raise our frequency to a higher level, we must first listen to our inner voice, our inner promptings. Then we must discern where these inner promptings and desires come from. Do they emanate from the conditioned mind, from a "lower self" that is desperate for a sense of security and love – or do they come from our "higher self," our soul, in alignment with our higher purpose? How can we tell the difference? We watch circumstance for clues. We observe the signs. We watch the actions of others. We watch our own actions. We trust our feelings, our intuition. We align with them, and then we take bold, committed action and go where the brave dare not go. As Connie says: *"Ask not for what you want from the Universe. Ask for what the Universe wants for you."*

Keep your feet on the Red Road
Your eyes looking Within
Your ears listening to the Silence
And Your Heart full of Love and Peace
Spiritwalker

IT'S A THREE-STEP PROCESS

Positive thinking, visualization techniques and the "Law of
Manifestation" are all well and good. They are an excellent start,
but they comprise only the second step in a three-step process,
a process that, to be successful, must begin with an accurate set
of assumptions. That is the first step, a preliminary phase, the
absence of which will sabotage all of one's best efforts. Many of
us have to overcome deep-seated beliefs that we do not deserve
an abundant life. We feel that we are unlovable. We seek control
of our lives, and attempt to compel the loving Universe to give us
what we want, using the power of our will. But, if we believe we
are unworthy, or are operating from a superficial belief overlay, no
real trust exists. We are faking it. We are in the wrong vibratory
frequency, and we will not reap the benefits we desire. We may
get a lot of stuff, but we will not be truly happy. We will always be
looking for more. We must ask ourselves, are today's millionaires
and billionaires any happier than we are? Really? To find lasting
happiness, we must, first of all, replace our hidden fear-based
assumptions with ideas like the ones this book offers. Having done
that, visualization techniques will have a better chance of working
in a truly beneficial way, but it is highly likely that we will simply let
such things go.

Once we have taken the first two steps correctly, there is a third essential step, one that few people understand. One has to put one's money where one's mouth is. It is not enough simply to hold a mental vision of what we want. It's not a matter of merely thinking or affirming that we trust the loving Universe and praying for whatever it is that we want, especially if deep down we don't really believe we deserve what we are asking for. We repeat: visualization is only one step in a three-step process. It also takes action, bold, committed action from a place of deep trust, and it is this final step in the process that actually triggers the desired outcome, by placing us in the frequency of love and abundance, the Trust Frequency, thus causing the explicate manifestation to emerge from the un-manifest implicate order. This is the creative process whereby the loving Universe responds to our requests. The tricky thing is that the Universe responds to our requests whether or not we are in the appropriate vibratory state to receive what we think we want. That is its unchangeable nature. The holographic Universe out-pictures a world precisely aligned with our inner reality. Hence the apparently negative manifestations we see all around us.

Until one is committed, there is hesitancy,
the chance to draw back, always ineffectiveness.
Concerning all acts of initiative and creation,
there is one elementary truth, the ignorance of
which kills countless ideas and splendid plans:
The moment one definitely commits oneself,

then Providence moves too*.
All sorts of things occur to help one that would
never otherwise have occurred. A whole stream
of events issues from the decision, raising in one's
favor all manner of unforeseen incidents and meetings
and material assistance which no man could have
dreamed would have come his way.
Whatever you can do, or dream you can,
begin it. Boldness has genius, power and magic in it.
Begin it now.

W. H. Murray, (mistakenly attributed to Goethe)

[* Providence doesn't really move. It's you who moves yourself into the Trust Frequency, where all manner of things exist that you could never have imagined in the lower frequencies.]

Don't we all want to live in a magical world where all manner of unforeseen incidents and meetings and material assistance await us? Things we couldn't have dreamed of? Wouldn't it be wonderful to walk confidently in the direction of our dreams and to experience a success unexpected in common hours? To have the laws expanded or new laws made in our favor, allowing us to live with the license of a higher order of beings? Could this be Heaven-on-Earth? Wouldn't we all love to live in the world described by Murray and Thoreau and not in the world our limited minds have created?

We must be willing to get rid of the life we've
planned so as to have the life that is waiting for us.
Joseph Campbell

Follow your bliss and the Universe will open
doors where there were only walls.
Joseph Campbell

DIFFERENT VIBRATORY PATTERNS

There is a very big difference, in terms of frequency, between
mentally visualizing something, and hoping and praying that
it will manifest, on the one hand, and deeply *knowing* that it is
so, and taking committed action accordingly, on the other. The
emotional and mental state, and therefore the vibratory state,
of the latter, is completely different from the former, and this
is what distinguishes the two. The two states reflect significantly
different frequency patterns, and will necessarily produce different
results. They are actually different worlds. Hoping and praying are
doubt-and-separation based activities, and contain within them the
distinct possibility of failure. Our hopes are often dashed, and our
prayers often go unanswered. Now we know why. Trust, on the
other hand, carries no trace of doubt, no subconscious, un-faced
fear that one does not deserve the desired outcome. Trust is the
essence of the Christian way, and of every other religion, needless
to say.

Trust in the Lord with all your heart, and
lean not on your own understanding.
Proverbs 3:5-6

God loves confidence in his loving power.
He will move mountains for those who trust
Him. Confidence in God can obtain anything

from His heart. It gives him so much glory when
we trust Him in darkness- not knowing where we
are going, but trusting that He does and He is leading.
Sister Immaculata

It is not God who moves mountains, it is the act of putting oneself into the Trust Frequency where there *are* no mountains, no obstacles, that is the key. We often manifest the opposite of what we think we are asking for, which is exactly the way it should be. We always get exactly what we *need* rather than what we think we want. This may seem terribly frustrating, but it serves a vital purpose: to cleanse us of fear and doubt on our soul's journey to wholeness. Only once all fear and doubt are gone will we truly live in the Trust Frequency. There is no way to fake it. The genuine *fakir** is anything but a faker.

* A fakir is a Muslim or Hindu religious ascetic who lives solely on alms.
And trust, needless to say.

Andrew grew up in Durban, the South African city where
Mahatma Gandhi lived as a young man. The population of Durban
includes hundreds of thousands of Indians, both Hindus and Muslims.
At the age of 16 or 17, on a Saturday night, he went to see a performance
by a "fakir", a famous Indian yogi who would allow himself to be nailed
into a coffin and lowered into a 6-ft deep grave. The grave was then filled
with dirt, and rocks were piled on the heap. Any normal person would
die of asphyxiation in no more than 6-12 hours. A guard was placed on
the site. The audience went away and returned a week later. As the crowd

watched, the grave was excavated. The coffin was hauled out and opened.
The yogi sat up, put his hands together in the namaste mudra, and rose
to his feet. When asked how he did it, he said simply: "I trust in God."
He smiled, bowed to left and right, and walked off into the night with his
friends. While remarkable, this experience was not particularly unusual.
Every Friday night in Durban, from that day to this, for example, one can
experience the phenomenon of fire-walking.

THERE IS NO FOOLING THE UNIVERSE

The mechanics of the Universe are extremely finely tuned. The
slightest fraction of a percent out of balance, and the universe
as we know it could not exist. There is no possibility for error,
no latitude, no fudge-factor. There is in fact no such thing as a
"mistake." Everything in the Universe is exactly as it should be.
It is actually the emotional components, the feelings around any
specific desire or intention, rather than the words we may say to
ourselves, and the committed actions we take, that perfect and
amplify the request and determine the outcome. And, we must
know that abundance, beauty, joy, ease and grace are our birthright.
We must know that each and every one of us is an inseparable
and essential part of the Loving Universe. If we have the slightest
inkling that we don't deserve the abundant life we are asking for,
that we are unworthy, or doubt the possibility of such a thing
actually happening, the Universe interprets this, quite correctly,
as a clear sign that we are not ready, we are not fully spiritually
prepared, and we do not see the results we are so fervently hoping
for. We are not in tune with our higher selves.

THAT LITTLE VOICE

To illustrate, here's a little story: You wake up one summer morning, ready to jump out of bed, brush your teeth, grab a cup of coffee and hit the freeway. You'd better not be late for work, or Fred will get the promotion you've been depending on to cover the mortgage on the new house. You've been following the same dull routine ever since graduating from college. Your job's OK, Fred's a good buddy, but somehow it's just not satisfying. To be honest, it's downright boring, and it's definitely not what you came to this planet to do. On the other hand, if you don't show up for work, you'll lose your job, you won't be able to pay the mortgage, you won't get the new car, and Sally won't want to date you anymore. Maybe Fred has his eye on her. But this particular morning, something seems strangely different. That little voice is a lot louder than usual, and it says: "Don't go to work. Just stay in bed. It's OK." So, a little bewildered, you roll over and go back to sleep. You dream of a palm tree on a warm tropical beach. You are reading a fascinating book, and a lovely girl is sitting next to you. You feel great.

At 9 a.m., just when you're "supposed" to be sitting down at your desk in town, you wake up, still feeling good from the dream, and call in with a stomach flu. You wander down the driveway to the mailbox, somewhat dazed, wondering what on earth is going on. You feel strangely elated. The mail is mostly bills and credit-card offers. While you are standing there, paging through the Victoria's Secret catalogue addressed to a previous tenant, here comes that guy down the road, Vincent, out for his morning jog. "Hey, good morning, I've been thinking about you." pants Vincent, his tank-top wet with sweat "Listen, you wouldn't be at all interested in re-locating to Honolulu and managing my business there, would you? I think you'd be just the guy…"

Vincent's proposal turns out to be precisely the thing you didn't even know you were waiting for. You chose to put yourself physically into the position where the loving Universe could give you more than you, yourself could have imagined. If you had dutifully climbed into your car and gone to work that morning, acting out of fear, you would not have been in precisely the right place at precisely the right time, Vincent would have left for Hawaii without you, and you'd never have learned to surf. You wouldn't be sitting here on the beach under this palm tree, reading this book. With Sally.

There is no time, only perfect timing.
C. S. Smith

As we have said, the Universe is incredibly finely tuned, infinitely more so than the 12-cylinder, 128-valve engine in my brother-in-law's latest Ferrari, but there is a parallel. It's all about timing. In the Ferrari's engine, hundreds or thousands of perfectly machined parts must move in perfect synchrony for the engine to run smoothly.

As the mechanic completes the tune-up, he shines the timing light down though the little hole in the housing, adjusts the screw, notes when the apparent movement ceases, and locks down the securing nut. The engine purrs contentedly, ready for anything. Each part now works in perfect synchrony with every other part, and so it is with us and the Universe. At times we all have that terrible feeling of being "out of sync," missing the train, misplacing our car keys, and showing up late for an important appointment.

Then again, all of us know that mysterious feeling of being "in sync," in harmony, attuned, where our timing seems perfect, and we just can't go wrong. A parking spot opens up precisely as you come around the corner, the person you were thinking about calling is in the check-out line at the supermarket, and you have exactly the right amount of cash in your pocket, no more, no less.

IT'S A MIRACLE

What is the difference? Can we pin it down? Certainly there is a difference in the emotional state, where the one feels just plain frustrating and stressful, and the other feels relaxed and divinely blessed. Aha! It's a difference in frequency, obviously. At times, our personal Universe purrs along like a well-tuned Ferrari. Other times, nothing we do seems to work. The astrology column tells us Mercury has gone retrograde, and there's nothing to be done.

Or is there? As Einstein famously said: "No problem was ever solved in the same consciousness in which it was created." We can choose to elevate our consciousness, and thereby improve our lives. As often as not, when things are going awry, if we look at our thoughts, we'll notice that they are not particularly positive. We're feeling incompetent, alone, insecure, off-balance. Fearful.

Insecure. And, when everything's going our way, we feel confident, connected, expansive, trusting that all will be well. Which comes first, the fear or the parking ticket, the trust or the city parking spot?

Laws that appear immutable in one frequency, for example "If I don't go to work, my kids will starve" are in fact quite real in that frequency. When we shift to a higher frequency, however, and make different choices, and then take committed action based on those choices, new laws apply to us, and "miracles" happen. Circumstances we never could have imagined come our way. The events we perceive as "miracles" are not exceptional at all, in the Trust Frequency. They are merely the way it is, in the higher vibratory realms.

PRACTICE MAKES PERFECT

By paying close attention to our assumptions and our attitudes, by replacing our outmoded unconscious beliefs with consciously-chosen ones, by aligning ourselves with our intuitive inner guidance, by placing our attention on the positive rather than the negative, by taking bold action and, finally, by letting go and allowing the Universe to deliver its gifts, in other words by consciously and intentionally examining and putting into practice each of the Seven A's, we attune ourselves to a higher reality and find ourselves living more and more in the Trust Frequency.

This is a very liberating experience. Amazingly so, in fact. It is precisely what the Buddha accomplished, when he set out in search of the end of suffering and eventually found himself in a state of Nirvana, free from all fear and attachment. There is no fundamental difference between the Trust Frequency and the liberated state of Nirvana, and it is readily available to each of us. There is nothing exclusive about buddha-hood. We are all *bodhisattvas*, awakened beings, in potential. It is our natural state, our birthright. It is the ultimate destiny of each one of us, once we awaken from the fear-driven dream that has possessed us for so long.

GRATITUDE IN THE ATTITUDE

The Seven A's, along with a healthy dose of acceptance, love, trust and gratitude, are your essential tools of transformation. Count your blessings. Be grateful for each opportunity that comes your way, including those that look and feel like problems. Be thankful for the people in your life who present you with challenges. Remember, there are no problems, only opportunities. Accept yourself, warts and all, and everyone in your life. The warts will go away, or transform themselves into flowers. Have compassion for those whose attitudes and behavior are still stuck in the Dark Ages. They too have not been playing with a full deck. They too have been operating from an erroneous set of assumptions. Everyone has.

As you begin to succeed in raising your individual vibratory level, you in fact succeed, by a phenomenon similar to osmosis*, in raising the vibratory level of the entire Universe, beginning with the people closest to you, your friends and family. How cool is that? Within the privacy of your own heart and mind, you are a secret agent, a secret change agent, a catalyst for cosmic change. This is an inescapable fact, an inevitable consequence of the interconnected quantum entanglement of all things.

The Universe *is* consciousness, the primordial energy behind all of Creation. In a sense, our individual human consciousness, filtered as it invariably is by our belief system, is an illusion, a shadow-play, a mere holographic projection. On the other hand, each of us plays a vital role as "roving sensory organs of the divine." As infinitesimal as each of us may appear to be, paradoxically, each of us is indispensable to the whole. Of the trillion trillion facets of the vast scintillating diamond of Reality, not one is of any less importance than any other. Not one facet has any less potential for splendor than any other. Not one facet has any more freedom than any other.

Osmosis: a process by which molecules tend to pass through a semi-permeable membrane from a less concentrated solution into a more concentrated one, thus equalizing the concentrations on each side of the membrane.

THE FIFTH ASSUMPTION

Free Will Is An Absolute Law Of The Universe.

Current Assumption

We have little or no control over our lives.
We are at the whim and mercy of others:
our parents, our partners, our leaders, our gods,
our circumstances.

Why have we so far failed to manifest an intelligent planetary society of liberated, equal, sovereign beings living together in harmony? One reason is this: we do not know that we are free. Few people realize that everything we do, think, or say is the result of our absolute freedom of choice, or that the loving Universe supports us unconditionally in this freedom, while obeying the unbreakable prime directive of non-interference.

*E*very human being longs for freedom. The deep desire for self-determination is one we are all very familiar with, but how many of us realize that we are, in fact, already free? We come from freedom. We are born free. We agreed to come to this life by the exercise of free choice. It is only our deeply ingrained, culturally-imposed assumptions to the contrary that makes us imagine otherwise. Free will is one of the fundamental characteristics of the Universe. It is one of the basic laws of human existence, despite the fact that most of us seem to have allowed ourselves to surrender and compromise our freedom to those who see themselves as more powerful or more important than we are.

Free will is also one of the basic characteristics of quantum physics. Science has yet to recognize the intertwined phenomena of consciousness and free will, two things that are fundamental to quantum theory in the context of the Observer Effect, but until this recognition occurs, a complete scientific understanding of the universe will remain impossible.

FREE WILL

The inalienable right to choose and modify one's
frequency, and hence one's reality.

As we have seen, we create the reality of our lives by the power of our consciousness, and consequently we have the freedom, the ability, the inalienable right, to consciously choose our frequency, and to attune ourselves to whatever reality we desire, from the lowest "Hell" to the highest "Heaven." We are the masters of our own destiny, although this can be difficult or impossible to believe from the perspective of the lower vibratory realms (*aka* everyday reality.) Our life experiences, very often, have conditioned us to feel helpless, powerless. We feel trapped. Our conditioned minds can see no way out.

MASTERS OF OUR OWN DESTINY

We humans were created, however that process took place, and set free, absolutely free, to create whatever world we choose, with no restrictions whatsoever. Free will, needless to say, includes the inalienable right *not* to align with one's inner promptings. We are free to defer progress on our destiny path, free to remain in the lower vibratory realms as long as we choose to, and free to ignore the intuitions of our higher selves.

Inevitably, as we grow up in our long-established families and communities, we accept the stories we are told and adapt to the environment in which we find ourselves. Whether we like it or not, we are programmed by the powerful ancestral conditioning systems created and propagated by our ancestors, our parents, teachers, culture heroes and peers. Most of us end up conforming, to a greater or lesser degree, to the consensus reality, and becoming very much like everyone else, despite our deeply buried but dimly conscious urges to the contrary. Conformity is the path of least resistance, and most of us take it by default. It is not easy to do otherwise. From a survival standpoint it is, it seems to most of us, our job, our duty, to fit in and survive, for the good of ourselves and our loved ones, and ultimately, the propagation of the species. It's that basic. We adapt or we die.

If a man does not keep pace with his companions,
perhaps it is because he hears a different drummer.
Let him step to the music which he hears,
however measured or far away.

Henry David Thoreau

A WORLDWIDE AWAKENING

Yet all of us know of a misfit or two, a maverick, someone who just did not fit in, or who chose a different path, an Einstein, a Thoreau, a John Lennon, a Gandhi, a Martin Luther King, or a Jesus, who marched to the beat of a different drummer.

Society does not look kindly on many of these visionaries, these misfits, and they often end up assassinated, or out on the street, or in an institution, while a very small percentage go on to become the folk heroes of the next generation, the way-showers. Quite remarkably, in the West in the 1960s we saw a large portion of an entire generation, tired of war and exploitation, take it upon itself to step outside the mainstream paradigm and diligently attempt to create a counter-culture based on peace and freedom and mutual respect. That unprecedented freedom movement is now several generations deep, and its influence continues to be profound, even though it is no longer front-page news.

Having said that, the Occupy Movement and other social activism organizations in the United States, and a series of revolutions in the Middle East, are rising into the mass consciousness just as this book approaches completion. It looks a lot like the stirrings of a worldwide awakening.

EACH DECISION LEADS TO THE NEXT

How many of us recognize the fact that our lives, and every aspect of the form they take, are the direct result of the free-will personal choices we have made every step of the way? Even the most conformist of us has made a conscious choice to conform. In so doing did we listen deeply to our own hearts? Did our parents or our teachers listen to us when we tried to tell them our truth? Probably not. Whether we go to school, do our homework, wear a tie, eat our breakfast, co-operate with our parents, get a job, join the Army, drive a car, pay our taxes, meditate, sail the Atlantic, get married, have kids, drop out, rebel, do it our own way regardless of the expectations of others, at every step we have been presented with a choice, and have made a decision, for better or worse, based on our fundamental assumptions about the nature of the Universe, and what we think will be best for us and those we care about. Each decision has led to the next, we have acted accordingly, and here we are. Think about it. We have created our own reality, consciously or not, every step of the way.

WHY ARE WE NOT FREE?

Free will is one of the fundamental laws of the universe, certainly as it applies to the human experience. The same principles apply to a greater or lesser degree to every sentient being on the planet. There are limits, of course. As a three-month-old baby I will not be free to go surfing, not just yet. Having manifested as a tree, I will not be able to fly. Having manifested as a bird, I will not be able to get a college degree. A dolphin cannot become a race-car driver. Not in this lifetime. A fifteenth Century Catholic nun cannot get a job at the Playboy mansion in 1967. But, aside from certain inherent restrictions of species and circumstance, of time and space, we are each free to make each of the decisions that determine the characteristics of our existence.

So, why are we not free? Why have we so far failed to manifest an intelligent planetary society of liberated, equal, sovereign beings living together in harmony? One reason is this: we do not know that we are free. Few people realize that everything we do, think, or say is the result of our absolute freedom of choice, or that the loving Universe supports us unconditionally in this freedom, while obeying the unbreakable prime directive of non-interference. Even our perceived lack of freedom comes from the exercise of our personal choice!

If indeed we are free, free to choose our lives at every step of the way, then obviously we are free to change our minds when new information comes along. At this point in history, as has been the case for thousands of years past, a large percentage of humanity seems trapped in a powerful web of deceit, of illusion, a sticky, tangled web of thoughts, traditions, attitudes, prejudices, conventions and social customs that acts as a sort of communal hypnotic trance that has kept things pretty much the same for centuries.

On the other hand, looking around us, it is obvious that something interesting is going on. New perspectives on the nature of the Universe are emerging, and we are not speaking merely of scientific progress. Books like this one are all over the New York

Times best-seller list, and films like *What The #$*! Do We (K)now!?* and *The Secret* were enormously popular. A great evolutionary awakening is in the works, the awakening that Teilhard de Chardin predicted and called the Omega Point, although at present we can only detect the results in a relatively small segment of the population, the so-called "culture creatives." The tip of the evolutionary iceberg. Once critical mass is reached, a tipping point, however, who can predict what changes we will see? One thing seems certain; radical change will occur rapidly, and things will never be the same.

WE AGREED TO TAKE THIS JOURNEY

What is humanity, ultimately? We are much more than just another living organism on a tiny planet lost somewhere in the vastness of space. The opening of the human heart is the primary purpose of all of Creation. Let us revisit a very important definition, one that we asked you to take as absolutely true. Remember? Let us remember the over-arching act of free will that brought us here in the first place.

HUMANITY

A collection of divine autonomous sovereign beings who chose to incarnate on Earth, each with a purpose and a gift, to learn and grow on their soul's journey to wholeness.

Before each of us incarnated, we made an agreement, a conscious choice, an over-arching act of free will. We agreed to come into the physical plane for two purposes, both to evolve and grow as sentient beings, *and* to bring a certain unique gift to the world, to contribute something important to the bigger picture. When we chose to materialize from the vast oneness into the physical, we gave permission to the loving energies on the planet to give us all of the experiences we would need to learn and grow on our soul's journey. This choice, this profound act of free will, overrides all the other choices, goals, and assumptions adopted by us and our parents, peers and society, most of whom, for the moment, continue to operate, at least to some degree, on the doubt/fear frequency.

NO MORE VICTIMS

By definition, then, if everything that unfolds in our life is a result of our free choice, there can be no such thing as a victim. Or a perpetrator, for that matter. We are presented with precisely the life experiences we agreed to, before we ever came here. We chose our parents, we chose the culture and the era into which we were born, and we chose the basic nature of the life we are here to live, the lessons we are here to learn. We are entirely, personally, responsible for everything in our lives. Even Ebenezer Scrooge learned that, in the end, although it took a series of paranormal visitations to get through to his closed heart.

> *I wear the chain I forged in life. I made it link by link,*
> *and yard by yard; I girded it on of my own free will,*
> *and of my own free will I wore it.*
> Charles Dickens, *A Christmas Carol*

This is a very liberating perspective, especially for those of us who have suffered or witnessed extreme abuse. As challenging as it may seem, we must be grateful to our "perpetrators," who are actually obliging our souls. At the highest spiritual level, we created them. They are us. By truly understanding and accepting the fact that we create our own reality, we are required to take responsibility for the events in our lives. Difficult as this concept might be for those overwhelmed by the compelling apparent reality of the lower frequencies, acceptance of the unconditionally loving nature of the Universe will inevitably result in emotional healing, individually and collectively. Everything, absolutely everything, serves the coming of peace and freedom on this planet. There is nothing but Love, no matter what it might look like on the surface.

You might ask a very relevant question: What's the point of going through all the pain and suffering inherent in being human? What purpose does it serve? It is to allow us to experience the consequences of our lower frequency thoughts and actions, and to help us develop the faculty of discernment, of self-reflection. The loving energies have cooperated, each step of the way. The grand experiment called humanity calls for cleansing ourselves of fear, and making the free will choice to act in total trust. By doing so, we bring Heaven-on-Earth into the physical plane, through our daily choices in society.

Life is a fascinating and often paradoxical balance of personal free will and what we experience as the "outer circumstances" that operate in behalf of our "higher selves," the events that accelerate and guide us on our journey to wholeness, our journey to self-love and self-acceptance, in harmony with our higher goals, desires and aspirations, and in spite of our current insecurities and our limiting beliefs about ourselves and the world.

First, you must understand that you are exactly where you have chosen to be. You are making exactly the amount of money you have chosen to make. You have exactly the kind of friends you have chosen to have. You are exactly the kind of parent you have chosen to be. For what you experience in life are the consequences of choices made deep within your mind, often subconsciously, but made in a part of your mind which is intelligent, knowing, and caring. Even your most miserable, painful, and devastating experiences are the results of choices you have made. Not the conscious you, but the "I" within you. This "I" controls all the orders within orders within your mind.
V. Vernon Woolf, PhD. *Holodynamics*

We are not *victims* of circumstance. Nothing could be further from the truth. We are, in fact, *beneficiaries* of circumstance. We are *blessed* by circumstance. Circumstance loves us more than we love ourselves. Circumstance is our unerring guide through the vicissitudes of life. Circumstance, manifesting as the "loving energies on the planet," is in fact a mechanism of our super-conscious "higher selves," the divine, connected part of each of us that knows all things and loves our "lower selves," our egos, unconditionally.

THE SIXTH ASSUMPTION

Circumstance Guides Us On Our Journey To Wholeness.

Current Assumption

We are all victims of circumstance, also known as fate.

Fate is blind, and its effects are random.

We are operating simultaneously on two or more different levels or frequencies. Our "higher self," our "full potential self," is creating the circumstance, while the "persona," the "lower self," the "ego," our everyday self, thinks it wants something else. To resolve the paradox, let's return to the definition of who we are: divine, autonomous, sovereign beings who have chosen to incarnate on Earth, to learn and grow on our soul's journey to wholeness, each with an individual purpose and a unique gift.

CIRCUMSTANCE

The seemingly uncontrollable outward events in our lives that determine and influence our decisions and direction in life.

*W*e opened this book with a rather unusual and elevated definition of the word "humanity." Remember? If we can accept the proposition, even theoretically, that the human journey begins with a pre-incarnation agreement to undertake our specific learning mission and to bring our unique gift to life on this planet, before we ever enter the birth canal, then our undertaking as we grow up and come to mature consciousness, is to remember (re-member) our higher purpose, to re-connect with our mission, and to discover the unique gift we promised to bring to the world, and to be grateful for the sometimes tough lessons that life presents along the way, knowing that each of our experiences is exactly what we need for our soul's growth.

This is rarely easy. For many of us, the challenges seem overwhelming. The whole adventure appears impossible, pointless, and even absurd. We put up resistance, and we suffer as a result. But, the fact is, we gave permission to the loving energies to take us on our journey, and the more challenging our path is, the more we learn, the more we grow in compassion, as long as we face life with acceptance, optimism and courage. And gratitude. For all of us, life is an interesting balance between the experience of free will on the one hand, and the compelling appearance of determinism on the other. It's a paradox. Many of us, at one time or another, feel that we are victims of circumstance. From our limited perspective, it looks as though circumstance is our enemy. However, it turns out that circumstance is our best friend. If we can *grok* that critical fact, we have another powerful tool in our evolutionary toolbox.

OF MICE AND MEN

The previous chapter notwithstanding, not all of us experience free will as the dominant factor in our lives. In fact many of us feel downright helpless at times. We feel that we are at the mercy of forces beyond our control. In all of our lives, from time to time, something occurs that we could not have anticipated. We might not have wished for it if we had predicted it. We are not good at expecting the unexpected, and as the Scottish poet Robbie Burns said: "the best-laid plans of mice and men go oft awry." A latter-day version of this is "If you want to make God laugh, tell Her your plans." Sometimes it almost feels as though someone or something is messing with us, testing us to the limits of our endurance. As a personal example, we have found, since beginning to write this book and develop the Trust Frequency workshops, that we have really been put through the wringer. We are being cleansed of every last vestige of fear and doubt. As we have learned, "Don't write the book unless you're ready to walk the talk.

THE HERO'S JOURNEY

Here's the kicker: When you embark on your journey toward alignment with the true nature of things, don't be surprised if there is a period of intense cleansing of old patterns, old thinking, old ways of acting. It may not feel like a whole lot of fun at times. The old operating system is many generations deep, and is ingrained at the deepest cellular level, both in our selves and in our society. You will very likely encounter a great deal of resistance, both inner and outer. The process, your personal voyage of discovery, is described in detail by Joseph Campbell in his book: *The Hero With A Thousand Faces*. Campbell calls this archetypal growth pattern, this path toward mastery, the "Hero's Journey." It occurs in the mythology of virtually all cultures, and is as relevant today as it was thousands of years in the past.

> *Yes, the past can hurt, but the way I see it,*
> *you either run from it, or you learn from it.*
> Rafiki, *The Lion King*

Of course, it does not always feel bad when the unexpected intervenes. Once we truly surrender to the loving Universe, the circumstances in our lives change in ways we could never have imagined. The main thing to keep in mind through all of the ups and downs and rounds and rounds, however they may feel at any given moment, is that circumstance loves us, and will continue to present us with situations that are perfectly designed to trigger the next phase of our growth.

> *Oh no! Not another learning experience!*
> Bumper sticker, California

At this time in history, we are undeniably in a period of accelerating change. It's obvious. The signs are all around us. The outdated systems are collapsing, as indeed they should. They were built on a false foundation, on fear and scarcity. All those things we were taught to put our trust in – money in the bank, a steady job, equity in our homes, education for our children, our retirement nest-egg, medical care for the elderly - we can no longer depend upon these old-paradigm things. We must now truly trust the loving Universe to provide for us. This is the essence of the American Dream - abundance for all. But, as they say in Connie's home state, Maine, *"You can't get theah from heah!"* It will require the kind of foundational shift that this book is suggesting.

True abundance is simply not possible in the fear/scarcity frequency, either for the individual or for society as a whole. As we have seen so clearly throughout history, no matter what political system is in fashion, material resources tend to accumulate in the hands of the powerful few, leaving the majority of the people impoverished. This out-of-balance neo-Darwinian situation inevitably leads to social unrest, to revolution. What is needed to make the change permanent and positive is evolution, not revolution. In order to realize our highest and noblest human potential, we must transition to a higher frequency where the laws are different, and circumstance will guide us every step of the way, as long as we pay close attention to the signs, and have the courage to act upon our guidance. We must change our attitude towards circumstance.

CIRCUMSTANCE LOVES US

We do our very best to figure out what we're meant to be doing with our lives, using every ounce of our intelligence, exercising our free will and carefully laying out our short-term goals and our lifetime strategy to get us from point A to point B. We work sixty hours a week, sacrificing our health and quality time with our families. We sincerely believe we are building security for the future. Then without warning the unpredictable happens. The car breaks down, someone dies, a relative gets sick, war breaks out, and the results of years of careful planning, prudent hoarding, and hard work lie in ashes. The stock market crashes, our marriage breaks up, the bank forecloses on the house, we are diagnosed with a scary disease, and suddenly everything is different. Horribly different.

> *One thing we do know: Life will give you whatever experience*
> *is most helpful for the evolution of your consciousness.*
> *How do you know this is the experience you need?*
> *Because this is the experience you are having at this moment.*
> Eckhardt Tolle, *The Power of Now*

At the moment disaster strikes, it feels as though our world has ended. We struggle and curse, pray for deliverance, go into denial, and search for someone or something to blame. We do everything in our power to return to the comfortable, secure state we thought we were in, but to no avail. Circumstance has intervened, and we, the hapless victims, are screwed. Again. Life's a bitch, we mutter under our breath.

And yet, time and again, after a few years have passed, and we can see the bigger picture, the "problem" turns out to have been an opportunity, a blessing in disguise, a turning-point without which our lives would have been less rich, less joyful, less rewarding. As the great yogi Paramahansa Yogananda famously said, *There are no problems, only opportunities.*

Joseph Campbell, one of the most influential thinkers of the 20th Century, realized toward the end of his remarkable, productive life, that the three greatest disasters in his life were the very turning-points that placed him exactly where he was meant to be, at exactly the time he was meant to be there. The great baseball bat in the sky came down, whacked him upside the head, and re-directed his course in life, with profoundly positive results.

It is vital that we re-assess the role of circumstance in our lives. Once we understand what is really going on, we realize that these apparently negative events are the loving Universe taking us on our journey. The appropriate response is not anger or frustration, it's gratitude.

Needless to say, it's equally possible that circumstance might intervene in a way that feels entirely positive. It all depends on the next lesson on one's journey. You might think you're well established on your rather dull path in life, and suddenly something happens or you meet someone who re-directs you in a much more exciting, inspiring direction, and you never look back.

IT'S A PARADOX

So, the seeming paradox is this: on the one hand we are absolutely free to create our own existence, and yet, from time to time, something will occur, some outer circumstance over which we have no control, some un-anticipated, unwanted event, which changes everything. This event might be relatively minor, like getting a flat tire on the way to a meeting, missing the meeting and yet marrying the person who stops to help, or world-shakingly huge, like crossing the Atlantic on the *Titanic*, and being one of the few survivors, or walking into the World Trade Center at 9 a.m. on September 11th, 2001. Certain pivotal events in one's life determine our course ever after, often triggering an epiphany of one kind or another.

In most cases, we end up looking back in gratitude. We see, with 20/20 hindsight, the critical decisions and actions that would never have happened had not circumstance intervened. There is an inspiring book entitled *Thank God I have Cancer* in which the writer expresses her profound gratitude for the enormous awakening which has occurred in her life. What is happening, when such events occur, is that our soul, our higher self, is magnetizing precisely the life experiences best suited to our growth.

You can't always get what you want,
but if you try sometime, you just might
find - you get what you need.
The Rolling Stones

FREE WILL OR DETERMINISM

The loving Universe sets you free, fulfilling your every request without judgment or question, and then, paradoxically, intervenes on your behalf just at the right moment, ensuring that you are exactly where you are meant to be exactly when you are meant to be there. So, who or what is running the show, you or the Universe? Is it some combination of the two, a cosmic balancing act?

RESOLVING THE PARADOX

Ultimately, we realize, we are divided beings, at this stage of our development, as a result of certain critical choices our ancestors made long ago. We are operating simultaneously on two or more different levels or frequencies. Our "higher self," our "full potential self" gave permission to the loving energies to take us on our journey to wholeness, and promised to bring a special gift to the world. This was our over-arching act of free will. Our "higher self" is creating the circumstance while the "persona", our "ego," our everyday self, may think it wants something else, in order to be successful and loved in the lower frequency that we incarnated into. Our ancestors chose to give more importance to the "material" world than to the "spiritual", and here we are.

To resolve the apparent paradox, let's return to the definition of who we are: divine, autonomous, sovereign beings who have chosen to incarnate on Earth, to learn and grow on our soul's journey to wholeness, each with an individual purpose and a unique gift. Remember, we gave permission to the loving energies on the planet to guide us on our journey, an over-arching act of free will, which we most likely forgot all about once we got here.

ALL IS GOING ACCORDING TO PLAN

How does this understanding resolve the paradox? How do we learn to use each unfolding circumstance as a guidepost? How can we be certain it's our higher guidance and not just our selfish ego driving our actions? We have to use another great human faculty – discernment. When circumstance intervenes, and our carefully laid plans lie in ruins, it's time to stop, take a dozen deep, connected breaths, remember who we are, and move back up into the Trust Frequency. Resist the habitual temptation of one's lower self to go into victim mode, and start looking for someone to blame. Poor pitiful me. Denial. Blame. Shame.

We then use a combination of acceptance and gratitude (which is not resignation) to determine our next steps, trusting that, despite appearances to the contrary, all is going according to plan. It's just that the plan is not what we thought it was, from our limited perspective. Once we see the big picture, we realize that the plan was far better than we had imagined.

THE BLACK SHEEP OF THE FAMILY

Your father wants you to become a doctor or an accountant or a lawyer, but circumstance disagrees. You just don't have that kind of temperament, or that kind of intelligence. You don't make the grade. So, instead, you end up becoming a poet and a musician. It's not making you any money, yet, but you love it. You may be the black sheep of the family, but, in fact, you are realizing your soul's purpose. You consider asking your poor, disappointed father, how many historically-important doctors, lawyers, accountants, or even multi-millionaires he can name. You can list them on the fingers of one hand. On the other hand, how many poets can you think of? Homer, Shakespeare, Milton, Wordsworth, T.S. Elliot, D.H. Lawrence, Dylan Thomas, Robert Bly, Rumi, Bob Dylan. The list goes on and on and on. How many musicians? Beethoven, Mozart, Chopin, Miles Davis, Elvis, the Beatles. Again, the list goes on and on and on. Apparently, history prefers poets and musicians over doctors and lawyers.

WATCH FOR THE SIGNS

Frequently, circumstance seems to be telling us one thing, giving us a certain set of instructions, and only later do we learn that the real message is something entirely different. We are offered a fantastic new job. We let go of our secure position with a mundane but successful company, sell our house and move to the opposite coast. The moment it's too late to pull back, the job opportunity evaporates. We have made a major, irreversible, expensive move that we would never otherwise have considered. It's a total disaster. What can we do? Listen carefully, pay attention, and act on what we hear. Watch for the signs. Trust the loving Universe. Something is going on that has not yet made itself clear. Pay close attention, then take bold committed action based on our inner guidance. Know that, even when it appears that all your efforts are for naught, you are loved.

EASE AND GRACE

All of Creation is counting on you to bring your gift to the party.

You are the only one on the planet who can provide your unique contribution. It is the very essence of who you are. Accept the parts of yourself that feel different, shameful or inferior. These are the aspects of your being that your journey to wholeness is asking you to love, accept and become.

Trust your feelings, Luke!
Obi Wan Kenobe, *Star Wars*

When we align with our higher purpose, our unique gift comes into being. When we trust our inner knowing, our inner promptings, our intuition, we move through life with ease and grace. Pain and suffering come from resistance, as any martial artist, any Buddhist, will tell you. When we act in trust, we don't run into the walls in the labyrinth. Instead, like Ariadne in the Greek myth, we unerringly follow the gossamer thread through the maze, unlike others who, exercising their free-will right *not* to align, continually wrestle with their challenges, failing to recognize the signposts that circumstance places in their path, and slamming into the wall at every turn. In the latter case, the negative consequences of the perceived "problems" are reinforced by complaints, which needless to say come from a negative attitude toward life, which comes from a negative set of assumptions.

How we respond to any particular circumstance is entirely up to us. It's all a matter of choice, free choice. It's the attitude factor, determined entirely by our assumptions about life. If we choose a negative response, we bitch and whine and complain. We look for someone to blame. The complaints are amplified by anxiety and worry, and gratitude, love and trust are nowhere to be found. On the other hand, if we understand that we are loved and supported on our soul's journey, every step of the way, we can choose to respond with gratitude to every circumstance, no matter what outer form it may take. Our attitude shifts from annoyance to acceptance. We accept apparent obstacles for the learning experiences and opportunities for growth that they are. Again, this is not necessarily easy. It takes practice. Is it any wonder that some lives seem divinely guided, while others hit potholes every mile along the way?

> *I want to know if you have touched the center of*
> *your own sorrow, if you have been opened by life's*
> *betrayals, or have become shriveled and closed from*
> *fear of further pain! I want to know if you can sit*
> *with pain, mine or your own, without moving to*
> *hide it or fade it, or fix it.*
>
> Oriah Mountain Dreamer, *The Invitation*

The inescapable fact is, to drive the point home one more time, the outer events and circumstances in our lives put us exactly where we need to be, exactly when we need to be there. Every single time, without exception. The challenge and the practice is to accept and trust that a "higher intelligence" is operating in our best interests. How often have we taken a committed action based on our then-current understanding of how things were going to turn out, only to have the rug pulled out from under us? Very frustrating, at the time. And yet, looking back, we realize that we would never have taken the action without the circumstance, and even though we might appear to have been deluded, to have been hoodwinked by an illusion, it was precisely the illusion that triggered the decision to act. If we had not acted, we would not have been where we are, right here, right now. The fact is, the loving Universe is never wrong. There are no mistakes. There really aren't. Once we understand circumstance, accept its central role in our lives, and remain alert to its unerring guidance, we will never again think of ourselves as victims of circumstance.

 THE SEVENTH ASSUMPTION

There Is Only NOW, This Precious Present Moment

Current Assumption

The past and the future are far more important
than the present. It is irresponsible not to learn
from the past and to plan for the future.

Very rarely do we even notice taking a breath. Can you remember the last breath you took? A thousand thousand miraculous inhalations come and go, un-remarked. It's all automatic, unconscious. This unconscious habitual activity, this living in the past or the future, completely separates us from the only true reality, which is
THIS PRESENT MOMENT.
The only thing that really exists is this very moment in time, this ephemeral moment that we call "the present."

If you are depressed, you are living in the past.
If you anxious, you are living in the future.
If you are at peace you are living in the now.
Lao Tzu (6th century BC)

Despite the important revolutions that have taken place
within physics, old ways of thinking continue to dominate
our relationship to nature. Time, we believe, is external to
our lives and carries us along with its flow; causality rules
the actions of nature with its iron hand and our consensus
reality is restricted to the surface of things and seems closer
to the rule-bound functioning of a machine than to the
subtle adaptability of an organism.
F. David Peat, PhD, physicist

For many of us, regrets, memories and nostalgia about the past,
and fears, hopes and plans for the future occupy most of our
waking thoughts, so we rarely put our full attention on the present
moment. We're too busy to sit around meditating. We don't have
"time," or at least, that is how it seems to us in our frenzied,
stressful lives, but let's stop for a second and ask ourselves: What
is time, in reality? The phenomenon we call time is, without doubt,
one of life's great mysteries.

We are told by the mystics: "time is just an illusion." In
that case, why are so many of us rushing around in all directions,
late for work, barely on "time" for our appointments, ruining
our health by gobbling bad food at fast-food joints, consuming
synthetic pharmaceuticals just to stay "healthy" and keep up our
energy level. Millions of us find ourselves sitting, drumming on

the steering wheel in gridlocked traffic during "rush hour," that misnomer for the times of day when everything seems to slow down and come to a grinding halt?

Attention! Here and now, boys! Here and now!
Aldous Huxley, *Island*

Other cultures operate on "Indian time" or "African time." Indigenous time seems to be something very different and less stressful than that experienced by the city dwellers in the so-called developed nations. Time, according to Einstein, is the 4th dimension, which along with the three dimensions of space, creates the space-time continuum we experience as the reality of our everyday lives. So how can time be an illusion, if it's such an essential part of reality? My iPhone tells me it's five minutes after noon, this fleeting moment that I think of as the present. Of course, it's gone already, before I have "time" to complete the thought. What about the past, yesterday, last week, the things we read about in our history books, the fascinating evolutionary unfoldment stretching all the way back to the alleged birth of the Universe 15 billion years ago? What about our ancestors, our predecessors in time, without whom we most definitely would not be here? What about our individual pasts, our stories, our personal histories, each of which is filled with the life experiences that have made us who we are? How can anyone deny the existence of the past, or its relevance to the present?

And then of course there's the future, a phantom realm that we can't quite put our finger on, but it certainly seems both real and very important. Next Wednesday at 10 a.m., I'll be sitting in the dentist's chair. On November 17, it will be my birthday. Again. Every four years, we inaugurate a new American president. Halley's comet will return to our skies on a very specific future date, and on and on and on. On December 21st, 2012, according to those who study these things, the Mayan Calendar came to an end. As you are reading this book, obviously, December 21st, 2012 was not the end of the world, as many had feared. It was merely the start of a new cycle of time. The ancient Mayan astronomers certainly believed in time. They were extraordinarily accurate when it came to predicting future celestial events. Of course, the Mayans performed their calculations in what we see as the distant past, so our immediate present was their distant future.

The trouble with our times is this:
the future is not what it used to be.
Paul Valery, philosopher

Time is experienced as an evolutionary sequence
of irreversible transformations.
Brian Swimme, cosmologist

For us humans, the future is generally perceived as an unknowable but somewhat predictable projection of the past. Based on past experience, we believe we can extrapolate a reasonable idea of what the future will look like. It has even been suggested that the future has already happened, and that it is this pre-existing state that draws us toward itself, thus giving us the illusion of time in motion. Aside from the philosophical questions, the future represents an extraordinary opportunity, the opportunity, at least as it applies to these authors, to bring everything we have learned in the past, all the undeniable experience we have accumulated in our combined 135 years on planet Earth, assimilate it, and find some way of contributing to the evolving human story, either through film or writing or in some other form of storytelling, perhaps just through the loving presence of our beings. We love time! But, on the other hand, we too never seem to have quite enough of it!

EVERYTHING IS PERFECT

Do you have a minute? We do. If you do as well, let us stop together, step out of time, and check into this present moment, right here, right now. Just for a minute. A timeless minute. Slow down. Stop everything. Breathe deeply, gently, and contemplate nothing but the Now. Feel the air. Listen to the wind. Don't allow any thought of past or future or anything else to intervene. What do you see? What do you feel? What is going on, right here and right now?

Except in the most extreme of circumstances, you will find that everything is pretty much perfect. While the past might not have lived up to your expectations, and while the future may be uncertain, possibly even frightening, right now everything is remarkably fine. No major emergency is upon you. You are alive, you are breathing, your life is not in imminent danger. The chances are, for the vast majority of readers, you are not starving to death, nor are you dying of some horrible disease. Not right now, at any rate. The bills are most likely paid, even though you may not be so sure about next month's. While next month's finances might turn out to be a "problem," worrying about next month today isn't going to help. Moreover, today's worry takes all the fun out of today, and as we have said elsewhere in this book, worry acts as a form of negative prayer, so the worry actively contributes to next month's rent "problem." As we now know, worry puts us firmly in the fear frequency, with predictable consequences.

On the other hand, if we are able to maintain our trust in the loving Universe, trusting in the unknown, and living in the present moment, putting one foot in front of the other, somehow next month's rent gets paid, effortlessly. It has everything to do with being here and now. An awful lot of us, if we're not spending our time worrying about or planning for the future, we're longing for, or regretting, the past. We are simply not present to the miracle of this precious moment. This moment that will never happen again, ever. We are totally engrossed in our personal drama, our time-based individual story, with all of its joys, conflicts, hopes and fears. Very rarely do we even notice taking a breath. Can you remember the last breath you took? A thousand thousand miraculous inhalations come and go, un-remarked. It's all automatic, unconscious. This unconscious habitual activity, this living in the past or the future, completely separates us from the only true reality, which is:

THIS PRESENT MOMENT

The only thing that really exists is this very moment in time, this ephemeral moment that we call "the present." Nothing else is real. Everything else is a figment of our imagination, no matter how compelling it might seem. The past exists only in our minds, in our memory. Our idea of the future is, at best, a projection, a passing thought-form, that has no tangible reality whatsoever. How many times have we lain awake at night, agonizing about some upcoming event, only to find that things are completely different when the dreaded day dawns? All of that fearful worrying was for naught.

There is deep interest in the subject of time and its effect on us, as evidenced by spiritual teacher Eckhardt Tolle's recent success with his non-fiction bestseller *The Power Of Now,* which talks about the importance of being in the present moment and not being caught up in thoughts of the past and future. While our use of time has a practical aspect, Tolle says, most people are "lost in time" and are only peripherally aware of the present moment.

Awareness is the power that is concealed within the present moment. The ultimate purpose of human existence, which is to say, your purpose, is to bring that power into this world.
Eckhart Tolle, *The Power Of Now*

Too much thinking about oneself is the greatest thing that keeps human identity from being fully present, for when you are constantly self-reflecting you are too caught up in past and future to notice the presence around you. You are doubting your own power. You

are not vibrating fast enough to channel the immense
energies of creation because your attention
is scattered and you are closed to the one
moment where the love that would quicken
you exists: the moment where you are.
Ken Carey. *Return Of The Bird Tribes*

TIME EQUALS STRESS

What is time? Obviously, time is one of the most important things in life. What else could it be? It's precious, and nobody has enough of it. Everybody wants more of it. Time is a lot like gold in that regard. Looking the word up in Wikipedia, we are told: "Time is a *concept* (emphasis ours) referring to the perceived flow of actions and events from the past to the future, or to its measurement." Oh! Time is a mere concept, a man-made mental construct. It's not even real. One would logically expect there to be a comprehensive scientific analysis and description of time, but even there we get no help. Says theoretical physicist Stephen Hawking "The laws of science do not distinguish between the past and the future," meaning that science, too, has little light to shed on the subject. If time is what separates past and future, and yet science does not differentiate between the two, why do time, and the management of time, play such dominant and central roles in contemporary life?

The only reason for time is so that everything doesn't happen at once.
Albert Einstein

What is the nature of time? Is it really just an illusion? And why is it important to know that? Thinking about it, we realize that time is, in a sense, a wholly man-made concept, a logical, left-brain attempt to get control of the forces of nature, to understand the cycles of the seasons and the movements of the planets. Nothing more. Somehow, though, our concept of time, and the importance we ascribe to it, has grown like a fungus or a cancer, until time (or the perceived lack of it) has become the single most stressful aspect of modern life. And that stress, we are discovering, is deadly dangerous to us. It is not too much to assert that time equals stress. It may well be the root cause of many of our most debilitating diseases. An illusion, making us ill? Killing us?

WHAT ARE OTHERS SAYING?

How do humans perceive time? Has it always been like this? How has time been perceived down through the ages? Here are a few historical thoughts on the subject:

> *People who believe in physics know that the distinction between past, present and future is only a stubbornly persistent illusion.*
> Albert Einstein

> *The swiftness of time is infinite, as is still more evident when we look back on the past.*
> Lucius Seneca (4 BC – 65 AD)

> *Dost thou love life, then do not squander time, for that's the stuff life is made of.*
> Benjamin Franklin

*The more business a man has to do, the more he is able
to accomplish, for he learns to economize his time.*
Sir Matthew Hale, 17th Century lord chief justice of England

He who knows most grieves most for wasted time.
Dante Alighieri (1265-1321)

Time is money!
Benjamin Franklin

Everyone, at least in the world's more technologically advanced societies, seems to take time very seriously indeed. And yet, the whole idea of time is man-made. Do you see the situation we have created for ourselves?

FISHING, ANYONE?

A few adventurous thinkers have waxed philosophical, and even playful, about the nature of time. *"Time and space are fragments of the infinite for the use of finite creatures"* mused 19th Century Swiss philosopher Henri Frederic Amiel. We have to confess that our favorite is the following: *"Time is but the stream I go a-fishin' in!"* wrote Henry David Thoreau. That's more like it! If time is but an infinite stream of perfect Now moments, in which we can "fish" as and when and if we please, we are approaching the relationship to time that humanity will develop once our new trust-based consciousness is firmly established. Looking at the spiritual traditions of the world, from the ancient Vedic traditions to the contemporary Zen Buddhist approach, we find that we can express the whole matter in three little words, three words that Harvard LSD proponent and professor-turned-guru Baba Ram Dass (*nee* Richard Alpert, PhD) used as the title to his influential 1971 hippie bible and spiritual guidebook.

BE HERE NOW

It's really very simple. Be as present as you possibly can. Pay attention. Breathe. If your mind drifts, that's OK. Bring it back, gently. Remember who you are. Be here now, in this very moment. Remember that you are a beloved, indispensable part of the most amazing thing in existence. Remember where you are: at the very center of the conscious, loving Universe. Put your total attention on what you are doing, feeling, and being, right here, right now, whether you are meditating, reading this book, cooking dinner, surfing, playing golf, or driving on the freeway.

> *Silence! Breath is a Godsend.*
> Javad Nurbhaksh, PhD, 20th Century Persian sufi poet

IN THE WORLD, BUT NOT OF THE WORLD

But wait! That's ridiculous. What are we supposed to *do?* We obviously can't just sit here and do nothing, expecting the loving Universe to take care of feeding the cats, mowing the lawn, and paying the mortgage. It doesn't work like that! Or does it? Well, no, it doesn't, not exactly. It's not about sitting around meditating all day. It's not about shaving your head and donning saffron robes. It's not about being passive, or opting out of society. There's wood to be chopped, and water to be carried. It's about paying attention.

It's about being present. It's about being in the moment. It's about breathing, about being aware of our intimate connection to the whole of Creation.

Before enlightenment, chop wood, carry water.
After enlightenment, chop wood, carry water.
Zen saying

OUT OF YOUR MIND

Listen carefully in the silence, pay close attention, and act on what you hear. As we've said before, life is about bold committed action, oftentimes going where the brave dare not go. Your actions may make no logical sense when viewed from the lower frequencies. Your friends and family may think you've flipped, that you've gone out of your mind. And, of course, you *have* gone out of your mind. You have gone out of your conditioned mind. You have chosen to walk away from the old, rigid aspect of your mind that kept you stuck in the fear-and-time-based paradigm. It takes courage to launch oneself into the unknown, into the unknowable, but there is no alternative, if we are to evolve. Trusting one's own inner knowing, one's intuition, one's "right thinking," is the key to "right action," as the Buddhists call it. Right action, however, is impossible in the absence of right thinking, and right thinking is difficult or impossible in a time-based reality, no matter how hard we try. Sad but true.

It's so easy to get all tangled up in our incessant thoughts, hypnotized by the compelling drama of our life's story, and to miss the boat. The party goes on without us, and we don't even know it's happening. Most of us have no idea what we're missing, or even that there's anything to be missed.

The Sufis put it like this: *"Be in the world, but not of the world."* In other words, we don't have to opt out of society, climb a distant mountain and sit all alone in a cave, chanting some archaic mantra. Instead, and it's a whole lot more fun, we are active, fully-engaged participants in life, but we engage with the world a little differently.

Living trustingly in the NOW,
we experience the true nature of the Universe.

Life is suddenly, radically different. We live more consciously, more efficiently, using ease and grace as our benchmarks. We have more fun than our time-controlled friends and family. We breathe and work and play and love and dance and remember who we are and that we are a precious, essential, inextricable part of the most amazing thing in Creation, the Creator, Life Itself. In a certain sense, yes, it's all an illusion anyway, so why not make life the best it can be, the best we can imagine? If we create our entire reality, let's enjoy it. If we write our own movie, let's make it a timeless classic, with a happy ending. An ending that lasts forever. The bottom line is, while we may be *in* time, we are not *controlled* by time, unless we choose to be. We are not slaves to time. If indeed there's going to be a future, and it certainly looks like there will be, let's make it the very best it can be. The future we experience then will still be Now, this precious present moment.

SPONTANEOUSLY IN THE NOW

Here is a challenging paragraph from a little-known book from the mid-1970s called *Endless Song of Infinite Balance*.

> *Our part is to live spontaneously in the Now, desire-less,*
> *without judgment and attachment, without concern for our*
> *destiny, without looking for compensation, rewards and answers,*
> *keeping our awareness on Truth, letting God's will be done.*

This little paragraph describes life in the Trust Frequency perfectly. At first glance it seems like an awfully tall order, even an impossible order, given our conditioned minds. Can we ever "let go and let God" to the degree this instruction seems to demand? Can we ever have that much unconditional trust? It's antithetical to everything we've been taught. Our first response is: we could never do that! It's simply not possible. But as we told you at the outset, if you take everything you believe to be true, including your assumptions about yourself, and flip it 180 degrees, you approach the true nature of things.

In fact, the Now is the gateway to the Trust Frequency, to Heaven-on-Earth, to Nirvana, where we truly can live according to the ideas suggested in the paragraph quoted above. The vibratory state of fear, blame, guilt, shame, worry, and anxiety, the emotions that are inevitable and automatic outcomes of the compelling concept of linear time and a doubt-based paradigm, place us firmly in the lower frequencies. It's just that simple. Each of these stressful mental activities has to do with either the past, (blame, guilt, shame), or the future (hope, worry, anxiety.) Such things do not and cannot exist in the present moment, if we are truly here and now. Those phenomena are features of the paradigm we have chosen to leave behind. If you go back over each of the Ten Assumptions presented in this book, and look at the "current assumptions" that accompany them, it is obvious why so many of us habitually indulge in these lower thoughts and emotions.

On the other hand, there is only Love and free will and this precious present moment, so where do blame, guilt, shame, worry and anxiety fit? Nowhere. They are gone. Poof! And with them, the analytical "memory mind" gives way to the all-knowing "intuitive mind." We re-connect to the Unified Field, we regain the "lost" powers of intuition and telepathic communication, and we, effortlessly, experience the world we dream of for our children, the world we've all been striving for, a world of peace, abundance, joy, love. An adventure beyond our wildest dreams awaits those of us with the courage and vision to take the plunge into a time-free, trust-based reality. As we have said repeatedly in this book, it is up to each and every one of us to consciously choose the reality we want to experience and to proceed accordingly.

OUR EVOLUTIONARY PURPOSE

Once a sufficient proportion, a critical mass, of our species has chosen to live in a state of open-hearted trust, in this timeless present moment, in the Trust Frequency, we will have reached a collective turning point, de Chardin's *Omega Point*. A spontaneous quantum leap in human consciousness will occur, a shift at least as significant as the transformation of *homo erectus* into *homo sapiens* that, according to current science, occurred some 70,000 years ago. This shift is of boundless significance. It's not just humanity that will make the leap. Quantum entanglement ensures that the entire ever-unfolding Universe and everything in It will transform along with us, as we fulfill our evolutionary purpose.

THE GIFT OF COLLAPSE

The early years of the 21st Century are tough times for many people. As the fear energy leaves the planet and the Earth moves more and more into the love vibration, the old survival systems that our predecessors put in place, based on their then-current assumptions, are collapsing. Look around you. It's pretty obvious. Our world is not what it was, even ten years ago, five years ago. Natural disasters, global warming, foreclosures, revolutions... No matter how attached we are to our possessions, our money, our illusions of power, no matter how much security we thought we were building as we compromised our very essence to survive, the things we thought we could depend on are deserting us, throwing us into the Now, where the only option is to trust unconditionally that everything will turn out better than we could possibly have imagined.

It is time to take bold, committed action, get our old ways of thinking and our conditioned minds out of the way, trust, relax, let go, and allow the innate intelligence of the Universe to unfold through us. It is precisely that unconditional trust that ensures that the future will be infinitely better than it would have been if the *status quo* had continued. The collapse pushes us beyond our imaginary limitations, beyond worry, beyond fear, beyond anxiety. Our challenge is to face our doubts and fears, move through them, and emerge on the other side. There is no other option. We burst through the door into the promised land, (which the Hopis call the 5th World,) just as the Hopi ancestors did when they entered this world through the underground *sipapu** deep in the Grand Canyon.

* Sipapu, a Hopi word, is a small hole or indentation in the floor of kivas used by the ancient Pueblo peoples and modern-day Puebloans. It symbolizes the portal through which their ancestors emerged from the 3rd World into the present time, which they call the 4th World.

TRUST THE LOVING UNIVERSE

Along with the collapse of our social and financial systems, as everything we thought was real and important becomes increasingly irrelevant, we may find ourselves in a state of confusion, not knowing what to do next. We might forget that we were angry at our neighbor or our mother, we might forget that we were afraid of the family next door who seemed weird, and we certainly have no idea of what we are "supposed" to do tomorrow. We have transitioned into the Now, into the Trust Frequency, where everything is already perfect. We have learned to trust the loving Universe.

Ease and grace have taken over, unless of course you are attached to the collapsing systems, unless your identity and your self-worth are tied up in the fortunes that are disappearing, the jobs you thought were going to give you the ticket to ride into status and security and freedom for you and your family. But since you've picked up this book, something in your soul wants to be free, wants to align with its highest purpose, is intrigued with possibilities that lie beyond your wildest imaginings. The Trust Frequency, your highest self, your purpose, your gift, the Conscious Loving Universe Itself, is calling to you. Can you hear It?

The Now, the conscious awareness of the present moment, is the gateway to the Trust Frequency, but we can't get there in the current left-brain mental construct we call the "memory mind," where the accumulation of everything in our life's experience is somehow stored in our individual brain, separate from everyone else's. As the evolutionary shift unfolds, we are moving into a new way of being that allows us to live more and more in the Now, in complete trust, with "effortless effort." The boundaries have dissolved, and we operate from the "intuitive mind" where all information is available as part of the Unified Field, the *Akashic Record*. Our memories of the past and our anxieties about the future melt away into a timeless oneness, a presence, a luminous state, a here-and-now awareness, from which we choose to take action spontaneously, aligning with our highest purpose, playing our part in the symphony of life.

We don't have to remember where we put the car keys. We simply put our hands on them whenever we need them. Cause and effect become blurred in an instantaneous access to the balance and beauty of ourselves and the world around us. Our internal

GPS is fully operational. Like Thoreau's Indian guide and the humble honeybee, we know exactly where we are, where we are going, and how to get there. We no longer need the iPad or an old-fashioned map to tell us where we are. Perhaps contemporary technology is training us to access the Unified Field, where all information exists, to access our true nature. We no longer have to "remember" anything because everything is stored in the "cloud." We can let it go, because we know we can access it anytime, anywhere.

Have you felt like your brain is made of Swiss cheese lately, that there are big gaps in your memory that you attribute to early-onset Alzheimer's, a brain freeze, a senior moment, senility? Here's the news! It is the evolutionary leap in consciousness putting us into the NOW! Once the process is complete, our uniqueness will be magnified, all the experiences that we've had that have honed us into who we are will remain a part of us, but the guilt/blame/shame game is over and we become the glorious vehicle of divine perfection we came here to be.

CONVERGENCE OF HIGHER AND LOWER SELF

Why is it important that we understand the effects of linear time? Why is awareness of the present moment essential to our development as humans? It is because our so-called ego, our "lower self," can only experience a time-based reality. The aspect of our being that Freud called the ego is completely entangled in time. It is not possible for the ego to experience timelessness, non-duality. On the other hand, our "higher self," our connected "divine" self, can never experience duality, can never experience a time-bound state. Our higher self exists in a state of permanent oneness with All-That-Is. This is another of the paradoxes of human existence.

We labor under the illusion that we are divided beings. As a result, partly, of Descartes' dualistic world-view, we have come to believe that we are split down the middle, that we have a "lower self" and a "higher self." The lower self we call the ego, and many spiritual paths seem dedicated to the idea that in order to be enlightened, the seeker must destroy, eliminate, eradicate, annihilate the ego. Only the higher self must be permitted to exist. And yet, the ego is our individuality. It is how we manifest in the world. Our individuality is a precious facet of the trillion-faceted diamond of Creation. It is who we are. It is I, it is You. Our individual ego self is the blossom on the glorious tree whose trunk is our divine, connected self, whose roots spread out and connect to everything in all of Creation. There is nothing inherently wrong with the ego, unless one suffers from insecurity, and who is truly free of insecurity in this fear-based paradigm? An insecure person tends to over-compensate, at which point the effects of an "inflated ego" become visible. We see the person as an "egotist," a boaster, a "control freak." Needless to say, the symptom of an inflated ego is actually a sign of a hurt little child, desperately pretending to be something other than what he thinks he is. In fact, needless to say, he is a divine, timeless, cosmic being, just like everyone else, but he has forgotten. For the moment.

IT'S ABOUT TIME

The fact is, the very act of incarnation results in an apparent split in our beings. From the undifferentiated oneness and non-duality of our pre-physical existence, we are born, at a certain moment and in a certain place, into a four-dimensional reality that is firmly governed by the laws of space and time. We become part of a fixed, predictable timeline. We emerge through the birth canal, forgetting everything we know. We experience our lives from infancy through childhood, adolescence and maturity, and eventually each of us drops the mantle of this physical body and melts into the undifferentiated oneness of the spirit world once more. During our earthly lifetime, part of us is here in the world, conscious but trapped in a time-bound ego, while another part remains eternally connected to the timeless matrix of all Being. That confusing and schizophrenic situation is about to change.

The time you enjoy wasting is not wasted time.
Bertrand Russell, PhD, philospher

WE ARE ONE

There is no such thing as wasted time. Everything in your life has served to prepare you for bringing your unique gift. There are no mistakes, no wrong choices. There is only Now. There is only Love. Remember, in the early decades of the 21st Century, *homo sapiens* is embarking on the adventure of evolving, consciously evolving, into *homo sapiens sapiens*, into Humanity 2.0, of manifesting the unlimited potential built into the DNA of our beings. This process has been described as a Great Awakening, a point in the evolutionary upward spiral when our lower and our higher selves converge, when we wake up and remember what we have always known: We are not divided. We are not separate. We are One.

THE EIGHTH ASSUMPTION

All Of Creation Is ONE.
Separation Is A Man-Made Illusion.

Current Assumption

We are inevitably and permanently
separate and disconnected from one another.
We are all alone in an uncaring universe.

How does the scientific fact of a 'hopelessly inter-connected universe' apply to us? Why does an understanding of the inter-connectedness and sacredness of all things matter so much? The answer is this: As a direct result of our ignorance of this fundamental fact, we humans have become profoundly confused. Dangerously so. No matter what ethnic or religious group we have come from, our inherited belief systems, individually and as communities, are severely flawed.

When the Eastern mystics tell us that they experience
all things and events as manifestations of a basic oneness,
this does not mean that they pronounce all things to be equal.
They recognize the individuality of things, but at the same
time they are aware that all differences and contrasts are
relative within an all-embracing unity. Since in our normal
state of consciousness, this unity of all contrasts, especially
the unity of opposites, is extremely hard to accept, it constitutes
one of the most puzzling features of Eastern philosophy.
Fritjof Capra, PhD, *The Tao of Physics*

When we see our fundamental unity with the processes of
nature and the functioning of the universe, as I so vividly
saw it from the Apollo spacecraft, the old ways of thinking
and behaving will disappear. Throughout history people
have sought to resolve the differences between their objective
methods and their subjective experience - between outer and inner.
Humanity needs to rise from the personal to the transpersonal,
from self-consciousness to cosmic consciousness.
Edgar Mitchell, PhD, astronaut

Unless you know yourself well, how can you know another?
And when you know yourself - you are the other.
Nisargadatta, mystic

The undivided unity of all things seems counter-intuitive. It is obvious, according to our physical senses, that the physical universe is comprised of a trillion trillion separate objects and entities and energies. It is absurd, as the rational-materialists tell us, and as our own senses confirm, to assert that all is one. The whole idea of non-duality makes no rational sense. The same logic applied to our understanding the nature of our planet, some hundreds of years ago. It was obvious, common sense and our physical senses told us then, as they tell us now, that the world was flat. Anyone suggesting otherwise was marginalized as a madman. You'd fall over the edge if you sailed too far. And then the paradigm shifted. No one today suggests that the world is flat. Well, not many people, at any rate*.

(*You may be surprised to learn that the International Flat Earth Society is still active, and claims to have been de-programming the masses since 1547. We're not kidding. Google them.)

BEYOND THE WORLD OF OPPOSITES

Non-duality is one of the great paradoxes of existence. On the one hand, here we are, each of us trapped in his or her own exclusive reality. I can never experience your universe, nor can you ever experience mine, no matter how close we are. I am a separate, autonomous being, with my own perspective. So are you. And yet... We must ask ourselves, what lies beyond the world of opposites?

> *And while I stood there, I saw more than I can tell, and I understood more than I saw; for I was seeing in a sacred manner the shapes of all things in the spirit, and the shape of all shapes as they must live together like one being.*
> Nicholas Black Elk

NOETIC SCIENCE

Quantum physics has established, through the theoretical, mathematical and experimental confirmation of the inter-connectedness of all things throughout time and space, the validity of unity or oneness consciousness, in effect confirming the world-view or cosmology of the yogis and the indigenous peoples of the world, and validating the often-unspoken inner essence of each and every one of the great religions. Furthermore, at this point in the history of science, the phenomenon of consciousness itself is at last beginning to get its day in the sun. A new scientific discipline has recently come into being. This emerging field is called *noetics*, from the Greek *noos* = mind. The noetic sciences are:

> *"explorations into the nature and potentials of consciousness using multiple ways of knowing, including intuition, feeling, reason, and the senses. Noetic sciences explore the "inner cosmos" of the mind (consciousness, soul, spirit) and how it relates to the 'outer cosmos' of the physical world."* Institute of Noetic Sciences, founded by astronaut Edgar Mitchell, PhD

ALL MY RELATIONS

How new are these revolutionary scientific concepts? Are they really new at all, or is Western science just catching up with the timeless wisdom of the world, at last? The Eastern mystics, for example, and the Native Americans, have always based their entire existence on these principles, as have most of the other indigenous peoples of the world. It wasn't until Newton, Descartes, and Darwin, the Age of Reason, that we Westerners fully separated, (although we many centuries previously bought into the idea of a separate God,) taking the radical dualist fork leading to the current rational-materialist paradigm. The Lakota phrase *Mitakuye Oyasin*, all my relations, at the opposite end of the cosmological spectrum, acknowledges and affirms that all things are inter-connected, every living creature, as well as the inanimate ones, the earth, the sun, the rocks, the sky.

When the Great Spirit is known within, in communities where truth and honesty are honored, people live in harmony with one another. They experience their own life and the life of the Creator as one. They know that our people are like the leaves and our tribes like the branches of a wondrous tree. They know that the life of the two-footed and four-footed and winged ones, the life of the plants and rivers and seas, the life even of the very sun, moon and stars grows also from that tree. All come from one single trunk of Being — the eternal being that we know as God. In this way, the Great Spirit lives within all things, within every plant and animal, every tree, every one of us here present.
Ken Carey, *Return of the Bird Tribes*

The trees wish to help us.
The rivers, the oceans, wish to help us.
The birds wish to help us.
All the other people we call animals, they wish to help us.
All we have to do is ask for help!
Chief Sonne Reyna, Yaqui-Carrizo elder
(from the authors' film *In Search Of The Future*)

THE ROLE OF THE WORLD WIDE WEB

As things stand at this time in history, at this moment in the evolution of the free mind, the only thing over which each of us has complete control is our own mind. At the same time, thanks to the breakthrough technological advances of the last few decades, we live in an unprecedented age of communication. Our individual minds are suddenly inter-connected in a digitally-enhanced group mind, something that has never happened before. This fact will inevitably have profound consequences. It already has. A new idea, a new attitude, a new understanding, a new belief system, can spread like wildfire. The potential exists for a sweeping change to flood through the collective consciousness of humanity, giving birth to an entirely new paradigm.

We are witnessing the seeds of global social change as this book is approaching completion, with rising demand worldwide for economic and social justice. As the printing press was to the 16th Century, so the World Wide Web is to the 21st Century, along with all the other communications media we now have. Add to that the awareness that there is infinitely more to life than the rather absurd reflections we see on television, a reality beyond anything we can imagine, and the knowledge that we are each free to make new choices, based on updated assumptions about the nature of reality, and the shackles are off. We can create whatever reality, whatever future, we choose, individually and collectively. We can dare to go forward in trust, making bold and confident moves, knowing that something is unfolding that is bigger than any one of us, bigger than all of us put together. The challenge is to decide what that means, to understand our central role and responsibility in co-creating, aligning and co-operating with that future, to step up to the plate, and to have the courage to become conscious evolutionists along with the rest of awakening humanity.

The World Wide Web can be seen as a new extension of the collective human brain, a technological phenomenon predicted more than half a century ago by Teilhard de Chardin. It seems that the new technology is training humanity, preparing us for the next phase of our evolution, giving us access to the unified field of all human knowledge, and simulating a direct connection to all information, all-that-is. The planet itself seems to be evolving, along with all life associated with it. The Earth in its entirety appears to be moving into a higher frequency, where love is more and more the dominant energy, and the old fear-based reality is gradually fading away. At some point in the near future, the old fear-based lower-vibration behavior will become impossible. We live on an "ascending" Earth, a planet that is moving upwards on the scale of vibratory frequency.

A DEEPER ORDER OF EXISTENCE

Everything, according to indigenous cosmology, is intimately related to every other thing, which is pretty much exactly what speculative quantum physicist and Einstein contemporary David Bohm realized in the early years of the 20th Century. Significantly, Bohm went on to pursue a passionate interest in human inter-connectedness, and spent the last decades of his life working with Native American thinkers on the multiple subjects of language, dialogue, cosmology and modes of communication in the quest for consensus.

> *The more Bohm thought about it the more convinced*
> *he became that the universe actually employed holographic*
> *principles in its operations; the universe itself is a kind of*
> *giant, flowing hologram. One of Bohm's most startling*
> *assertions is that the tangible reality of our everyday*
> *lives is really a kind of illusion, like a holographic image.*
> *Underlying it is a deeper order of existence, a vast and*
> *more primary level of reality that gives birth to all the*
> *objects and appearances of our physical world in much the*
> *same way that a piece of holographic film gives birth to a*
> *hologram. Bohm calls this deeper level of reality the*
> *implicate (which means "enfolded") order, and he refers to*
> *our own level of existence as the explicate, or unfolded, order.*
> Michael Talbot, *The Holographic Universe*

AN UNBROKEN WEB

While the Lakota pray to the six directions, North, West, South, East, Sky and Earth, knowing and acknowledging that all things are intimately connected and part of a greater, conscious whole called *Tunkashila*, or Grandfather, with whom they each have an intimate personal relationship, quantum science found itself approaching the situation from an apparently very different perspective.

> *In his general theory of relativity Einstein astounded the*
> *world when he said that space and time are not separate*
> *entities, but are smoothly linked and part of a larger whole*

*he called the space-time continuum. Bohm takes this idea a
giant step further. He states that everything in the universe
is part of a continuum. Despite the apparent separateness
of things at the explicate level, everything is a seamless
extension of everything else, and ultimately, the implicate
and explicate orders blend into each other. Take a moment
to consider this. Look at your hand. Now look at the light
streaming from the lamp beside you. And at the dog resting
at your feet. You are not merely made of the same things.
You are the same thing. One thing. Unbroken. One
enormous something that has extended its uncountable arms
and appendages into all the apparent objects, atoms, restless
oceans, and twinkling stars in the cosmos.*
Michael Talbot, *The Holographic Universe*

The wise ones, the shamans, the spiritual masters, the
founders of religions and the visionaries of all ages and cultures,
and now, our quantum physicists, maintain that we are all One.
Everything is One, despite the compelling evidence of our senses
to the contrary. The trillion trillion things are merely facets of an
unbroken whole. Separation is a man-made illusion, the result of a
limited perspective.

*We live in succession, in division, in parts and
particles. Meantime, within man, is the soul of
the whole; the wise silence; the universal beauty
to which every part and particle is equally related;
the Eternal One.*
Ralph Waldo Emerson, *The Over-Soul*

A HOPELESSLY INTERCONNECTED UNIVERSE

Quantum physics has long sought after a "theory of everything", a single mathematical equation that could account for all the physical laws in the universe. In *Science and the Akashic Field*, the Hungarian scientist and futurist Ervin Laszlo proposes that a genuine "theory of everything" is now achievable. The consequences of such a theory are profound, once it is integrated into our collective worldview.

> *Western scientists are beginning to discover what has been documented by Eastern sages and mystics for thousands of years; that within nature exists an interconnecting field that interweaves every atom, cell, organism, and mind, throughout time, the Akashic Record*. This field acts as "the memory of the universe" and continuously interacts with matter at every level from subatomic to cosmic to influence the way every living thing grows, adapts, and evolves.*
> Ervin Laszlo, philosopher of science

> *Ervin Laszlo has, probably more than any person alive, intricately spelled out a staggering but often neglected fact: we live in a hopelessly interconnected universe, with each and every single thing connected in almost miraculous ways to each and every other thing.*
> Ken Wilber, philosopher

* In Laszlo's book *Science And The Akashic Field*, akasha is described as "the aether from which all matter is formed."

How does the scientific fact of a "hopelessly inter-connected universe" apply to us? Why does an understanding of the inter-connectedness and sacredness of all things matter so much? The answer is this: As a direct result of our ignorance of this fundamental fact, we humans have become profoundly confused. Dangerously so. No matter what ethnic or religious groups we have come from, our inherited belief systems, individually and as communities, are severely flawed. The old, limited paradigm no longer serves us. It is a house of cards built on a false foundation, and the obvious signs of collapse are all around us.

At the species level, there is only one race, the human race, *homo sapiens*, and yet the world we have created is divided in extraordinary and largely un-examined ways to ensure permanent separation, from birth to death, from generation to generation, by language, skin pigmentation, class, caste, gender, religion, sect, place of birth, ethnicity, economic status, political affiliation, and arbitrary national boundaries that have nothing whatsoever to do with the reality that we are all divine sovereign beings, members of the same remarkable species, living on a single unified planet, a manifestation of the unified consciousness of Love. Let's look, for a minute, at the consequences of this most fundamental and erroneous of human cultural assumptions.

AN ABSURD AND TRAGIC MISBELIEF

One of the fundamental organizing principles of every human society on the planet, one that everyone takes for granted, is this: it is natural, normal and "patriotic" to see ourselves as American,

British, Chinese, French, Iranian, Indian, Russian, Zulu, Maya
or Wabanaki, or any of a hundred thousand different national,
ethnic and tribal groups, depending on where we happened to be
born, and that this is a good thing. When do we ever question the
correctness, the appropriateness, of one of the most fundamental
concepts underlying today's world: *nationalism*? What has happened
to us as humans, and why have we created these divisive systems
that are so integrated into our societies that we rarely if ever stop
to examine them? If deep down we know that we are all one, why
do we find ourselves so divided? Who came up with these fear-
based ideas, and why do we blindly go along with them? Between
the twin forces of religion and nationalism, we find ourselves
divided and fragmented like the scattered shards of a beautiful but
broken mirror. We have lost the ability to see beyond the illusions
we have created.

What difference does it make where we were born? Why
do I need a "passport" to come to "your" "country," just because
I was born on a different island than you were? What could be
more ridiculous? We were all, each and every one of us, born on
this beautiful planet Earth, and it is absurd and tragic that this
fundamental fact goes unrecognized. It is unimaginably foolish
and fantastically expensive. It is nothing less than social and
economic madness. The prevailing paradigm dictates that we
are all inevitably, permanently separate, by the simple quirk of
fate that determined the place of our birth. And it's not just the
Western world that has bought into the delusion of separateness.

For whatever reason, it seems to be universal. If I happened to be born into the Hutu tribe, somewhere in Central Africa, I am forever and profoundly different from someone who was born into the Tutsi tribe just a few miles to the south, despite the fact that our appearance, language, costume and culture are indistinguishable to an outsider. To a member of the Hutu, a Tutsi is perceived as less than human, and *vice versa*. The ancestors of the Hutu and the Tutsi were, probably, a pair of brothers who argued and went their separate ways to found different clans, which later grew into the warring tribes we know today.

Somehow, worldwide, variants of this ancient tribalism devolved into nationalism, and today the entire planet is in the grip of a rigid, all-pervasive illusion, tenaciously enforced at staggering cost to the populace. Have you ever stopped to think about the economic and social cost of maintaining and defending all of the borders of all of the so-called countries in the world, all of the armies, the navies, the air forces, the border posts, the immigration officers, the detention camps for "illegal aliens?" It is nothing less than insane, a profound perversion of reality, and yet who ever looks at the ridiculous situation we have created for ourselves? Has anyone ever looked at the global *status quo* from a higher perspective, and wondered whether there could be a better way to expend our precious energy?

> *Being able to shift to a higher realm of perception can help us find solutions to our problems, resolve conflicts, heal disease, and experience oneness with all of creation.* Alberto Villoldo, PhD

Can you think of anyone who has written or spoken on this most obvious and fundamental of subjects, other than Garry Davis? Wait a minute. Who is Garry Davis? Well might you ask. Garry Davis should be a household name. Garry, who turned 92 in 2011, is the American air force gunner who had an epiphany while bombing innocent German women and children during WWII. After the war, Garry relinquished his United States citizenship and started the World Citizen movement. He has seen the inside of 38 prisons as a result, but he perseveres to this day. You can apply for your World Citizen's passport through his offices in Washington, right now. Garry has freed thousands of stateless refugees around the world by issuing them World Citizen passports. You can experience the story of this extraordinary former American in the award-winning 2012 documentary *JUST ONE: The Garry Davis Story. No Borders. No Boundaries. No Fear.*

Why is Garry Davis almost the only activist working to change the system? Why has his work been ignored? Why is this not the number one item on the United Nations' agenda? Does the phrase "United Nations" mean anything? How can we change this disastrous situation? Can we change it? Well, since the only constant in the Universe is change, and since life is indeed an evolutionary upward spiral, why should we think that the current paradigm will remain in place forever? There must be some way to dismantle the rigid current setup, to let go of the fear and mistrust that created all of this in the first place, and create a world free of national boundaries and tribal and religious divisions, where the splendid diversity of humanity is celebrated and honored rather than mistrusted and feared. All that is needed is a new idea, an idea based on truth, not fear-induced fiction.

> *These ideas suggest an inner unity of human consciousness*
> *that extends beyond the diversity of individually evolved forms.*
> *The current belief in many disciplines seems to be that violence*
> *is inherent, and therefore, inevitable. If the new view is correct,*
> *however, then our separateness - the major source of the selfishness*
> *and callousness that leads to violence - is an illusion.*
> *Beyond this illusion, the separateness that is in appearance only,*
> *stands the unitive reality of inseparability.*
>
> Amit Goswami, PhD, physicist

NO EMPIRE LASTS FOREVER

All change begins with an idea. In fact all the tribes, all the nation-states, all the religions, all the divisions in our species, are nothing more than ideas themselves, and ideas can be replaced or modified at will. The American or the British or the French or the Iranian flags, for instance, like every other national flag, are nothing more than symbols for an idea, and a divisive, defective, and dangerous idea at that.

The fact is, anything that started as an idea can be replaced by another idea, and looking back through history at the continual ebb and flow of social systems over time, it is clear that no single social, political or religious system has ever held sway for very long. In fact, looking back through history, it is obvious that major change is occurring at shorter and shorter intervals. As soon as a new idea comes along, after some initial resistance, the old paradigm melts away. The Babylonians and the Romans and the

Mayans and the Romans, the Inca and the French and the Zulu, the Portuguese and the Aztecs and the Spanish and the British empires came and went as dominant forces in their geographical regions. Feudalism and monarchism came and went, the Berlin Wall came down, the Soviet Union collapsed and apartheid went away. The American empire appears to be crumbling. Empires do not last forever. A new paradigm is not only possible, it is inevitable, as the cycles of birth, death and rebirth go on.

> *Even among bourgeois economists, there is hardly a serious thinker who will deny that it is possible, by means of currently existing material and intellectual forces of production, to put an end to hunger and poverty, and that the present state of things is due to the socio-political organization of the world.*
> Herbert Marcuse, *The End of Utopia*

IMAGINE

Clearly the socio-political structure of the world could use a little re-inventing. As must be obvious by now, it is the fundamental assumptions that underlie our social and political systems that so desperately need an upgrade. Politics-as-usual is not going to fix the situation, not "democracy" nor "socialism" nor any other artificial social system, especially if that system is subject to manipulation by the rich and the powerful. Only a radical re-birth of the individual and collective human spirit, a true quantum leap in consciousness, a new unitive concept of humanity, a real shift toward a higher vision of reality, is going to bring about the needed change, and because this is the only way out of the morass, that is indeed the way it will happen. Change, it seems, is inevitable. The question is: how do we make sure that the coming change will be for the better?

> *If we, in our separate, fragmented egos, want to be whole again, we not only have to understand the situation intellectually, we must also delve into our inner reaches to experience the whole... How can we re-enter that enchanted state of wholeness? I am speaking not of a regression to childhood or to some golden age, nor am I speaking of salvation in eternal life after death. No, the question is, how can we transcend the ego level, the level of fragmented being? How can we achieve freedom but at the same time live in the world of experience?*
> Amit Goswami, PhD, physicist

It is essential that some of our most fundamental assumptions be replaced. Our fear-based world-view must be replaced by a cosmology based on trust. It is really that simple, although we are not suggesting that the transformation will necessarily happen overnight. The seeds of the new unitive ideas have long been planted and are spreading, germinating invisibly in the collective human heart and mind. The Internet, Facebook, YouTube, Twitter and all the other social media phenomena are playing a major role. Our *imaginal* DNA is being activated. The shift is hitting the fan! A great awakening is in progress. It is in the process of going viral.

A NEO-TRIBAL VISION?

Once we truly awaken, and rub the sleep from our eyes, what will the world look like? What kind of society will we create, once we have finally evolved into *homo sapiens sapiens*, "wise man?" It seems possible that our new social structures and groupings might look tribal or neo-tribal on the surface, but based on a consensus reality very different from the old exclusionary, fearful, defensive ethnic and religious hierarchies. Can you picture a tribe based on the concepts in John Lennon's song *Imagine*, a society operating from a higher conscience? No countries. No flags. No religions. No chiefs or warriors. No military budget. No priests or judges. No elites. No enforcers. No criminals. No separation. A society of disciplined, self-assured, responsible equals. In *Civil Disobedience*, Henry David Thoreau envisions just such a society:

> *Thoreau's real view toward government is, "That government is best which governs least, and consequently, that government is best which governs not at all." He puts a period at the end of that sentence, but really to understand what he's talking about, you need to say, "That government is best which governs not at all, because in such a government, all the citizens govern themselves." That's the key. What Thoreau wants is self-governors, everyone their own king and governor and congress and senate. You do not need laws to control you because you have an inner law that manifests itself in your outer conduct. Thoreau's idea of government is not anarchism. It is basically, at the most individual level, self-government.*
> Bradley P. Dean, PhD, scholar. (From the authors' film *The American Evolution: Voices of America*. Part 1)

IT BEGAN IN THE 1960'S

Thoreau envisioned a time when individuals would operate from their higher conscience in society and create a world in balance. Imagine a world of flexible, trust-based communities, based on Thoreau's principles of self-governance, operating from a higher conscience and creating a world in balance. What a concept. A tribe (it's hard to think of a more appropriate word in the English language) or a society like that would welcome members from all races, philosophies, pigmentations and geographical origins. We would celebrate, honor, respect and admire our differences. Participation would be entirely voluntary, with groups and individuals and families coming and going freely, moving from community to community and place to place when and if they wanted to.

Ultimately, there is only one tribe, US! Imagine the new human tribe, broken up into countless voluntary clans, based entirely on affinity and friendship, not compulsion or law. Significantly, perhaps, aspects of this neo-tribal lifestyle have been evolving in a variety of experimental forms for several generations, ever since the 1960s, in the so-called counter-culture, which is now a well-established, world-wide phenomenon, though it rarely makes the news these days. Consider the Burning Man "tribe," as one rather extreme, part-time, but remarkably successful 50,000-member example.

THE GODS MUST BE CRAZY

Is there no precedent for such a society? Has any human culture ever modeled such an intelligent way of being in the world? Can you think of such a thing, throughout all the 200,000 years of human history? No, you say? Wait. Are you aware of the San Bushmen, the first people of Africa? The little, peppercorn-haired, apricot-colored people who carry the world's oldest human DNA? Do you remember the popular film *The Gods Must Be Crazy*? For countless millennia, long before the advent of the black cattle-herding tribes who emerged from West Africa about 10,000 years ago, the little orange-skinned hunter-gatherers now known as "Bushmen" roamed the entire African continent, and developed an egalitarian, peaceful social system that has no equal in history.

They never developed weapons of war. They had better things to do. They invented almost every musical instrument known to man. They left us a precious heritage in the form of the world's most prolific and sophisticated rock art, from Egypt in the north to the Cape of Good Hope at the southern tip. They developed effective strategies to prevent the rise of an elite. They had no leaders. Anyone could become a healer. Men had precisely the same rights as women, as did children. There is a large body of literature on these extraordinary people, if you'd like to learn more about them. The Bushmen have a lot to teach us, when it comes to the art of being human.

You need a good heart, mentally and physically,
to be well. This is also necessary in healing others.
The Bushmen of the Kalahari know each other's hearts.

We also know the hearts of all the other people in the
world. You must open your heart to have a good heart.
There can be no jealousy or bad intentions inside you.
You must go with an open heart to your neighbor and
everyone around you. You must look after everyone.
Open your heart and serve one another. This is our way.
This is the key to healing.

From: *Kalahari Bushman Healers*, edited by Bradford Keeney, PhD

A WORLD WITHOUT POVERTY

Ultimately, we foresee, once the new "wise man", the true human, is firmly established, there will be no borders, no guards, no passports, no armies, no prisons, no police. No military budget. No separate countries. Such absurdities will be inconceivable, because humanity will have awakened. An understanding of the forgotten inter-connectedness and sacredness of all things will re-emerge and peace will come to prevail on Earth! The terrible, incredibly expensive illusion of separateness will dissolve, and we will live in the reality of one world, one people, celebrating the splendidly diverse and remarkable species that we have always been. We will put all of our resources toward creating a world without poverty, without illness, without homelessness, and have tons of time to enjoy it.

LAY DOWN THE WEAPONS OF WAR

Oneness and abundance are the true nature of things. Once we awaken to that fact, the systems and behaviors based on separation and scarcity will disappear. Humanity will lay down the weapons of war, as the five warring Iroquois tribes did over 500 years ago, when they heeded the words of the Peacemaker, Deganawida, adopted The Great Law, buried their weapons beneath the Tree of Peace and created the Iroquois League of Nations.

Right now some of the people are in transition
into a higher level of understanding. I call it
the shift of the worlds.
Grandmother Bertha Grove, Ute Elder.
(from the authors' film *In Search Of The Future*)

The current consensus reality is just an illusion, an aberration, in its worst aspects an imaginary, fear-based, bizarre and primitive collective hallucination. It prevents us from seeing the deeper truth: the world is already perfect. When we decide to wake up, the hypnotic nightmare will fade away, as all dreams do. We won't even bother trying to remember the details, the way we are taught to remember our history today, with its endless catalogue of dates, battles, body-counts, assassinations and bloody conquests. What a silly waste of time that would be, when there's wood to be chopped, water to be carried, music to be played, love to be made, fun to be had, and children to be nurtured? Life was like that back in Bushman times, for a hundred thousand years. It will be like that again. All we have to do is do it!

We will each bring our piece of the hoop,
and together create the hoop of life.
Grandmother Kitty, Nakota Elder

THE NINTH ASSUMPTION

Humanity Is On An Evolutionary Upward Spiral.

Current Assumption

We're going to hell in a hand-basket. Look around you!

We have learned nothing over the past centuries.

The world would be better off without us.

Looking back through the millions of years of human development, it is evident that our evolving species is on an upward spiral. And the process is accelerating. We have come a long way in the past century alone. As the trend continues, as we awaken, we are lead inexorably to a higher consciousness, a higher reality, a state of being which, ultimately, will become the Trust Frequency, or Heaven-on-Earth.

*W*hat kind of future are "We the People" creating, intentionally or otherwise? Consider Hollywood's sci-fi vision of the future of our planet: ever more militarization, ever more bondage, less and less freedom. *Brave New World, 1984, Robocop, Total Recall, Terminator, Star Wars, The Matrix, Avatar, Mortal Kombat, Tron: Legacy.* An isolated few in a desperate fight for freedom. Against overwhelming odds, our heroes triumph over the corrupt System, which has been taken over by the Dark Side.

IN SEARCH OF THE FUTURE

These blockbusters paint a scary picture, but they also serve a higher purpose. We get to play out our shadow side in a collective cleansing. We face our darkest fantasies, moving through them to the higher truths portrayed of these stories. Central to these films are eternal truths, truths we know in our heart of hearts. The Divine has always spoken through story, and Hollywood is using its enormous power to inspire social change, giving us the courage to undertake our own "Hero's Journey" in the battle with our personal and collective Dark Side. Since we create reality via the power of our consciousness, we clearly have a choice as to what kind of future we bring into being. Do we tacitly agree with science-fiction's dark consensus, or do we know that a higher truth will triumph in the end? Are we going to Hell in a hand-basket, once we figure out what a hand-basket is? No! Something entirely different lies in our immediate future. We are waking up. Each of us has a role to play in creating the future: the thousand years of peace, love, beauty and abundance described in the prophecies.

In man the perpetual progress is from the
Individual to the Universal, from that which
is human, to that which is divine.
Ralph Waldo Emerson

IT'S WAKE-UP TIME

Whether you believe in divine creation, extraterrestrial seeding (as do many of the indigenous peoples of the Earth), or in "hard science's" descent-from-the-apes version of the origin of our species, there is one thing a lot of us can agree on if we place our attention on the positive. Looking back through the millions of years of human development, it is evident that our evolving species is on an evolutionary upward spiral. And the process is accelerating. We have come a long way in the past century. As the trend continues, as we awaken, we are lead inexorably to a higher consciousness, a higher reality, a state of being which, ultimately, will become the Trust Frequency, or Heaven-on-Earth. Whatever time may mean to you, it seems certain that something positive is unfolding as time goes by.

We're not talking about going back to some idyllic past, to some Garden of Eden which existed in a previous time, and to which we can return. It's not about going back at all. There is no such thing as "back." There is only Now, and in the Now that we currently think of as "the future," we might look "back" upon these rather primitive times and wonder how we could have been so blind, so foolish. We will look back at ourselves from a higher perspective, because in a sense, life is a spiral, and though we might find ourselves coming "back" around to a familiar place we seem to have known before, we'll be an evolutionary step upward in the forward-and-upward moving spiral of awakening.

As Aluna Joy Yax'kin, the guide, author, and mystic, said in our 2007 film *In Search Of The Future:* "People think the end of the Mayan calendar (in 2012) is going to be the end of the world, but it's not. It's not the end of the Mayan calendar either. It's the end of a cycle of time that comes back round again and starts over. Now, when it comes back around it's like a serpent, but the serpent never catches its tail. It's an evolutionary notch up, it's a spiral. So, what we're coming back around to feels very familiar on a very deep level inside of us. We have learned so much in that 104,000-year cycle, and now we're going to take it another notch up and become creators of a new reality."

THE NOOSPHERE

The visionary Jesuit priest and paleontologist Pierre Teilhard de Chardin (1881–1955), in the mid-1900s, proposed that the sphere of consciousness surrounding our planet, the *noosphere** as he called it, would continue to develop, and would one day reach critical mass, with the result that a worldwide 100th monkey* phenomenon would occur, an Omega Point would be reached, and the whole of humanity would spontaneously elevate to a higher state. De Chardin in fact also foresaw the technological advance that we now know as the World Wide Web, the computer-based, non-centralized "nervous system" that has recently evolved in Earth's biosphere, connecting billions of people in previously inconceivable ways.

The noosphere is best described as a sort of 'collective consciousness' of human beings. It emerges from the interaction of human minds. The noosphere has grown in step with the organization of the human mass in relation to itself as it populates the earth. As mankind organizes itself in more complex social networks, the higher the noosphere will grow in awareness. This is an extension of the Law of Complexity Consciousness, the law describing the nature of evolution in the Universe. The noosphere is growing towards an ever-greater integration and unification, culminating in the Omega Point - which is the goal of history.

Pierre Teilhard de Chardin, *The Future of Man*

The Internet can be thought of as an extension of the human mind, of the *noosphere*, a merging of planetary consciousness, with the potential to trigger and facilitate an enormous evolutionary acceleration. It is not yet known exactly what shape the metamorphosis will take, but there is little doubt that the phenomenal explosion of information-availability brought about by the Internet will play a major part. There is an interesting convergence occurring in the opening years of the 21st Century, with the end of the Mayan Calendar in 2012, apparently tied to a rare astronomical alignment in our home galaxy, the so-called Age of Aquarius dawning, the Hopi's "Great Purification" and "Fifth World" expected any moment, and a number of other prophecies all pointing to a coming shift around the same time, and the fact that human technology has reached the point where, for instance, the information contained in this book is instantaneously available to everyone on the planet with access to a computer. Whether or not we buy into the predictions of the prophets, we clearly live in a time where profound and irreversible change seems inevitable, whether as a result of disastrous global warming, some "outside" intervention, or of a great inner awakening and consciousness expansion on the part of the human species.

We also live in a time when we in the West have finally recognized the value of the indigenous perspectives on the world, a time when ancient and modern cosmologies are coming together and affirming one another. A synthesis of contemporary quantum science, ancient spiritual wisdom and indigenous cosmology and inner knowing/intuition is occurring. The pieces of the puzzle are coming together in a whole new way. For the first time in recorded history, we have access to a picture of the "true" nature of the Universe, one that is accessible both to our intuitive and our intellectual minds, to both left and right brain. The resulting integration of all knowledge and understanding pierces the veil of illusion and allows us to imagine, en-vision, and then to co-create a "new" world, which could just be the "Heaven-on-Earth" foreseen by the prophets of old. That vision is what forms the basis and the inspiration for this book.

Since the mid-1960s, in a worldwide movement that has been termed the "counterculture," small experimental groups have been living alternative lifestyles, expanding their consciousness individually and collectively through contemplation, communication, meditation and entheogenic "plant helpers," and developing ways to live in harmony with each other and with nature. These experiments have directly and indirectly influenced the lives of hundreds of thousands of people, and several generations have now been born into these new and expanded realities. We hear about the "Indigo Children," new arrivals on this planet, who seem to be and know something both different, more loving, and beginning their lives at a higher level of consciousness than those who have gone before.

> *Many changes in the 1960s have become fixtures*
> *of European and American society. This was*
> *apparently the result of conscious effort by a large*
> *number of people to affect the future by working*
> *on themselves and working together to create a society*
> *that was more harmonious, more loving, and more in*
> *harmony with the environment.*
> Ralph Abraham, PhD
> (from the authors' film *In Search Of The Future*)

> *Humanity comes to this world to participate in*
> *the elaboration of a superior project. We are here*
> *participating in this project generation after generation,*
> *and each time, each generation, we have more abilities.*
> *Our mission is marked by the following way of*
> *thinking about destiny: mankind comes to the world*
> *with the end of seeking perfection by means of*
> *personal development. Perfection will come when*
> *mankind has developed the ability to create all we*
> *have the capacity to conceive. Each of the generations*
> *has within themselves memory genes in each body.*
> *All the experiences of the anterior generations*
> *are inherited by each of the individuals. Each of*

these individuals, with the experiences of their own
lives, enriches this genetic treasure.
Tlakaelel, Mexica-Tolteka elder

(from the authors' film *In Search Of The Future*)

SPEAK OF THE DEVIL

Once we wake up, we are no longer under the oppressive illusions propagated by the traditional religions and the various social systems, such as "communism" or "capitalism." As a species, we are growing up, coming into a mature understanding of the nature of the Universe, so we no longer automatically believe in the existence of separate, anthropomorphic entities such as "God" or the "Devil." As little children, we believe everything our parents tell us. We have no alternative. Our elders are like gods to us. All through our educational process, we are trained to reflect back the vision of reality portrayed by our teachers and professors. We are rewarded for this reflection by high school diplomas, college degrees, jobs, and the illusion of security. The same principles apply in our "religious" and "spiritual" training. We are rewarded if we conform, if we study and obey the Bible or the Koran or the Torah, do our mantras and our prayers, and become acceptable members of the community. The same process applies in most of the native traditions, as well as in all the guru-dominated spiritual paths. However, we have become more and more aware that all of the various traditions, lovely as some of them are, are in fact traps, keeping us in bondage generation after generation, and holding up evolutionary progress. At some point in each of our lives, we are presented with a choice: graduate into adulthood and become our true selves, or remain stuck forever in the lower grades, essentially as slaves to a system invented by others, frequently with a powerful controlling motivation.

QUESTION AUTHORITY

As more and more of us awaken into the next phase of human evolution, we inevitably move on from the limitations of the past. The "Age of the Masters" is over, as surely as the "Age of the Monarchs," once all-powerful, has long ago faded away. Those of us who are awake are now beginning to take responsibility for ourselves, for our own lives, for our own view of the world. No longer is it appropriate to give our power away to authority figures, whether political, medical, legal or spiritual. We exercise our inalienable free will, we take charge of our own minds, and we become exponentially more human in the process. This is a sure sign of the onset of maturity.

THE SECRET PURPOSE OF HISTORY

To summarize then, humanity is on an evolutionary upward path, a spiral leading inexorably to a higher reality, to Heaven-on-Earth. A master key to this evolution is the Trust Frequency described in these pages. There has been a hidden purpose to history. Every action, every event, has had two purposes, no matter what it may have looked like on the surface. Remember, there is nothing but Love. One purpose occurs on the illusory lower plane, obedient to the laws of space-time, human law and the dominant fear frequency. But since there is only Love, that action also inevitably serves a higher purpose, our journey to wholeness, the coming of peace on Earth, Heaven-on-Earth. This is an absolute. It is the consciousness of unconditional Love (God if you will) coming to understand Itself through physical experience, thereby expanding, growing, and evolving with every breath each one of us takes. Each of us is a roving sensory organ of the Divine, which is the undivided All-That-Is.

The "hundredth monkey" phenomenon concerns the manner in which a behavior or thought spreads rapidly from one group to all related groups once a critical number of initiates is reached. Similar to the concept of the "tipping point," it means the rapid spreading of an idea or ability to the remainder of a population once a certain portion of that population has grokked the new idea or learned the new ability.

THE TENTH ASSUMPTION

The Trust Frequency Is Real.
It Is Available To Anyone,
Anywhere, Anytime.

Current Assumption

Life's a bitch and then you die.

The Trust Frequency is, quite literally, that place or that state described in the world's sacred literature as Heaven, Shambhala, Nirvana, or Samadhi, and is presided over by the most powerful creative force in the Universe, LOVE.

THE TRUST FREQUENCY

An elevated state of being where the soul's destiny awaits,
with more abundance, balance, freedom and joy than we
can imagine. It is where the true nature of the Universe
is experienced. It is available to anyone, anywhere, anytime.

The Universe, once it is seen and experienced from the elevated perspective of the Trust Frequency, is one of unlimited abundance and perfect balance. It is the "problem-free reality" described in the well-known Swahili phrase *hakuna matata*. It sounds like heaven to us. How do we get there? The foregoing nine assumptions, and the Seven A's, are all the tools we need. Once we *know*, without any shadow of doubt, that this higher reality is not only possible, but is the natural order of things, we automatically transition into a state of gratitude, love, and trust, which are our primary vehicles to the Trust Frequency, to Nirvana, to Heaven-on-Earth. The more we open up and integrate these three things into our everyday lives, the happier we will be. Inevitably. It is the high road to happiness!

THE INDIGENOUS WAY OF LIFE

The Native Americans, traditionally, give daily thanks to the plants and the trees and the animals for supporting them, as well as to Father Sky and the Earth Mother. Gratitude is ever-present. As they do this, they are vibrating in the Trust Frequency, whereas we Westerners seem, for the most part, to have forgotten where everything comes from. We rarely acknowledge the source of our well-being other than the occasional "grace" before dinner, or an exclamation of "Thank God!" when things are going our way. Our vibrational frequency is more often on the level of anxiety than gratitude.

On the economic front, to the Native American, the "giveaway" is a core aspect of their traditional way of life. This concept is evidence of an abundance-and-trust-based paradigm. Hoarding or saving, those universal practices in the "developed" world, are foreign to the native way. If you have it, share it. There will be more tomorrow. Trust the loving Universe. This is an axiom of true indigenous cosmology.

Keep a spin on those frogskins!
Grandmother Kitty, Nakota Elder

HOW MANY REALITIES ARE THERE?

There are no limits. The Multi-verse, another word for the All-That-Is, consists of an infinitely vast and variable, ever-evolving quantum field containing all possibilities, throughout all of time and space, in all dimensions, both manifest and un-manifest, including countless multiple universes, perhaps as many as 10 to the power of 100, according to physicist Ervin Lazslo. That inconceivably huge number has recently been upgraded to 10 to the power of 500. That's 10 with 500 zeroes, equivalent, quite possibly, to all of the sentient beings that have ever existed, or will ever exist, in all of the universes put together. It seems quite possible, therefore, that we each get our own reality, our own exclusive universe, of which we are the sole creator and sustainer, but that's a discussion for another day.

Modern science agrees, and the Hopi people have known forever, that everything, without exception, is made up of electromagnetic energy vibrating at different frequencies. While those vibrations make up a spectrum of *all* possible frequencies, we as humans can only experience a certain limited range as we currently exist. This particular Universe, the one we experience in our daily lives, vibrates at a certain frequency, or more accurately a nested collection containing a limited spectrum of frequencies, to which our beings, both physical and metaphysical, are carefully calibrated and attuned. Aside from the occasional courageous shaman, or the inter-dimensional traveler of science fiction, each of us must remain within the frequency spectrum of this particular universe, or risk insanity.

> *We are in the field of quantum mechanics. Science has discovered a kind of law that we do not understand at the moment. Applying quantum mechanics to the microcosm, and relativity to the macrocosm, we have the unified field theory. Unifying quantum mechanics and relativity, we can talk about the reality where we can travel in different dimensions that exist here and now. These realities co-exist in different frequencies, different vibrational states. This corresponds to each of the dimensions. In this dimension in which we live now, we are vibrating in a certain wavelength in which this whole universe vibrates. Our senses are only able to receive this frequency. But occasionally some people can pass beyond this frequency and see what there is on the other side.*
> Tlakaelel, Mexica-Tolteka elder
> (from the authors' film *In Search Of The Future*)

The remainder, which represents the vast proportion of what is actually in existence, remains unknown and unknowable to us in this stage of our development. Interestingly, much of the invisible material of the physical universe has recently become detectable by our scientific measuring instruments. Examples of this are the phenomena we call "dark matter" and "dark energy," the apparently missing 96% of the mass of the detectable universe. There is certainly much more to this Universe than meets the eye. How, for instance, did Jesus perform the miracle of the loaves and the fishes? Did he somehow reach into the boundless realm of the un-manifest, into dark matter, and draw out an abundance of food for the multitude who came to hear him speak?

> *And he commanded them to make all sit down by companies upon the green grass. And they sat down in ranks, by hundreds, and by fifties. And when he had taken the five loaves and the two fishes, he looked up to Heaven, and blessed, and brake the loaves, and gave them to his disciples to set before them; and the two fishes divided he among them all. And they did all eat, and were filled. And they took up twelve baskets full of the fragments, and of the fishes. And they that did eat of the loaves were about five thousand men.*
> Jesus Feeds the Five Thousand: (Mark 6:30-44)

Whether this story is literally true or merely metaphorical, one thing is certain: there is vastly more to this existence than we have ever dared to imagine. Shamanic and psychedelic journeys take certain individuals to some of these alternative realities, but the simple fact is, there is infinitely more to Reality with a capital "R" than we can currently fathom. Speculative physics, especially when combined with ancient Vedic and indigenous cosmology, is at present in an explosively expansive mode, with brand-new visions and ideas emerging almost daily. It is the most exciting of times to be alive! And it is not only academics with PhDs who have access to the new vision. Far from it.

> *They joke about me, they laugh about me because I never went to school. I'm capable to interpret and translate because I speak from the universal mind. The animals taught me. They were my mentors, they were my teachers. Jesus never taught me how to pray. The animals taught me how to pray. If you understand this language you will be able to talk with the eagles and the four-leggeds and creepers and crawlers, fish people; you could talk to them. I am capable of speaking to all living. So, I am living proof.*
> Wallace Black Elk, Lakota elder

Existence is limitless, far beyond any one individual's ability to *grok* it in all its aspects. However, even if we limit ourselves just to this one Universe, the one we actually experience, we still find ourselves in an unimaginably vast and incomprehensible environment, barely detectable in its entirety by our six senses, although the sixth sense, that one not quite yet acknowledged by mainstream science, gives us an intuitive sense of just how amazing this existence may be. There is little doubt that there are other realms inter-acting with us every breath of every day, realms both "dark" and "light," realms vibrating on every level of the frequency spectrum, that influence our thoughts and our feelings, and to a greater or lesser degree determine what we feel, do and say in this life.

There may very well be other life-forms, UFOs and extraterrestrials, the beings that we think of as the spirits and the angels and the gods, with whom we are interconnected simply because there is no alternative. Quantum entanglement is a universal phenomenon. Nothing exists outside of the matrix of All-That-Is. How could it?

> *Each individual describes and perceives from*
> *different points along the great Medicine Wheel*
> *of eternal being, but each one does so within*
> *the context of certain basic recognitions. Chief*
> *among these recognitions is that all creatures*
> *inhabit and live within a single field of shared*
> *consciousness, that all are projections of a single*
> *Being, and that all of us - angels, humans, animals,*
> *vegetables, microbes and minerals - are differentiated*
> *aspects of one conscious and coherent whole.*
>
> Ken Carey, *Return of the Bird Tribes*

If everything in the Universe is deeply entangled or interconnected in the matrix of the Quantum Field, then we are by definition intimately connected to everything that exists, and it is only our species-specific limiting *homo sapiens* vibratory filter system that prevents us from simultaneous awareness of all these other realities and the accompanying sensory overload that would no doubt accompany such awareness.

The Universe we do experience, this everyday reality with all its ups and downs, is different for each and every one of us. There is no way any one of us can experience another's reality, no matter how close we might be. Our individual realities are mutually exclusive, and consist of a shifting spectrum of vibratory frequencies, which emotionally we might experience at different times as "low vibes," "good vibes" or "high vibes" in 1960s parlance. At times we feel "good". At other times we feel "bad."

Most of the time we don't even notice how we feel, we're so busy trying to keep up. Each of these vibratory levels, however, has its own set of laws and characteristics, and the rules that apply to one level of consciousness are not necessarily applicable to the others. If we do not know this, we are missing out on the greatest opportunity available to humankind. The highest "vibe" we can experience is the vibratory state we call the Trust Frequency. Is there anything higher? It is impossible to say. The Trust Frequency is a sacred place, an elevated state of being, where fear can not and does not enter, where scarcity, poverty, violence and disease are simply non-existent.

LOVE IS ALL THERE IS

The Trust Frequency is, quite literally, that place or that state described in the world's sacred literature as Heaven, Shambhala, Nirvana, or Samadhi, and is presided over by the most powerful creative force in the Universe, Love. It has been our free-will-choice to visit this limited Earthly reality and to experience the opportunities and lessons that this life has to offer. The Trust

Frequency, once we become aware of its existence, is available to each and every one of us, and can be accessed by the relatively simple combination of understanding, awareness, intention and conscious choice described in this book.

HEAVEN IS RIGHT HERE, RIGHT NOW

Once we understand the true nature of the Universe, once we have the correct information, we realize that it is entirely up to us, exercising our inalienable right of Free Will, to decide the frequency we wish to vibrate on. In other words, we can consciously choose to move into higher consciousness, to be happy, to be satisfied, to be joyful, to be fulfilled, using these Ten Assumptions and the Seven "A"s as our tools. Putting all seven of the A-words into a single sentence, just for the fun of it, we get the following: with focused Awareness and accurate Assumptions, we can choose positive Attitudes, decide where to place our Attention, and Align with our highest inner promptings, take committed Action, and then Allow the loving Universe to manifest beyond our wildest dreams. Alternatively, we are equally free to choose to be miserable, stressed, frustrated, sick, resentful and angry. It is entirely up to us. Such is freedom.

Nobody can tell us what to think or how to feel, not even in the most authoritarian of situations. If we consciously choose the Trust Frequency, and by diligent practice, by rooting out and replacing any negative core beliefs lurking in the dark corners of our psyches, by opening our hearts and minds, by letting go and truly learning to trust the loving Universe, we find ourselves spending more and more of our time in an elevated state of consciousness. We find ourselves, quite literally, in Heaven-on-Earth. For some this may come as a spontaneous epiphany. A switch gets flipped, and life changes forever.

For most of us, it takes deep introspection and no small amount of courage. It can take time and hard work, at the beginning. It may not be easy. We are talking about deep, permanent psychological transformation here. It is best not to expect instant nirvana, but it is highly likely that even the most skeptical among us will have some encouraging glimpses, some flashes of inspiration, some sudden shivers of delight, upon reading this book.

Contrary to popular belief and dogma in certain circles, it's not about dying first and then going to heaven. There is no "then." Heaven is right here, right now, once we have present moment awareness and consciously choose it to be so. It is about awakening to that fact. After death, who knows? There is only here and now. Most of the religions of the world come close to understanding this, as their originators may well have done. If the religions of the world were to undergo just a simple re-focusing of attention, a return to the basic message of their founders, and that of the masters, saints and prophets of all ages, the divisiveness would disappear and the fun would appear in *fun*damentalism.

THE DEMISE OF ORGANIZED RELIGION

It would require an ever-so-subtle tweak for the religions to align with Universal Truth, to actually do what they believe they are doing. Needless to say, there is much resistance to this, as such a re-alignment would inevitably bring about the demise of the rigid dogma, structure, patriarchy and hierarchy that has overtaken and ruled the major religions for centuries. In the essence of the teachings of every religion lies the demise of the religious hierarchy itself. As divisive as nationalism is, so too is organized religion divisive, in its present form, but that era is over. The "new human" does not need power and control over others. We are all divine, autonomous sovereign beings who can choose to act from our highest conscience, independently but in harmony with those around us.

Thankfully, we live in a remarkable and unprecedented age. Communication technology, indigenous cosmology, quantum science, our own awakening, and the mystical inner traditions of the major spiritual paths are all contributing to a universal understanding of the oneness, sacredness and inter-relatedness of all things, replacing the need for organized religion, which is after all, merely an artificial construct of the human imagination, despite its huge and undeniable, if controversial, contribution to the evolution of civilization.

THE AMERICAN MIND

As we said earlier, the "Age of the Masters" is past. We no longer need an intercessor. We are now able to access all the wisdom of the Universe directly, with no need for a priestly caste to intercede with, or interpret, the Divine on our behalf. This is exactly what the Mayflower Pilgrims set out to do back in the early 1600s.

The Pilgrims separated from the Church of England at risk of their lives and freedom, fled to Holland, and then made history by establishing the Plymouth colony in present-day Massachusetts. They understood that humanity was intended to relate directly with the divine, in alignment with their own higher conscience, an understanding remarkably similar, as they discovered to their surprise, to that of the Native Americans with whom they lived in peace and friendship for the first fifty years after their arrival in Plymouth.

In New England, a synthesis of English and native cultures gave birth to the American Mind. The founding of America signaled a true quantum shift in the evolution of the free mind. In the opening decades of the 21st Century, we find ourselves at another such turning point. Four hundred years after the landing at Cape Cod, we as a species have arrived at another decisive moment of historic change, an inner event some have called the "Shift," heralding a new age of freedom, an age during which humanity heals its split personality and comes into a new phase of maturity as a species. It is a true coming-of-age. The student does not stay in school forever. Eventually, with a little work, we graduate and move onward and upward into adulthood, and this option is now available to each and every human on this planet.

After all, that is our true nature, if we can just remember who and what we really are. The obvious question is: how do we do that? It has to do with our understanding, our conscious choices. It has to do with accessing the Trust Frequency in whatever manner we choose to do so. It has to do with healing the imaginary split in our psyches, with the convergence of the ego with the divine self. As we transform ourselves, we transform society.

THERE'S A PARTY GOING ON

The Trust Frequency can be likened to an extraordinary celebration. We could call it the Eternity Party. You received your invitation at birth, but you do not have to show up. Ever. At least not in this lifetime. Free will is the order of the day. There is no compulsion.

Have you ever been invited to a wonderful festivity, but did not attend for some trivial reason? You just didn't feel like it. You were having a bad hair day. Later in the week, you ran into a friend who was at the party. It was the social gathering of a lifetime, and you missed it! Amazing people you hadn't seen in years, wonderful food, your favorite band, fabulous free gifts, and you weren't there! Why would anyone choose to miss the party of a lifetime if we knew where and when it was happening, and we knew how to get there?

As we have seen, we are born into a world governed by a lower frequency, the insidious realm of fear, doubt and scarcity. Most of our society's current assumptions and social systems are fear-and-scarcity-based. Our entire economic system is based upon competition for ever-more-scarce resources. We are conditioned to believe that this is all there is. Anything else is pie-in-the-sky. On the other hand, in the higher vibratory planes, there is a place where everything exists that we could possibly desire, and more than we can fathom, our soul's destiny, our gift, our purpose, everything the Conscious Loving Universe wants for us. It is like an eternal and heavenly party going on – and on – without us. Until we make the free-will choice to show up. Free will allows us the right not to attend, but only a masochist would consciously choose such a path. Right? You'd have to be nuts.

THE DIRECTIONS TO THE PARTY

The pathway to the party becomes clear through trust in our own intuitive knowing, our own inner promptings. When we listen to that inner voice, and act upon what we hear, when we trust our feelings, trust our new "best friend," circumstance, when we honor ourselves and act accordingly, the world comes into balance around us. If we are operating in the higher frequencies, when we serve ourselves we automatically serve others, and when we serve others we automatically serve ourselves. A win-win situation. We have arrived at the party. Let the celebration commence!

Needless to say, we don't actually have to "travel" to the party, and we can never be late. The party is right here, right now. Always. It's eternal. It is we who are trapped in the illusion of time. It is merely a question of waking up and finding ourselves here and now.

HONOR THYSELF

From the perspective of the lower frequencies, honoring oneself may seem selfish and ego-centered, but until each person serves himself/herself first, following one's inner guidance regardless of expectations, of "commitments" to others, the world will stay out of balance. Reluctantly saying "yes" when meaning "no," being "nice," honoring commitments when one's feelings are screaming at us to do otherwise, simply throws the world around us out of balance. It takes us off the path to the party, and derails everyone around us, even though we think we are doing it to serve them.

> *It doesn't interest me if the story you*
> *are telling me is true. I want to know*
> *if you can disappoint another to be*
> *true to yourself; if you can bear the*
> *accusation of betrayal and not betray*
> *your own soul; if you can be faithless*
> *and therefore trustworthy.*
> Oriah Mountain Dreamer, *The Invitation*

We each have to choose to play our part in the symphony, trusting that the conductor will cue us at exactly the right moment, and knowing that our part might change at any time. We can't know what another's part in that symphony is, nor the nature of that person's soul's journey. When the conductor's baton points at us, all we can do is to play our part with the utmost joy and abandon, responding to instructions from our higher self. If we each do that, the great orchestra of life will play a symphony the likes of which no one has ever heard.

CHOOSE A HIGHER STATE OF BEING

Let's return to the subject of frequencies. Throughout this book, we have asked you to look at this Universe in terms of vibrational frequency, to agree that the Universe, as science would readily confirm, consists of an unlimited spectrum of frequencies, from the lowest to the highest. We have asked you to accept the idea that we can, with practice, use our free will and our conscious attention to attune to the frequency level of our choice, to consciously "plug into" any point on the frequency spectrum. With practice, we can intentionally disconnect from wherever we are right now, choose a higher state of being, tune in at that level, and find ourselves vibrating at a whole other frequency. We find ourselves in an alternative universe with a completely different set of rules and laws. By the laws of free will, your twin sister, your father, your children may choose another reality. That's perfectly OK. Remember, we each get our own universe. The consensus reality will carry on as usual, for the time being. In the meantime, you will find that the reality you resonate to has become real, for you. Life is a whole new ballgame.

To reiterate the most fundamental fact revealed in this book, we humans have the power to consciously control the frequency we experience, by choosing our assumptions, attitudes and actions. We do that anyway, but we tend to do it unconsciously. Our feelings of gratitude, love and trust are our vehicles to the Trust Frequency. Our old belief system told us we had little or no control over the life we lead and the way we respond to it, that we are at the mercy of forces and people greater than ourselves. We have been conditioned to believe that life is a Darwinian contest for survival of the fittest. That belief has turned out to be quite untrue, even in the realm of biology, where we now know that it is cooperation, not competition, that leads to survival. In order to thrive, we must collaborate and cooperate, following the example of the multitudinous micro-organisms that make up our own bodies. The neo-Darwinian view results from a very limited perspective. Once the larger picture is seen, it becomes obvious that even seemingly competitive species, as in the predator-prey relationship, are collaborating in an extremely intelligent manner which ensures optimum health and population for both predator and prey. It is a win-win situation.

In our individual everyday lives, most of us fluctuate up and down emotionally, several times a day, depending on what's going on in our outer lives. Outer events often trigger changes in our vibratory state. We experience mood swings. An unexpected smile from a passer-by might elevate our state of mind enormously, or an undeserved traffic ticket might do the opposite. We often find ourselves vibrating at a lower frequency, having made an unconscious choice to allow ourselves to do so. The challenge then is to stop, look around, re-member who we are, take a deep breath, and choose to re-connect with the loving Universe at a higher level. We are, ultimately, all-knowing, all-loving, all-creative beings. We created this reality in the first place, so what are we doing down here in this low vibratory reality? The answer is this: We are learning. We are growing. We are exploring the astonishing beauty and diversity of our own beings.

ANYONE CAN GET THERE

The conscious ability to choose our individual vibratory rate is a major consequence of our free will. Once we understand the true nature of the Universe and our intimate relationship to it, we can choose to tune ourselves to the highest frequency we can imagine at any particular moment. This is something we can learn. It's a process. It takes practice to become adept at keeping our thoughts aligned with the highest possible frequency. It takes remembering the true nature of the Universe, and remembering who we really are, how loved we are, how precious we are. With every breath. Mostly, what it takes is trust, that little five-letter word that is at the opposite end of the scale from fear and doubt. Eventually, once our basic assumptions have been upgraded, trust become automatic, and we cease to go up and down with every new experience. The roller-coaster ride is over. We have reached what the Sufis call the "station," the plateau, where our ever-fluctuating states stabilize.

As we rise higher and higher on the scale of vibrations, with fear and anger and all the darker emotions way down there at the bottom, we rise from emotion to emotion, all of the feelings inherent in being human passing by, until, way up here, we find the place where trust resides, a place of contentment, confidence, acceptance and love. We have found happiness. We are in a boundless domain of vibratory possibility, where abundance, beauty, peace, joy, kindness, inspiration, creativity and friendship dwell, the Trust Frequency. When we act from that timeless place, we affect everything around us. We elevate the fiber of the entire Universe.

The Trust Frequency is the highest state of awareness,

possibly beyond our ability to conceive at this time, from our current perspective. It is a state of oneness, a state of boundary-less integration with All-That-Is, a state of total connectedness with the quantum field, with the *Akasha*. It is a state of being that is emotionally and spiritually related to the feelings we experience when we are in love. In fact, that's exactly what it is. We are literally "in" Love. There is no other place to be, is there? It is only the fact of our absolute freedom that allows us to imagine otherwise. In other words, we are imbedded in a Universe that consists entirely of Love, with a capital "L," and once we awaken to that state, our vision expands, our heart opens, and we truly know what it means to be en-lightened. Closing our eyes, we are filled with light, a luminosity that has no boundaries. We have dissolved our sense of separateness and become one with all things, a transcendental state that has been described by the sages and luminaries of all ages. We have connected to our true essence.

The cool thing is that this state is available to everyone, not just the ones who have been meditating for years or doing yoga or chanting mantras. It is the natural state of the human being. It is the state of the divine child. Anyone can access this state, at any time, and almost everyone has, at one time or another. Henry David Thoreau had such an experience on Mount Katahdin in Maine. We call these states "peak experiences," no pun intended. We all have such experiences, and we remember them throughout our lives. The question is: can we integrate these states into our everyday existence, and learn to operate from a higher place? The answer is a resounding YES! Once we have upgraded our fundamental assumptions, our core beliefs, once we know that we are in fact divine sovereign beings who are an inextricable part of a loving Universe, everything shifts, and eventually, this becomes a permanent state, if we so choose.

The other remarkable consequence of living in the Trust Frequency is that we become much more functional. Being in an elevated state of trust does not impair us in any way. Quite the opposite, in fact. It vastly enhances our abilities, allowing us to focus and concentrate on the task at hand, with boundless energy, enthusiasm and optimism. Work ceases to feel like a chore. It becomes play. It becomes a dance.

KEYS TO THE FUTURE

The question is: once we have accepted that the Trust Frequency is real, how do we go about getting there? To transport ourselves from A to B in the material world, we usually need some sort of vehicle, a skateboard, an ox-cart, a Prius, a rocket ship. In the world of consciousness, there are also vehicles which will take us from one "place" to another, but these vehicles exist in a different dimension. There are in fact, no such things as time and space. Time and space are mental constructs that have no reality at the highest level of existence. The Trust Frequency is not some heavenly place far, far away, in some distant, unreachable future. It is right here, right now. It always has been. It always will be. In fact, the Trust Frequency is all there is. It is simply Reality, viewed from the highest perspective. Anything else is a man-made, fear-based illusion, completely artificial and delusory. As we have seen, the vast majority of mankind has bought into the illusion, to the point where a book like this is probably seen as madness, pie-in-the-sky dreaming. But, we ask you, who is the psychopath? Who is the deluded one?

Once again, we remind you that the vehicles that deliver us to the Trust Frequency are gratitude, love and trust, the three inter-related child-like states of being that lie at the heart of the entire spiritual undertaking. These simple, universally accessible vibratory states or mind-sets are the keys to the future of each of us as individuals, and, ultimately, the keys to the future of our species, of our planet. All of the complex and often confusing mysticism developed and promulgated throughout history, all the countless words ever written or spoken on the subject, come down to these three things: gratitude, love and trust.

ROVING SENSORY ORGANS OF THE DIVINE

On a personal level, we can think of ourselves as roving sensory or experiential organs of the ever-unfolding and ever-evolving Divine. Everything we think, do, feel, or sense, without exception, gets reported back to Central Headquarters, becomes part of the *Akashic Record*, the totality of the experience of the ever-evolving Conscious Loving Universe in the Eternal Now. It is the most amazing adventure, and the greatest privilege imaginable. We are at the very epicenter of the evolving Universe, watching the cosmic drama unfold from the best seats in the house. Could anything be more profound, more exciting? Could anything be more inspiring? Could anything be more REAL?

A NOTE ON CONSCIOUSNESS

(and a short story)

*Within a single neuron, the combined microtubule activity
equals potentially 1,000 trillion operations per second in
computing power. Consciousness arises through these countless
quantum computations amplifying, or magnifying,
the latent field of conscious awareness embedded in the
fabric of spacetime itself.*
Stuart Hameroff, MD, research scientist

*At one time, conscious awareness was alive in only a
tiny fraction of the existing humans. But the destiny
of the species was forever altered when this form of consciousness
 emerged in increasing numbers until in time it became the
determining characteristic of humanity. So too with us.
A new form of consciousness is beginning to emerge in a
small slice of contemporary homo sapiens. As with the early
self-aware primates, we are astounded by the new awareness,
and when we go to speak of it, we discover that we
have no easy or established or efficient way of transmitting
this mode of consciousness.*
 Brian Swimme, PhD, cosmologist

Consciousness IS the Unified Field.
John Hagelin, PhD, physicist.

HUMAN CONSCIOUSNESS

There are two fundamental and inter-twined types of consciousness that are relevant to this discussion: the super-aware life-force of the living Universe Itself, and the limited self-referential experience of the (individual and collective) human mind. Science, thus far, only recognizes the latter, and has encountered extreme difficulty in accurately defining and describing the phenomenon. What is consciousness, human consciousness? We can describe it as the combination of awareness, assumption, attitude, attention, alignment, action and allowing (the "7A's") that determines our individual and collective frequency, and hence our reality.

At its core, this book is about consciousness, human consciousness, our individual and collective consciousness. It is about the potential for us to expand that consciousness; in other words, intentionally to elevate our frequency, the vibratory level from which we experience our life, and in doing so, to move us to a higher, happier level of being. Let us take a moment to think about this vital but neglected subject.

Most psychological analysts and scientific researchers think of consciousness as a reflexive, purely human phenomenon, "us" realizing that we are "us," "we the people" looking into the mirror and recognizing the fact that we are people. They believe that this faculty of self-awareness came about as a result of the evolution of ever-more complex organisms over time. *I am a complex organism, therefore I think*, as Descartes might have said. Consciousness is equated with the act of thinking, a function of the brain. The more complex the brain, the more clearly we can think, and it is this act of thinking that somehow brings us into being. As highly complex organisms, the theory goes, humans are able to entertain complex thoughts, and accordingly come into existence.

> *At its core, consciousness is self-referential awareness,*
> *the self's sense of its own existence. It is consciousness*
> *that is trying to explain consciousness.*
> **Tom Seigfried,** *science writer*

According to the narrow focus of science, consciousness is seen as human self-awareness, nothing more. What, then, about the consciousness of the trees, of the birds, of the dolphins? Of the higher primates? Of the jellyfish? Of any sentient being? Of Planet Earth? Of the Universe itself? What about the consciousness of a great spiritual master, or that of a shaman under the influence of *ayahuasca*? Is it merely self-awareness, or is it "cosmic consciousness." Is the awareness of a long-time meditator any different from the average Joe's? Could it be that science is examining the subject through the wrong end of the telescope?

The fact is, consciousness is vastly more than physics or psychology have yet dared to imagine. Consciousness lies at the deepest root level of the universe, predating everything in creation.

Consciousness was, before anything came into Being

If there really was such a thing as the Big Bang, it can best be described as the un-manifest becoming manifest, the implicate becoming explicate, the unborn-but-living Universe awakening into self-awareness, with each and every sentient being throughout all of time and space contributing, through what science calls quantum entanglement, to that ever-unfolding awareness.

The genesis of the Universe is non-physical consciousness (energy) exploding into physical existence (matter) and coming to know itself. $E = mc^2$. Energy becoming matter becoming life. Energy becoming life becoming matter. This is not mere abstract speculation or philosophical fantasy. It is biological reality of the highest order. It is how our Universe works.

In the classical realm of physics, at the tip of the iceberg of reality, it is true that matter appears very concrete and lifeless. But if you scratch beneath the surface you find the molecular level, the atomic level, the nuclear level, the grand unified and super-unified levels. At every stage nature wakes up, nature comes alive. The concreteness and objectivity of the universe vanishes and ultimately one is left with pure abstraction, pure self-interacting, self-aware intelligence.
John Hagelin, PhD. physicist

This is big picture thinking indeed, thinking that continues to challenge our species' greatest thinkers. For the purposes of this book, thankfully, all we need to understand is the nature of human consciousness, what forms it takes, and what types it may be grouped into, and how this understanding can help us to elevate our frequency. Broadly speaking, we can identify two fundamental kinds of human consciousness, passive and active. For example, the act of becoming aware of something is a passive act, the mere act of observation, whereas to take an action based on that observation is an active manifestation of consciousness. To think about that observation before acting is yet another manifestation of consciousness. To illustrate, here is a little story from long ago and far away:

IN THE TIME BEFORE TIME
(The Lion, the Leopard, and the Owl)

*I*t is the time before time. Time, whatever that word means, will not be invented for another ten thousand years, but that means nothing to you. You are a person in the time before time. In your world, there is only Now, this timeless present moment. You are a young man of the First People, the Harmless People, the rock artists, the African bushman hunter-gatherer clan who call themselves *Ju/ 'hoansi* or *!Xam*. Both of these words, in the ancient click languages, mean simply, "Real People." There are no other two-legged people. The Tick People are not Real People. Nothing in your world has changed since Mantis created Eland from a discarded scrap of leather. Of course, days have always turned into night and winters into spring. Herds of eland have come and gone. It has rained and the sun has shone. The moon has lived and died. Babies have been born, and elders have returned to the spirit world, but otherwise, everything is exactly as it was at the moment of creation. Animals are people, and people are animals. Everything is alive. The Big God lives in his house in the sky, and the Little God walks on the Earth disguised as a praying mantis, making mischief wherever he goes.

Last night, for the first time, you went to the Big God's house. You climbed up a rope, into the sky. It was terrifying, but also, it was wonderful. You understand so much more the purpose of *N!um Tchai*, the trance dance. Even the wordless songs now make perfect sense. On your way home to the little camp in the red sand dunes, shaking from exhaustion but elated as never before, you saw in the darkness a small herd of antelope not far way, just over the next gentle rise in the rolling landscape. This morning, before sleeping, you decide to go hunting. You will feed the whole family tonight. Silently, you pick up your little bow and the quiver of poisoned arrows, look down at the naked brown sleepers around the dying fire, smile gently, and walk off into the rising sun. Grandmother and grandfather are getting old, you think to yourself. There is a single spreading acacia tree between you and the golden, glowing sunrise.

The antelope herd is exactly where you saw it in last night's trance vision. Their horns glisten in the morning sun. The birds in the acacia sing their raucous song. Far away, a lion grunts. The antelope herd is moving slowly off to the south, so you move swiftly in that direction, keeping the morning breeze in your face. Soon, you are in position. You hide in deep shadow in the space between two large overhanging rocks, under an ancient painting depicting a scene much like the one in front of you. You calm your breathing, and wait. Now! Your tiny arrow flies true. It pierces the rump of a fat little buck. His horns are just beginning to sprout. The buck jumps, startled at the sting. The herd moves off, grazing contentedly, the little buck with them, and you follow from a safe distance.

After an hour, the little buck begins to totter a little. He falls behind the herd, and wanders off on his own. You follow, keeping him in your line of view, but taking care not to startle him. He could easily run for an hour before dropping to his knees, and you would never find him, in spite of the tracking skills taught to you by your grandfather. It is getting hot. The herd moves off to the south, and the little buck stops and looks around, a puzzled look on his face. It won't be long now.

There is a patch of shade next to a tall, weatherworn rock. You lie down for a moment, confident that you will easily find the buck after your nap. You fall asleep and dream a strange dream of pale flying people and giant metal fish. After a timeless time, you are startled awake by the echoing grunt of the lion. It is closer this time. Much closer. You sit up and listen carefully. Is that the cough of a leopard, as well? It is still hot, but the sun is now low in the west. You slept too long. You stand up cautiously and rub your eyes. All right, you tell yourself, it is time to find that tasty little buck and get back to camp. The people are hungry. Lion grunts again, not fifty meters away. There he is, right there through the tall grass on top of the nearest dune. He has not yet seen you, but he probably smells a hint of something tasty in the air. You look at the tall rock which had shaded your sleep. No. In the distance, the top of the acacia is just visible.

You make up your mind. You break cover and sprint towards the acacia. Lion sees you the moment you move, and lumbers into action. He is closing in, fast, but you have no time to look over your shoulder. Will you be able to climb the tree in time? Will your lungs burst before you ever get there? You reach the tree and clamber up like a terrified monkey. You hear Lion's breath right behind you. It's loud. You reach the safety of the fork in the tree and look down at last. Lion is huge. He is standing on his hind legs, reaching up as far as he can with a gigantic forepaw. You could reach down and shake hands with him, but that does not seem like a very good idea. Lion watches you for a long time. His huge yellow eyes are chilling. Then he gets down and walks around the tree. He gives a roar of disgust and walks off into the sunset. You are bathed in sweat, but your skin is icy. You gradually stop shaking and settle into the fork to rest a while. You breathe and you watch. Lion is heading directly for the little buck, who has finally died and lies there waiting for you. All of your effort today will be in vain, you think.

Just before disappearing from sight, Lion stops and lets out another roar. He sounds less sure than before. The sun is going down. Half of it is already gone.

Would you kindly go away, Mr. Lion? I have a family to feed.

Lion does not go off. Instead, he hesitates, changes his mind, turns around, trots back over to the acacia and flops down under the tree. No more than ten feet below you. He looks up at you, hungrily, then puts his huge head in his paws. In minutes, the lion is fast asleep. He snores. After a long while a strange jabbering starts up. It is the hyena family, all twenty of them. They materialize out of the gathering dusk and place themselves in a circle, patiently awaiting the inevitable. Is that Leopard's cough you hear, behind all of the hyena chattering? Lions cannot climb trees, but it is a different story when it comes to leopards.

There is nothing you can do. The camp is too far away for a shout to be heard. The birds above you in the tree are making a headache-inducing racket as they recount the countless stories of their day before settling down for the night. Your mouth feels like the bottom of a dried-out waterhole, full of dust and elephant urine and buffalo dung. Your hands refuse to stop shaking. The predators on the ground below have infinite patience. There is no hurry in the timeless time. Once you fall asleep, you will probably tumble from the tree, and dinner will be served. There is nothing you can do, except to relax and recover your energy. Breathe, you tell yourself. It has been a long day. You could almost fall asleep, right here in the fork of this tree, like you did when you were little. The birds are quietening down at last. There is a lingering luminous glow in the western sky, but pretty soon it will be dark. Very dark. You breathe deeply, and your racing heart settles down. You fall asleep, and dream you are a little boy back in camp, at your mother's breast. It's peaceful.

Suddenly you wake up. Your eyes are wide in the gloom. It is almost completely dark. What was that? Was that the cough of Leopard, right below you? You look down. There she is, looking up at you! *Oh grandfather! Where are you?* Leopard's eyes glow yellow in the semi-darkness. You make eye contact with her. All it will take is a single bound, and Leopard will be right up there with you, in the fork of the acacia, her powerful jaws crushing the life out of your young body. And yet, Leopard does not move. Not yet. She fixes you with her hypnotic gaze. You stare back, petrified. Even though there is no time, time stops. Nothing moves. The silence is deafening. Even though it is almost dark, it does not get any darker. In fact, it seems to get lighter. Your consciousness expands. You begin to remember.

Leopard appears to nod at you. Her spots blur in the gloom and her eyes seem to move up and down, just a tiny bit. Your memory comes back in a flood. Of course! *What* were you thinking? *Why* were you thinking? *Why* were you so afraid? Had you forgotten? Did you let fear take over completely? Had you stopped breathing? After a while, a little smile illuminates your face. You have *remembered*. Leopard smiles back, or at least, that's what it looks like in the dusk. You straighten up, open your beak, blink your huge eyes at Leopard, give out a little *hu - hu*, spread your owl-wings and glide silently out of the acacia. You land in a small explosion of dust right where the little buck lies, waiting for you. He is *your* little buck, and he will be coming home with you tonight. You fold your wings, adjust your crooked loincloth, pick up the buck, sling him over your shoulders, and stride swiftly back to camp in the last of the light. You sing a little song that comes to you, a song of the ancestors, a song of thanks to the stars, who are blazing in the sky above you.

Behind you, the solitary acacia tree is now a black silhouette against the last of the deep-red glow in the western sky. The hyenas are still sitting there. They have not yet realized that their dinner has flown away. Leopard is hanging out in the fork of the tree. Lion looks up at her from the ground. Their eyes meet and something like a smile passes between them. Leopard slips sinuously down to the ground, a shadow flowing against shadows. She looks at Lion.

"He's going to be good!" says Lion, in the ancient click language of Africa. The two big cats resume their human forms. Their old, wrinkled faces are barely discernible to one another, but they do not need to look. They have been together since the beginning.

"He's a good boy." says the bushman grandmother we know as Leopard. *"We'd better get home before he wonders where we are. He might think the lions got us!"*

The grandfather known as Lion nods. They walk off into the west, holding hands. They stop for a moment, change their forms into night-vultures, and flap off noisily. A happy cackle of laughter is the last we hear of them as they disappear into the starry night.

END

Andrew Cameron Bailey 2012.

This little tale can be used to illustrate many aspects of what we term "consciousness." We, the readers, "see," in our imagination, a young bushman and a lion, somewhere in Africa in an earlier time. We "experience" the drama of the story as it unfolds. We "participate" in the events vicariously, using our power of "imagination," another aspect of our consciousness. The boy sees a lion coming towards him through the bush. This is a passive act of observation. He thinks about the situation for a moment or two. He sprints to the nearest tree and clambers up to safety. The lion, having observed the boy as soon as he moves, arrives at the base of the tree a fraction of a second too late. Each of the foregoing sentences describes a different manifestation of consciousness, active or passive. As the lion paces about under the tree, the boy experiences the "emotion" of relief, yet another aspect of his consciousness. The disappointed lion, too, is conscious. He too has emotions. He may express his frustration by roaring in anger and stomping off into the sunset. Alternatively the lion may think about the situation for a moment, change his mind and lie down under the tree for a nap. Perhaps the boy will fall asleep and tumble from the tree.

Dinner is served. Good choice, Mr. Lion!

Half an hour after the lion falls asleep, a pack of hungry hyaenas shows up, and sits patiently, awaiting the inevitable. How do the hyaenas know? Instinct? What on earth is instinct? It's another form of consciousness, needless to say, closely akin to intuition. Memory, our ability to access information and feelings from the past, and imagination, our ability to close our eyes and "see" things from the past, or invent things that do not yet exist, or to "fantasize" about things that will never exist, these are all vital aspects of the consciousness that we experience in our daily lives. And then there are the various states or levels of consciousness. Presumably, an enlightened saint is in a higher state of consciousness than a Charles Manson or a sedated inmate in an asylum. Presumably, the Dalai Lama is in a higher state than one of his novice monks. Presumably, a shamanic healer, like the shape-shifting indigenous elders described in the story above, manifests a higher type of consciousness than the average man-in-the-street, enabling the shaman to take different physical forms at will. It seems there is no limit to the variety and power of human consciousness.

Clearly, this subject could easily fill many fascinating volumes. Such an in-depth analysis is beyond the scope of the present book. Despite all of the above, however, science in its narrow focus does seem to be on the right track as far as the human potential for conscious evolution is concerned. It is specifically the self-referential aspect of our consciousness, our self-awareness, that allows us to examine and assess our state of being. It is the mechanism whereby we are able to look into the mirror, examine our core beliefs, and consciously choose to change them. Our mind is the only thing that has the capacity to change our mind. In this complex world that we humans have created, using our collective consciousness, our minds are the one thing over which the individual still retains complete control, which is a very good thing. It is essential to the further evolution of our species and to the future of life on this planet.

CONCLUSION

*T*o summarize, the essence of the Trust Frequency perspective on human existence is this: we live in a conscious, loving Universe, a Universe which loves us unconditionally. It is the inherent nature of the Universe to give us everything we ask for, in other words, to faithfully reflect in our outer reality the contents of our consciousness, namely our thoughts, beliefs, assumptions, desires and so on. Another way of saying this is that we create the world we experience by the power of our consciousness, by the Seven A's. This ongoing creative act is the inevitable result of the phenomenon quantum science calls the Observer Effect, which is subject to our inalienable free will.

We can choose whether or not to function as the "observer" in any given situation, and we select the degree and quality of that observation, and the nature of what manifests as a result, by the state of our consciousness. The only reality is that experienced in the immediate present moment, and reality is not dualistic, it is unitive. We are One. In the context of this non-dualistic, ever-present reality, humanity is seen to be evolving in an upward spiral. There is no reason to doubt the reality of the Trust Frequency. In fact, the only thing between humanity and Heaven-on-Earth is the very doubt that such a wonderful thing is possible.

STANDING ON THE SHOULDERS OF THE ANCESTORS (an exercise)

Picture this: Here you are, (as are all of us if we only knew it), standing erect with your head way up in the stars, beyond the atmosphere, beyond any earthbound considerations. You are more awake than you have ever been. You are a super-conscious entity somewhere in a vast cosmos of stars and galaxies. There are no boundaries. You are consciousness itself. You are at the very center of that vast cosmos. You inhale, quietly. The only sound is the gentle passing of your breath. The view from here is amazing. You want to do your best to tell the world, to "report back all that you see." It will not be easy. There are no words in any known language to do justice to the vastness, to the splendor, to the beauty. Let it go. Just be here, in this timeless moment.

Lest anyone should think you are "spaced out," that you have your head in the stars, let me tell you where your feet are. They are firmly planted on the shoulders of your ancestors, who form a great pyramid which goes all the way down through time and space to the center of the Earth, to the center of the Universe. Your mind is merged with all that is, melded into the quantum field of all reality. You are in boundary-less real-time contact with everything that is, everything that ever was, everything that will ever be. Your naked feet are channels for the upwelling wisdom of the ages, which comes to you from the elders of all times, since the very beginning, which is Now, just as it was then. A helical river of light is gushing around the axis of your spinal cord in both directions, up from the ground, and down from the Universe. You like it. It feels good. It is peaceful. It is good to be back. Home.

$\mathcal{P}$ART II

$\mathcal{F}$OOD FOR THOUGHT

*F*OOD FOR THOUGHT

*P*art One took us on quite a journey, did it not? Whew! A little like crossing the Great Divide. But, here we are, on the Other Side. We have explored the entire phenomenon of human consciousness. We have taken a deep look into our innermost souls. We have seen what might be holding us back from a life lived at a higher level, and we have learned what to do about the situation. Finally, we have taken off into a higher dimension, and that is the elevated perspective we'd like you to remain in, as we present a series of essays and stories that, collectively, we call "food for thought." These short transformative pieces take us deeper into certain aspects of the Trust Frequency, and suggest how to implement the ideas in our lives, both individually and in society. Enjoy!

A MEDITATION ON PRAYER

While we're up here, in this expanded state, there are a few things that it would be useful to contemplate, from this higher perspective. The first has to do with prayer and meditation. What is prayer? Why do humans pray? What does prayer do? What is the relation of prayer to "focused visualization." We shall ask the same questions about meditation, but first, let us address the uniquely human phenomenon of prayer. No other creature prays, as far as we are aware. The dolphin, like the human, plays, but we do not believe they pray. The dolphins are the most intelligent creatures on Earth, or at least they have the largest brain-to-body ratio.

And yet we never see them gathered on the beach, down on their ventral fins, facing East, chanting through their spouts. Why is that? If they are so intelligent, how come they don't seem to have the ritual of prayer?

Humans, on the other hand, have been praying for a very long time. No one knows exactly when the phenomenon of prayer was first invented, but it was probably around the time of the first priesthood, whenever that was and however that came into being. A long long time ago, possibly in Babylonian or Sumerian times, or even much earlier. However, the timing is not important except in a historical context, because, as you will see, the very phenomenon of prayer launched our species into a mode from which it has yet to emerge. The consequences have been enormous, so huge that it is impossible to see them unless you are standing with your head in the stars.

So, what exactly is prayer? How do people pray? Is prayer different from meditation? First, let's have a look at two well-known prayers, think about the men who are said to have created them, and see if we can get a picture of the effects these prayers might have had upon the countless millions who have diligently repeated them over the centuries, often on pain of death. That is correct. Forced prayer has been the rule, not the exception. Voluntary prayer is a relatively recent innovation.

First, consider this: to pray, one generally has to pray *to* something. Furthermore, one generally prays *for* something. The "something" to which one addresses one's prayers could be a graven image, say a golden calf. It could be a carved statue of the

Virgin Mary. It could be a picture of Lord Krishna. It could be
an enormous gold-plated sculpture of Gautama the Buddha. It
could be the Sun. It could be a giant old oak tree, if you happened
to be an ancient Celt. It could be a huge cube of black rock. It
could be a photograph of an Indian guru. It could be a statue of
a beautiful long-haired young man nailed to a wooden cross. If
you were one of the countless faithful in one of the monotheistic
religions, which include Judaism, Christianity and Islam, you would
most likely pray to Jahweh, God, or Allah, who as far as one can
tell from the literature on the subject, are omnipotent male deities
living in a faraway place called Heaven. Finally, just for the fun of
it, if you happened to be a devil-worshipper, you might pray to
a handsome, red-skinned, horned male individual who lives in a
faraway place called Hell.

As you can see from the sample above, there are many,
many forms that prayer can take, depending on the historical and
geographical circumstances that put you here on Planet Earth.
What do all of these forms of prayer have in common? Clearly,
in each case, a lowly human being is sitting, standing, dancing
or kneeling in a state of sacred focus, sincerely attempting to
communicate with something or someone else, a separate being of
infinitely greater importance and power than the humble devotee.

Let's look at the Lord's Prayer, that lovely recitation of faith
that is said to have come down to us from Jesus himself. We shall
only examine the opening phrase, and then we shall move on to
the central prayer of Islam. *"Our Father, which art in Heaven..."* So
begins the Lord's Prayer. Keeping in mind the fact that the spoken

word carries enormous creative power, what are these words really saying? What are they doing? What are they reinforcing? On one level, the surface, they are acknowledging an unimaginably great power, the Father or Creator, who is somewhere that is not here, in a beautiful place called "Heaven," a place that the humble devotee hopes to get to some day, if only he or she is good enough. And good enough in this context usually means... obedient enough.

On a deeper and extremely effective level, the phrase *"Our Father, which art in Heaven..."* makes it absolutely certain that *"we"* see ourselves as separate from a masculine entity called *"Our Father,"* and that *"we"* are not *"in Heaven."* This certainty is re-affirmed and reinforced every time we repeat the prayer. Who really wrote these words, and with what intention was their repetition enforced? What assumptions underlie the words? What has been the effect on the millions of believers who have repeated them? And, *please* do not feel offended, if you are one of those believers. This is a perspective you may not have considered before, but if you have read this far, you know that our un-examined assumptions, including the assumption that all forms of prayer are a good thing, have landed our species in a lot of trouble,

Let's look at the primary prayer of Islam, and see whether it is any different. It comes from the same roots, from the same part of the world, the Middle East, the home of the three Abrahamic religions. The Prophet Mohammed's prayer opens: *"Bismillah, er rahman er rahmin. Alhumdalillah ay rabbil al amin."* Translated from the Arabic, it goes like this: *"In the name of Allah, the Merciful, the*

Compassionate. All praise be to Allah, the Lord of all the worlds." If we know that the word "Allah" can also be understood as "All, Ah!" and we know that All, Ah! can only mean the conscious loving Universe, we are in good shape. But how many of us know that? How many Muslims see it that way? Perhaps the Islamic prayer is a step in the right direction, but the deity is still seen as a separate, masculine entity, and the concept of a separate heaven populated by gorgeous willing virgins remains strong. The faithful male follower will be rewarded, if and only if he is perfectly obedient. If not, he will be judged and punished, apparently for eternity.

DO YOU SEE THE SITUATION?

How many followers of the Abrahamic religions, for example, know that they live in a conscious, loving Universe? That we are all One? What are the consequences of this lack of knowing? At the risk of getting too esoteric, let's dig a little deeper. In Islam, one has to go to the Sufis to escape these illusions of separation. Sufism is, if you will, the inner heart of Islam, as perhaps the Essene path is to Christianity. The basic Sufi practice is the *zikhr*, which means, simply, remembrance. The repetition of the phrase *"La illaha ill Allah"* is the Sufi's path to the elimination of the "nafs", the false illusory self or ego. The phrase *"La illaha ill Allah"* can be interpreted to mean "There is no god but God." The phrase consists of two parts, a denial and an affirmation. The Sufi therefore denies that there is any reality but Reality. Nothing is real except the Real. The Real is affirmed, while illusion drops away. There is nothing but God, nothing but Love!

If there is nothing but God, if there is nothing but Love, then the question is: who or what are you? How can you possibly be separate, unless you yourself do not really exist? Unless you are merely part of the ephemeral dynamic interplay of creation? Is the *zikhr* a prayer? No, it is most emphatically not. The *zikhr* is a sacred practice, a remembrance, which is something completely different. It is a sacred practice designed to banish the illusion of separateness, to trigger the inherent divinity and freedom of the individual, which might account for the persecution the Sufis have suffered over the centuries at the hands of their fellow Muslims.

The point about the power of prayer, in case it has not been obvious, is this: prayer, as it is commonly practiced, is an extraordinarily powerful mechanism for keeping us trapped in the illusion of separation, and therefore controllable by those who know more than we do. Was this the intention of those who composed the prayers and enforced our use of them? I think that's an interesting question for another forum, but we do not need to go into it here. The purpose of this book is to liberate us from illusion, including the illusion that praying to an imaginary, separate "god" will be of benefit to us. The realized Sufi master can not, in good conscience, perform the five obligatory daily prayers of Islam. The master has banished his illusions. He has annihilated his lower ego. He (or she) is one with the Divine. There is no one present but God, and for God to get down on his own knees and pray to himself... well, you see the absurdity.

MEDITATION

It is in meditation that our thoughts are clarified, by the very process of stopping our ceaselessly chattering thinking monkey minds and merging into the silence where all wisdom awaits. Meditation is emphatically not prayer, although the two activities are often confused. Prayer might be described as a one-way conversation with an imaginary friend, something commonly done by children. Which is lovely, needless to say. Meditation, on the other hand, is a process of silencing the inner conversation that most of us conduct with ourselves (and our imaginary friends) every waking moment of our lives. Meditation is about dissolving the illusions of time and space, and becoming One with the Universe. Meditation is for grown-ups.

Is it necessary to meditate? Yes it is, although the form of one's meditation can vary widely. The universal goal of meditation is to find oneself in a state of oneness, of unity, of connectedness. There are those who are there already, but the rest of us need a strategy for getting there, in this busy world. There are countless avenues to the state of oneness, from the silent (and often painful) sitting *zazen* of Zen, to a Thoreauvian epiphany while hiking in nature, to simply sitting with a cup of coffee on the edge of the ocean and melting into the sound of the waves. Yoga will get you there. Certain psychotropic substances, properly used, will get you there, temporarily. Connected breathing will get you there. The goal is to be fully present with every breath, every heartbeat, fully alive, fully aware. Sitting silently is good training, and is valuable for stress management, but ultimately, if we are to become fully realized humans, we need to become what Victor Vernon Woolf calls our "full potential self," all day, every day. Only then are we fully, truly human, *homo sapiens sapiens*. It is about remembering, as the Sufis know so well. It is about being as aware as we possibly can be of our connectedness to All-That-Is. The ancient Sanskrit phrases *Tat Tvam Asi* and *Om Tat Sat* express it perfectly. I Am That. The Supreme Truth.

WHAT IS MEDITATION?

The state of meditation can occur at any time and place, not merely when one is sitting silent in a sacred spot. Meditation is, ultimately, that state where we are totally and permanently connected, where the veil has lifted and we are one with the Universe. The *practice* of meditation is how we get there. It is, simply, a path to an elevated state of being. To some it comes naturally. There are those among us who seem gifted with a calm, contemplative nature in the midst of the chaos of modern existence. For most of us, though, it takes discipline and sometimes it feels like hard work. Eventually, we all get there, if we persevere. As the Zen master said: *Before enlightenment, chop wood, carry water. After enlightenment, chop wood, carry water.*

THE HEART OF THE MATTER

The heart of the matter is this: we are infinitely greater than we have ever dared to dream. There is no limit to our greatness. We can be wildly, joyously certain of this. The limited reality that we adopted as children came down to us from people who also lived in a limited reality. It was not their fault, any more than it was the fault of the child who believed what it was told. The cultural and philosophical programming and conditioning that we unknowingly accepted and then deployed as the basis for our lives was faulty. The paradigm we inherited from our forebears was based upon erroneous assumptions, upon core beliefs that were very often the polar opposite of what is really true. We can change all that. All we need is the information in this book, and a copious dollop of courage along with a sprinkling of patience.

What is astonishing and delightful about this present time is the fact that, thanks to the confluence of a number of social, spiritual and technological factors, we can now re-invent ourselves, both individually and collectively, in any way we desire. We are free. We are powerful. We are intelligent, creative, unlimited. We know this, those of us who are awake. Our species is spontaneously, consciously, evolving. The *imaginal* cells in our DNA are being activated. There is nothing to stop us except... ourselves. Look around you. The old way is collapsing, brought down by its own lack of foundation. The house of cards is trembling.

EINSTEIN AND HUBBLE

What was the greatest scientific discovery of the 20th Century? Albert Einstein's 1907 Theory of Relativity, you'd most likely say, the revelation that triggered the last great paradigm shift in the physical sciences. And you'd be correct. However, Einstein himself could not believe the mind-boggling implications of his discovery, which contradicted some of his most basic beliefs about the nature of reality. So what did Einstein do? He fudged the equations, adding a term he called the "cosmological constant." Toward the end of his life, Einstein confessed that this act was the greatest mistake of his scientific career. It was the astronomer Edwin Hubble in 1929, two decades after Einstein's paradigm-shattering early work, who awakened the world's greatest genius to the fact that his original intuition had been correct: we live in an expanding universe!

> ... ironically, science itself has now begun to step into the realm of the mystics. The "new sciences" story finds biologists and neuroscientists astounded by the hitherto unstudied capacities of the human brain and heart, indicating our ability to intentionally amplify love and compassion. It finds psychologists exploring the territory of contemplatives and revealing a map of human consciousness far beyond the individual ego-self. It finds physicists discovering that the presumed separation of observed and observer doesn't exist.
>
> Judith Thompson, PhD. *The Social Healing Project*

Now folks, before you glaze over, this is not a science book, although it is science, quantum science to be precise, that is opening up the vision for the new paradigm. This is a simple book, a practical book, an accessible book, about spirit, about the spiritual nature of the Universe, about the human potential. So why is the above discovery important to our thesis? Firstly, let us remind ourselves that science and spirit, physics and metaphysics are not really separate. That is just another illusion perpetuated by our current left-brain mechanistic world-view. In this particular case, science answers the central question of the spiritual quest. How so? What in Heaven's name does an expanding universe have to do with Spirit? Let's approach the question from another angle. There is an old Sufi saying, in answer to the ageless question; *where is God? God is closer to you than your own jugular vein.* That's pretty close, isn't it? The Native Americans have a similar articulation.

> *The first peace, which is the most important, is that which comes within the souls of people when they realize their relationship, their oneness, with the universe and all its powers, and when they realize that at the center of the universe dwells the Great Spirit, and that this center is really everywhere, it is within each of us.*
> Nicholas Black Elk, Oglala Sioux

THE OMNICENTRIC UNIVERSE

Now let's get back to Einstein and Hubble, and see why the fact of an expanding universe has such profound spiritual and cosmological implications. There's an inescapable consequence to Hubble's discovery. Careful measurement of the movements of the galaxies reveals that all of them, without exception, are moving away from us. In fact, as Hubble explained to Einstein, everything is moving away from everything else. If everything in the universe is moving away from everything else, where does that place us? Where does it place you? Aha! You get it! You are at the center. The fourteen billion light-year journey to the center of the universe puts you right here, right now. At the center of the Universe. Reading this book.

The Universe is omnicentric, meaning simply, that the center of the universe is everywhere. This makes no sense in a three-dimensional Newtonian world. We simply can't visualize it. It's sort of like being on the surface of an enormous balloon as it is blown up. As the balloon expands, every point on its surface moves away from every other point and yet every point remains the center of the balloon. There is no way to picture such a reality in the 3D world, but that is simply the way it is in this multi-dimensional Universe. You are at the very center of the Universe. So am I. So is everyone on planet Earth. So is the moon. So is Mars. So is the Andromeda Galaxy. So is the most distant celestial object thus far discovered by the Hubble Space Telescope. This has profound implications for our world-view, challenging as it may be to make the shift in perspective from what we have been taught to believe.

Traditional science, upon which the entire "developed" world bases its reality, paints an undignified picture of the human species as an insignificant cluster of tiny, inconsequential entities on a tiny, inconsequential planet in a tiny, inconsequential solar system somewhere on the outskirts of an obscure galaxy lost among countless billions of similar galaxies in a vast, lifeless, mechanical universe. No wonder so many of us feel powerless and see our lives as meaningless. However, as set forth above, the truth is the polar opposite of the "scientific" view. Neither science nor religion seems to have the faintest clue as to the boundless magnificence of the actual situation.

> *If humans, in order to become fully human, truly do need to ponder the Universe to discover their place in nature, and if this three-hundred-thousand-year tradition is rooted in the requirements of our genetic makeup, then we will find our way to ideas concerning the proper human role in the universe one way or another. And if the institutions of education and religion have, for whatever well-defended reasons, decided to abdicate that role, someone somewhere else is going to step forward and provide it.*
> Brian Swimme, PhD, cosmologist

Where are we? At the center of the Universe, right here, right now. Where is "God," the Creator of all things, whatever you may choose to call It? Same answer. Right here, right now. *Closer than your own jugular vein.* Think about it. If you and I and the Creator of all things occupy precisely the same space and time, what does that imply about who and what I am, about who and what you are? The fact is, incredible and incomprehensible as it might sound at first, each and every one of us is not only *at* the very center of the Universe, we *are* the Universe Itself. There is not now, and there never has been, any *real* separation between us as "individuals" and the "outer" reality we live in, despite compelling sensory evidence to the contrary. Space and time, it turns out, are illusory in the larger picture.

> *It transcends all proving. It is Itself the ground of*
> *being; and I see that It is not one and I another,*
> *but this is the Life of my life. That is one fact then;*
> *that in certain moments I have known that I exist*
> *directly from God, and am, as it were, His organ.*
> *And in my ultimate consciousness, I am He.*
> Ralph Waldo Emerson, Journal Entry (1837)

PAN-INDIGENOUSNESS AND ITS RELEVANCE FOR THE FUTURE: ENVISIONING A NEW WORLD

The principles found in indigenous thought - the way of life of the native peoples of the Americas and the essence of most tribal or "traditional" cultures throughout the world - are principles which resonate to the deepest aspirations of all of humanity, and can thus be thought of as Pan-Indigenous. They form common threads that tie the heart of humanity together in a vision of a world in balance.

The following compares and contrasts concepts found in indigenous cosmology as applied to life in society, with the characteristics of a society based upon the Newtonian/Cartesian/ Darwinian paradigm:

Sharing
vs. Hoarding or saving
Concern for the common good
vs. Individualism at the expense of the common good.
Cooperation
vs. Competition
Concern for the future impacts of present action
vs. Instant gratification
Respect and reverence for all of life
vs. Dominance of concern for profit
Trust in the love of a Higher Power manifested in all action

vs. Fear, doubt

Living in balance with the rhythms of life

vs. Being driven by a man-made concept of time

Understanding the interrelatedness of all things and all actions

vs. Separation

Understanding and trusting Abundance

vs. Fear of scarcity

An understanding of the co-creative power of thought

vs. Random coincidence

Equality between all aspects of life

vs. Human dominance

Incorporation of the metaphysical into physical reality

vs. Bound to the limits of physical reality

Note: This is distilled from personal observation and experience with indigenous peoples and from an important essay by Donald L. Fixico, professor of history at the School of Historical, Philosophical and Religious Studies at Arizona State University. "Call for Native Genius and Indigenous Intellectualism" *Indigenous Nations Studies Journal*, Vol. 1, No. 1, Spring 2000. It is available on the internet.

Let's envision a world in which these principles are put into action in the everyday interactions of humanity. Let's ponder the ways in which various cultures from around the world employ, or could employ, these principles at home, in the workplace and in schools. Following is an economic model which is based on these principles:

A New Economic Theory

The dominant Western cultures currently base actions and decisions on a model of economics which has the bottom line as its principal determining factor. This is the profit-based model of a growth-oriented economy in a world of scarce resources, using supply and demand as the "invisible hand" to regulate and control the outcome, determining "profit," success and survival in the short term. This might be called "Bottom-Line Economics"

Proposed below is a model called "Top-Line Economics." This model takes the highest aspirations of humanity and places them as the dominant features in the interactions between individuals who are in the process of flourishing in a world of abundance. It is based upon the above "givens," values or basic assumptions intrinsic in indigenous thought as well as the concepts presented in this book.

Top-Line Economics

When the principles of trust, integrity, generosity, respect, inspiration, love, cooperation and gratitude are actually the dominant determining factors of human interaction in the workplace, at home and in schools, the resulting abundance will allow all aspects of the world to flourish in a manner heretofore unimaginable.

How might we implement these principles today in our daily actions? What might our governments look like? Our schools?

Our workplace? Can you think of an actual behavioral change you could implement in your life that would reflect these principles? How would the implementation of these principles affect the relationship between cultures, between nations?

The above can be accomplished once we commit to treating each member of the human family with the following understanding:

The Expanded Family
Global/National/Workplace/Schools/Home/Self
A unit of independent, autonomous individuals, all seeking their unique destinies within the context of caring, consideration and respect for others achieved through conversation, listening, patience, kindness, empathy, compassion, playfulness and truthfulness, allowing the Universal Laws of perfect balance, abundance, harmony and win/win to manifest through letting go of fear, separation and doubt, moving into total trust of a universe driven by unconditional love.

A New Energy
All of this is possible because there is a new energy available on Earth which supports the manifestation of the infinite balance, abundance and unconditional love that are at the foundation of Universal Law. Individuals are beginning to experience this in their lives which, step-by step will influence them to make new choices on how they will live day-by-day:

Spontaneously:
Trust will replace fear.
Ease will replace struggle.
Serenity will replace tension.
Generosity will replace hoarding.
Abundance will replace scarcity.
Unity will replace separation.
New Systems will develop.
New Relationships will replace out-moded ways of being.
An understanding of the interconnectedness and
sacredness
of all things will begin to emerge.

It is in this way that true peace and profound freedom will come to prevail on Earth.

Connie Baxter Marlow. 1991.

*H*OW MANY WILL IT TAKE?

*N*ow that you have read this book and absorbed the contents, you very likely find yourself in a new reality. That is wonderful! It will make a huge difference in your future life, and the life of those around you. Now let's consider the larger picture. How many of us will it take, having transformed ourselves, to re-think and transform our world? A billion? A million? A hundred thousand? A thousand? Well, let's have a look at history. How many people contributed the foundational ideas that underlie our current societies? Firstly, let's remind ourselves that we humans put together the "civilized" world as we experience it today. Humans created this multi-faceted reality, with all of its beauty and ugliness. Therefore, logically, humans can change it. Now, let's look at exactly how many people it took, idea-wise, to get us to this point.

> *Rome wasn't built in a day.*
> *It just looks that way.*
> Anonymous

The pyramids were not built as a result of a hundred thousand slaves waking up one morning with a brilliant idea: "Hey, guys, let's go get some hundred-ton rocks on the other side of those mountains, and build ourselves a gigantic, mysterious structure!" The pyramids were built as the result of the vision of one person, a single Pharaoh who decided to leave a monument to himself. The next thing anyone knew, there stood a huge edifice, gleaming in the desert sun. It's still there, thousands of years later.

Clearly then, this world is the result of the ideas of a very small group of men. Yes, that is correct. Men! Every one of them. Who were they? Let's list them. Let's see if we can identify, say, thirteen men, a baker's dozen, of idea-people like the above-mentioned Pharaoh, the great visionaries who provided the ideas upon which our current civilization is constructed. Who were the architects of this reality, this seemingly permanent way of seeing and doing things, just as the Atlanteans and the Mayans must have thought their ephemeral civilizations were permanent?

Let's name some names. Going back through recorded history, let's start the list with, say, Abraham, about four thousand years ago. Then Aristotle, Julius Caesar, Newton, Descartes, Darwin, Einstein, umm...Who else? That's a pretty short list, whichever way you look at it. How about Henry the Eighth? He broke away from the Roman Church. Jefferson? He broke away from England. We're up to eight. Any more? Going, going... How about Hitler? His ideas are still very popular in certain circles. Maybe not! How about Carl Marx? I guess we could stick Moses in there, but he's sort of included in Abraham, as are Jesus and Mahommed. How about Shakespeare? Not really. The Pope? Which one? He also comes along with Abraham, sort of. This should be easy, but it's not, is it? We're looking for the founding fathers of the current paradigm, the ones who un-arguably co-created our view of the world. Ronald Reagan? Chaka Zulu? Chairman Mao? Mick Jagger? Yeah, right! Excuse me? We can't even get to ten? Well, come to think of it, let's add John Lennon to the list. He wrote *Imagine*, after all. Hooray, we're up to ten. Well, nine and a half, anyway. Oh, let's add Buddha. Ten and a half! Going, going, gone!

The point, if it isn't already obvious, is that our current reality is built upon the ideas of an extremely small cadre of men, men who lived at different times historically, but whose ideas, whether or not they were in alignment with ultimate reality, remain incredibly strong to this day. Therefore, it is not impossible that a tiny group of men *and* women, the very ones mentioned by Margaret Mead in her much-quoted statement, can change the world. It's not the men, neither is it the women, who will bring about the change, however. It's the *ideas* they base their activities on. Look at the hundreds of thousands of intelligent, well-meaning men and women who have given their all in search of a better world. Nothing seems to have worked, so far. Not capitalism, not communism, not the United Nations. Not a thousand wars. Not Christianity. Not Buddhism. Not Islam. Why not?

You know the answer, dear reader. They had the wrong ideas, the wrong assumptions, the wrong opinions. All of those good people, without exception, based their efforts on a world-view, a set of ideas, a cosmology, that they had inherited from the short list of idea-people listed above. Not one of those men (except, presumably, Jesus and Buddha) lived in anything resembling the Trust Frequency. Their fundamental assumptions were fatally flawed. It's a dilemma that no one, to this day, has been able to solve. Until now. Unless we are mistaken, there's a job to be done, and we now have the wherewithal to do it. It's up to us!

THE PARADOX OF EXISTENCE

The great and confusing paradox of the human experience is this: we are simultaneously an infinitesimally tiny and insignificant speck lost in the vastness of creation, and we are, at the same time, the whole of Creation itself.

We are the drop and we are the ocean

Our life experience tends, powerfully, to teach and reinforce the former, but as life goes on, we are able more and more to expand our consciousness, to dissolve the illusory bonds of separation, to include not only the whole of humanity, but also the entire planet and all its teeming life-forms, and ultimately the entire Universe, in our being. It is our choice. The fact that the vast majority of our fellow humans at this point in our evolutionary spiral seem to choose the limited existence in no way diminishes the larger reality. We emerge through the birth canal from the Oneness, we become an individual, forgetting everything we once knew, and then we gradually rediscover the reality of this amazing and unified existence. It is the greatest adventure ever undertaken. As Nelson Mandela famously declared in his 1994 inauguration speech, repeating the words of Marianne Williamson:

> *Our deepest fear is not that we are inadequate.*
> *Our deepest fear is that we are powerful beyond*
> *measure. It is our light, not our darkness that*

most frightens us. We ask ourselves, who am I
to be brilliant, gorgeous, talented, fabulous?
Actually, who are you not to be?
You are a child of God. Your playing small does
not serve the world. There is nothing enlightened
about shrinking so that other people won't feel
insecure around you. We are all meant to shine, as
children do. We were born to make manifest the glory
of God that is within us. It's not just in some of us;
it's in everyone. And as we let our own light shine, we
unconsciously give other people permission to do the same.
As we are liberated from our own fear, our presence
automatically liberates others.

Marianne Williamson, spiritual teacher

Our part is to live spontaneously in the now, desire-less,
without judgment and attachment, without concern for our
destiny, without looking for compensation, rewards and
answers, keeping our awareness on Truth.

O'Dell, Lucille & Arnold, Robin: *Endless Song of Infinite Balance*

*P*RESCRIPTION FOR PEACE

The instructions could not be simpler: Read the lyrics to John Lennon's visionary song *Imagine*. Open your mind to the possibility that these are much more than just the words of a popular song. Realize that they describe the true nature of things. Pierce through the illusion of fear, separation and scarcity. Begin to live as though the world described in the song is real. Because it is! Allow yourself to imagine...

Imagine there's no heaven...
Imagine there's no countries...
Imagine all the people living life in peace...
Imagine no possessions...
Imagine all the people sharing all the world...

You may say I'm a dreamer,
but I'm not the only one.
I hope some day you'll join us
And the world will live as one.
John Lennon, visionary

Teach the children that this is the world they are preparing for, the world we will all bring to pass on Earth.

"Let there be peace on earth, and let it begin with me"

PART III

APPENDIX

REMEMBER
If ever you find yourself in doubt or fear
TRUST THE LOVING UNIVERSE!

*I*T'S STORY TIME!

*W*ell, dear friends, you have worked hard, and it's time for a break. You deserve it! Here are some stories, some of them fictional, some of them true, and a poem. In one way or another, each of these short pieces illustrates various aspects of the Trust Frequency, of the Reality we have described in this book. Enjoy!

A POEM

I AM INDIGENOUS

UNDER PAINTED SKIES

IN A PAINTED DESERT

I AM INDIGENOUS...

I LIVE

IN ANY ONE

OF A HUNDRED MILLION ETERNAL UNIVERSES

I APPEAR

AND I PONDER....

I LIVE ON THAT LITTLE PLANET

WAY OVER YONDER...

I AM INDIGENOUS

UNDER PAINTED SKIES

IN A PAINTED DESERT

I AM INDIGENOUS.

Andrew Cameron Bailey,
Sedona 9.30.2006

A LAND WITHIN A LAND

*O*nce, when the world was different, but still very much the same, there was a land within a land - a desert within a wasteland - and there were people who lived in these lands and who walked side-by-side, one not knowing the other. The desert people knew much sustenance from the land. They lived simply, joyfully, in a place where time and money had no meaning. They gave of themselves and received what they needed when they needed it, effortlessly. But in the desert there was no water. The desert people gleaned just enough fluid to stay alive from the moisture that gathered overnight on the leaves of the scrub that dotted the desert.

The people of the wasteland knew no sustenance from the land, for they lived on concrete. To them life was hard work and a struggle. They spent their lives always running to catch up, but through their mechanized systems water came in adequate quantities to sustain them.

The languages these people spoke were foreign to each other's ears. They couldn't understand one another and the wasteland people feared the desert people because they had been taught to hate anything they could not understand, to distrust anything that was different from themselves. So although the desert people and the wastelanders looked alike, they were different – they couldn't understand how or why the other could survive. Life went on this way for many thousands of years.

And then a time came when a curiosity, a deep un-namable desire, began to stir in the wastelanders. A distant memory, a feeling, a need to be one, led some of them to explore the ways and language of the desert people, for indeed once they had all been one people.

On one bright sunny day one of the wastelanders came in contact with a desert person while venturing out on the fringes of the wasteland. He was feeling good that day, open to the possibilities of life and when he saw the desert woman he was fascinated by her free energy. It reminded him of something he once knew and felt. This memory stirred him that day, to the point where he actually approached her, smiled at her, touched her and even went so far as to offer her a drink of water from a flask he was carrying, not remembering that she had never known water the way he knew it. She drank from his cup and they looked in each other's eyes and remembered each other. She drank with a boundless thirst, for her body was drinking in an essential life force that it had grown accustomed to living without.

They came together there on the edge of the wasteland many times when they would hear a call that came to each from a silence within. Each time she drank as though she couldn't get enough, as though she might replenish her parched body at each meeting. He, too, was replenishing himself, basking in the memory of his life as a desert person. Parts of him came alive that he had forgotten ever existed. It was a thrill for him to be more wholly alive, if it was only briefly for these encounters there on the edge. He had grown so accustomed to the ways of the wasteland. He had become somewhat comfortable there, especially before the memory, before the encounters. Now, however, he would think of her out there, and dream sometimes of being there with her and she would join in these dreams and they would be excited and happy. In these dreams they went beyond the wasteland and the desert to a place neither of them knew, a place where life pulsed with a wholeness and oneness no one had ever known.

But between dreams he would forget all about her, forget that he had ever been a desert person. He put all his energy into showing up for the expectations of the wasteland. In the busy, scheduled life of the wasteland there was not time for dreams, seldom time to wander on the edge and many times he didn't hear the call. And sometimes he would hear and he would remember and he would want to go and meet the desert woman and dream and remember. He would go, but often he forgot to bring her the precious water she had discovered when she met him and drunk from his cup. She was always happy to see him, for her body was thirsty and anticipating the joy she felt when she satiated that thirst. Sometimes he not only forgot the water, but he also forgot to smile, to touch her, to look in her eyes. He forgot to remember that there was time for everything, because in the wasteland time was money and there wasn't enough time or money to do all the things the wasteland expected of you, let alone walk and talk and love way out there on the edge.

She would always respond to the call, looking forward to seeing him, because she loved his smile, his eyes and his touch. The thirst he had awakened in her body was ever-present now and the desert could not satisfy it, there was no water there. Sometimes she encountered other wastelanders who offered her a drink, but she would remember his smile, his touch and the way she felt when she drank with him and she would wait for him. But try as he might he could not seem to release the idea that he had no time and he would respond to the call out of a deep desire to be free, but would then remember, or forget to remember, and would go so far as to offer her a drink, but then become distracted and walk away barely saying good bye. And she would watch him disappear into the wasteland and wonder and wait.

Connie Baxter Marlow

Snowmass, Colorado 1996.

$\mathcal{T}$HE BIG BASEBALL GAME

$\mathcal{O}$nce, when the world was young, all the people, the four-legged people, the winged people, the crawling ones, the finned ones and the two-legged people played the game of life together joyfully. Each played a special part in the game and everything was in perfect balance. They played like this for thousands of years until one day many of the two-legged ones discovered they were different from the other creatures and decided not to play with everyone else any more. They decided to start their own game. They discovered that they could think and manipulate things, so they designed a game where they could use their brain power and manipulate the world to their advantage.

They called the new game "baseball," and they walked away from the Coach of the Universal Game and came up with rules that would serve them better than the Universal Laws that governed the game that the rest of Creation was playing.

In this new game, it would be each person for him/herself. Everyone would choose a position. There would be pitchers, catchers, basemen, outfielders, batters and umpires. They decided that instead of everyone benefiting from the game equally, there would be winners and losers. The winners would be the ones who scored the most runs, and for every run they would get a prize, and the losers would usually get a little something, just for playing the game. This, they figured would keep everyone interested in playing this new game.

The two-leggeds played this game for thousands of years. When new two-legged were born they came into the world expecting to play the game with the rest of Creation, but their mothers and fathers would begin at birth to teach them the rules of the baseball game. Survival being of utmost importance to all creatures, the little two-leggeds quickly learned the rules, and took their positions.

This baseball game became very intense. The two-leggeds were really into it. They pitched, caught, batted, ran and collected their prizes when they won and felt sorry for themselves when they lost. They started to lose players. Injuries and disease began to take their toll. These two-leggeds forgot what it was like when they were one with the rest of Creation. They forgot that everything that they ever wanted or needed had just come to them automatically, without worrying or thinking about it, in a joyful way.

So, on they played, and they became dependent upon their special brain power. This game of baseball didn't comply with the Universal Laws that came naturally; so they had all they could do to keep on top of all the rules and plays. When they weren't actually playing ball they were busy re-arranging, caring for and repairing the stuff they had accumulated.

Then, one day, one of the two-leggeds who was out of the game due to an injury happened to notice the rest of Creation through the wire mesh of the baseball field fence. He thought that since he couldn't play baseball, he'd go check out what was going on amongst the four-legged, finned and winged ones.

What he discovered was that everything outside the field was moving in perfect harmony, without the frantic feeling of the baseball game. He sat in peace looking back through the fence wondering what made the two-leggeds think that all that frenzy was so much fun. He noticed that even the winners didn't look like winning the game was so great.

He started to ask himself how the two-leggeds could regain the joy, balance and abundance that the rest of Creation enjoyed. And to his surprise an answer came. A voice spoke to him, not one he could hear with his ears, but still, a voice, and the voice told him:

"You two-leggeds were right. You are very special and very different from the rest of Creation, but not separate from it. You thought you could walk away from the Universal Game and make up your own rules and play this game alone, but as each of you gets hurt or sick and has a moment to reflect and remember, you know somewhere in your hears that playing the game with all of Creation was more satisfying. I am going to remind you of the rules of the Universal Game and perhaps you can apply them to your baseball game and you will regain your connection to the whole:"

"First of all: You will all continue to play the same positions, only your purpose will be different. You will not be playing simply to further your own interests, you will be contributing to the whole with everything you do."

"Secondly: Everyone will always win. There will only be winners, no losers."

"Thirdly: The position of umpire will be eliminated. There

will be no such thing as a foul ball or error. Every action will contribute to the successful outcome of the game. There will be no judgment or blame."

"Fourth: You must rehire the coach. You will not be able to see or talk with Him/Her directly. This Coach will be the only one who can see the full scope of the game and He/She will call all the plays. You must trust Him/Her. and the only way you will hear what you are to do is to listen to your own inner promptings. You must trust yourself, your own knowing and that is how the coach will communicate with you and tell you your next move."

"Fifth: Circumstance will direct you.

"Now go back to your fellow two-leggeds and tell them what you have discovered, see if they are ready to play their game of baseball by the Universal Laws I have shared with you. If they are, they must leave all the old rules behind and everyone, absolutely everyone, who wants to play the Universal Baseball Game must understand and align with the five conditions I have presented to you."

The injured player went back to the field and tried to get the attention of his fellow two-leggeds. But they were too busy. Some glanced his way, but most played on, heedless of the crazy lame one who was trying to be heard over the din.

A few heard, and they were overjoyed. They weren't having any fun anyway. All the promises of what the prizes would bring them were empty. They didn't bring any joy, just stuff, useless stuff.

Little by little, more and more two-leggeds heard what the

injured one was saying and they were relieved. But, they wanted to be sure of one thing, was the umpire position truly eliminated? The one who was judging and blaming everyone, would he really have no place in the new game?

"But what about our brains?" many of them asked. "If we're taking orders from the coach through our inner knowing, what do we have these incredible minds for?"

"For the betterment of all Creation," a voice answered.

THE BEGINNING

Connie Baxter Marlow,
Snowmass, Colorado 1991.

$\mathcal{L}$ARRY'S CHOICE
by Andrew Cameron Bailey

"$\mathcal{T}$he Archivist explained it to me. It was a little like this a long, long time ago. Well, not really, but it's the closest I can get." The *croupier's** voice was silky, almost feminine. "Back then, the people, you included, came to Las Vegas in the hope of hitting the jackpot. In the hope of becoming fabulously rich. They gathered in huge glittering halls like this one, tens of thousands of them. Each of them intent on the shining machine in front of them."

Sir Lawrence Olivier stood gazing into the screen. What am I doing here, he wondered. How did I get here? The screen was not really a screen, in the physical sense. It was more of a holographic, floating apparition. The display was divided into seven sections, laid out along the horizontal axis of a twisted Möbius strip, a figure-eight infinity symbol. It was extremely beautiful, an exquisite work of art. To the left of the grouping was a vague blurry circle or sphere that represented the infra-red. So it seemed to the former Shakespearean actor. Next came seven vertical rectangles or bands, which glowed red, orange, yellow, green, blue, indigo and violet. To the right of the violet band was another vague blur, strangely similar to, but somehow completely different from, the one all the way to the left. That, he thought, must be the ultra-violet domain.

Standing on one leg, Sir Lawrence (he thought of himself

as "Larry") tapped the toe of his right shoe on the shiny glass floor beneath him. The scuffed patent leather had seen better days. Larry touched an icon on the screen above the main display. The icon was in the shape of a tall slender mushroom. A translucent column rose gently from the floor between Larry's legs, expanding into a mushroom-like stool perfectly fitted to his lower anatomy. He settled into the seat, and closed his eyes. This place is absolutely silent, he realized. No it's not. Listening very carefully, beyond the rattle of his busy mind, there was a deep quiet hum, like the sound contented bees make on a summer afternoon. There was a faint smell, as well, a subtle aroma that reminded him of a glade in the forest near his boyhood family home.

"At this stage in the evolutionary spiral it is different," continued the *croupier*. "No longer do you come here in search of mere material wealth. Instead, and of course you know this, or you would not be here, you come in search of the greatest treasure in the universe. Remember, do not exceed sixty seconds."

"One minute. I will not forget." Larry opened his eyes. The *croupier* floated off down the aisle. Beyond the slim, formally-dressed figure, an infinite array of identical screens receded off into the distance. To left and right, it was the same. Above and below, the pattern was repeated, visible through the transparent floor and ceiling. *Ad infinitum*. Before each screen stood, or sat, an individual, most of them sharp and well-defined, others a little blurry at the edges. Many wore Western attire, others African, Middle Eastern or Biblical clothing. There were Tibetan monks and Andean alpaca herders. Ah, that feels good, thought Larry.

The stool emitted gentle warming vibrations that undulated up his spinal cord in exquisite tremors. His seven *chakras* lit up one after the other as the tremors ascended.

Nineteen seconds. I have plenty of time, thought Larry. All the time in the world. He looked off in the opposite direction from the one in which the *croupier* had gone. In that direction, too, the rows of screens went off into infinity, left and right, above and below. The person standing right next to Larry was a brassy woman in a long black evening gown. Platinum blonde. Dark roots. Buxom. He had never met her, but she stirred a recollection from the days of the silent movies. Two screens down from the blonde, Vivienne Leigh was sitting on her translucent stool, holding tight to the two-inch-thick flexiglass counter beneath her screen. The counter had no visible means of support. Tentatively, she touched the screen in front of her. She shimmered. Between the two women, a turbaned Indian swami sat cross-legged on his stool, intent on the information before him. The swami stroked his long grey beard with one hand. The other reached, hesitantly, toward the display in front of him. Up and down. Left and right.

Bringing his eyes back to his own screen, Larry wondered: why does everyone want to be a celebrity? Why, five or six spots down from his station, there was Adolph Hitler! Why would anyone want to come back as Hitler? Who would I choose? Henry the Eighth? Jesus Christ? Francis Bacon? Sri Aurobindo? What if I came back as me? Myself? Larry chuckled. He looked at the screen. He hovered his right forefinger over the glowing emerald rectangle at the mid-point of the display. The tremors from the stool activated his heart *chakra*. Bright green. Then it faded.

Twenty-two seconds. So, let's see, how does this work? Larry was getting the hang of it. He hovered his forefinger over the red rectangle to the left. The action triggered a change in the display. The Möbius strip rotated, or rather, it mutated. The red rectangle grew and moved to the center of the display. The green band went away. Above the central red rectangle, another series of colored bands appeared, orange, yellow, green, blue, indigo and violet. Above the violet rectangle, a vague circular blur was the ultra-violet. That is what it seemed to Larry. Below the red central band, another set of colored rectangles went down. Larry moved his finger to the violet rectangle near the top. He touched the screen. His finger met no resistance. There was nothing there, or at least, he felt nothing. The display changed. An entirely different reality opened up all around him. Angelic. Heavenly. Wonderful music. The hall of the infinite screens was gone. Larry put his hands behind him. He was back in the hall of the infinite screens. Adolph Hitler was still there, and Napoleon had taken a seat next to him. Bob Dylan looked away from a nearby display for a moment and winked over at Larry before returning his attention to the challenge in front of him. Dylan looked very old, at least ninety. His face was craggy, weathered, like an ancient mountain range, like his voice in the later recordings.

"Thirty seconds," called the *croupier*.
"I won't forget," replied Larry. "By the way, do you happen to know how many realities there are, in total? How many universes?"
"Do the math," said the *croupier*, turning to the sun-tanned young

woman in the miniscule white bikini standing to his left. The girl was away from her screen for some reason. Larry closed his eyes and pondered. He had never been particularly good at mental arithmetic. If there are seven fundamental universes, and each of those universes has seven upper and seven lower harmonics, how many is that? And then each of these fourteen individual harmonics each has its own set of seven upper and seven lower realities. How many is that? Times seven for each of the original basic seven. And what about the vague blurry areas at each end of the spectrum? Do they each have seven upper and seven lower harmonics themselves, or is the physics different in the non-visible realms? Why should it be? Are those dimensions blurry as well? If indeed they do exist. What would it take to experience them? Who would dare?

Larry shook his head, and opened his eyes. He looked at the digital readout at the top of his screen. Forty seconds. He glanced to the left. Adolph Hitler was still there. But wait, wasn't he off to the right, the last time he looked? He glanced right. Yes. There, too, stood Hitler. The dictator had not thought to activate his pleasure stool. Did he know what he was missing? There can't be two Adolph Hitlers, thought Larry. Can there?

"Thirty-five seconds," whispered a voice near Larry's ear. For the first time, he realized that the *croupier* was female. The outfit had fooled him. He looked at her face for the first time. Dark, almost black hair. Skin the texture of rich cream. Startling blue eyes. Self-consciously, he turned and looked at his reflection in the glass screen. The display hovered a foot above the flexiglass counter. Behind him, the reflected images of row upon row of identi-cal screens stretched off into infinity, each with its human figure standing or sitting before it. Getting a little grey around the edges, Larry thought. And I'm only forty-five. He shot a smiling glance at the receding *croupier*.

"Thanks," he called.

She turned. "Do you have a question?"

"I'd like to speak to the man upstairs, if that's at all possible."

"There is no man upstairs. In fact, there is no upstairs."

"Are you saying that this is all there is?"

"This is it."

"Well, somebody must be in charge."

"That would be me."

"But you are... I mean..."

"You are correct. I am not really in charge. I am more of a guide. Mandelbrot** and Escher put the system in place, and left me to explain matters to folks like you."

"Mandelbrot? Escher? M. C. Escher? Where are they? I would like to meet them."

"They are long gone."

"Long gone? Where?"

"I have no idea. They got the job done in something like thirty-nine seconds."

"You mean they...? All of this?"

"Yes."

"Did Möbius have anything to do with it? Do you know how I would find Möbius?"

"You would have to ask the Archivist." The *croupier's* voice was kind, but firm.

"The Archivist?"

"Speaking of thirty nine seconds..." The croupier twinkled over her shoulder as she glided three aisles over and six or seven rows to Larry's right. Was that Steve McQueen? Next to Henry the Eighth? I have to concentrate, or I'll never catch up with Mandelbrot.

"Don't you be worrying about Mandelbrot." The voice had a strong Australian inflection. Larry looked to his left. It was the brown-skinned girl in the white bikini. He had never seen the young woman before. Had he? Her eyes were the kind of eyes that he had never been able to resist. They had violet overtones, like Liz Taylor's.

"You could come back to Sydney if you like, Ziggy. We miss you. Fair dinkum we do!"

He seemed to remember that voice from a recent life-time. From the shadow of a dream. There was the echo of an echo in his body.

"Thank you," said Sir Lawrence. "I will think about it."

Did she call him… Ziggy?

"G'day Zig," the woman called as she strolled leisurely off down the aisle, back to her station. No, she did not seem to have a station. All the places were occupied. She must have over-stayed her time, and was trapped in this hall forever. The girl was young and tanned and dressed only in a very skimpy bathing suit. Bathing suit? This hall of mirrors is not exactly Bondi Beach, Larry thought. He determinedly put his attention back on the screen before him. Was he hallucinating, or were there now three Adolph Hitlers within a thirty-foot radius of where he sat?

He took a deep breath. If Mandelbrot and Escher designed this system, he reflected, that explains a lot. Every time I touch one of the colored rectangles, another sixteen (or is it eighteen?) of them open up. And any one of those will do the same. It goes on forever, doesn't it? Forty-five seconds, read the display, which had turned from green to orange and had begun to flash on and off, subtly. Ooh. I have used up three-fourths of my time, and I have not yet begun. Decisions, decisions. The display reverted to its default setting. Larry hovered his forefinger over the central green rectangle, the one corresponding to the *anahata**** *chakra*. The stool quivered deliciously under him. His own heart *chakra* pulsed in emerald resonance with the simulation. He closed his eyes for a moment and smiled. The pine-forest aroma from his youth grew stronger. As with the other rectangles, sixteen (or was it eighteen?) additional rectangles opened up, both above and below the central green one. Each color was represented, in the correct order. ROYGBIV. He remembered the acronym from high school back in England. Above and below were the strange blurry spheres, the top one ultra-violet, the bottom one infra-red. Symmetry. Super-symmetry. Going on and on into infinity. "E = M.C. Escher," he thought with a giggle, recalling something he had once come across in Google Images.

Larry opened his eyes and stared, fascinated. His forefinger moved first up and then down the column. As it moved, each of

the rectangles lit up in turn. Tentatively, he tapped the red rectangle at the very bottom. A whole new reality opened up. Tibetan.
Demonic. The realm of Kali. Utterly terrifying. He put his hands
behind his back, quick as a flash. Instantly, he was back in the mir-
rored hall, sitting on the pulsating mushroom stool.

"Fifty seconds." intoned one of the five Hitlers standing in
an arc in front of him. Why had they left their stations?
"It's your choice." said another of the Hitlers. He could not tell
which. None of the little moustaches had so much as quivered.

Larry ignored the Hitlers. I have less than ten seconds,
he thought. My tuxedo needs dry-cleaning. I have not shaved in,
how long has it been? I need a bath. Where are my good shoes?
What am I thinking? Looking up, Larry noticed that Bob Dylan
was looking his way again. The musician looked to be about thirty
years old. He had a guitar slung over his back. He winked at Larry,
turned to his screen, and punched at it decisively. Bob Dylan
vanished in a gentle flash of bright blue light. The space before
his screen was vacant. The screen went away. Larry realized that he
had been seeing similar flashes all along, in each of the colors of
the rainbow. He had not noticed them before.

"Fifty five seconds." The *croupier* was back, pushing though
the encircling crowd of Adolph Hitlers. "Are you all right?" she
asked. She seemed concerned.
"I'm fine," he replied. "I've just never been very good at making
decisions."
"Do you have any questions? Your time is almost up."
"Yes. Let me think. Why would anyone want to come back as

Adolph Hitler?"

"Excellent question. Let me put it this way. If you don't hit one of those buttons in the next three seconds, you will have plenty of time to find out. All the time in the world." She turned and glided off, sinuously, as though she was sliding along the polished glass floor on silent, oiled roller skates. Her tuxedo was immaculate. Her dark hair formed itself into a perky little duck's tail behind her head.

There must have been fifty Adolph Hitlers pressing in on the former actor as his attention returned to the screen in front of him. "Two seconds," hissed the Hitlers, in unison.

Larry's right forefinger hovered over the center of the screen. Alternative universes opened up each time he moved his finger. His finger shook. Even the most miniscule movement changed everything.

"Fair dinkum, Ziggy!" The Australian woman's voice came echoing. "One second," she called from an infinite distance away. "See you in Sydney. I hope?"

Sir Lawrence Olivier made his decision. He made up his mind. His finger moved. Every one else had gone. Mae West. Clint Eastwood. Winston Churchill. Marilyn Monroe. Isaac Newton. Vivienne Leigh. Mahatma Gandhi. John Lennon. Albert Einstein. William Shakespeare. Madonna. Julius Caesar. Hundreds of others he could not name. Bob Dylan, of course. The hall was full of Hitlers, thousands of them, holding their collective breath.

"You are ours," the Hitlers whispered, internally. "Ours."

The unspoken words echoed sibilantly around the vast auditorium.

One half-second. Larry's finger came down upon the screen, landing decisively on the blurry spherical area directly above the central green rectangle, above the *anahata* and beyond each of the alternative universes that had emanated, however briefly, from it. As the Hitlers moved in, triumphantly, Larry dissolved in a crackling fume of ultra-violet. There was a muted bang, a brief aroma of honeyed ozone, just the merest of hints, and then nothing. His station was empty. The station blinked into non-being.

"One minute," said the Australian. "Down to the wire. Whew!"

"One minute," agreed the *croupier*. "Exactly sixty seconds."

"Perfect!" breathed a million Hitlers. They snapped to attention, formed themselves into disciplined fractal ranks, and goose-stepped off into the curving infinity. They disappeared in the misty echoing distance. The staccato sound of their marching jackboots faded and died.

Silence, except for the quiet humming of summer bees. For a long moment, the infinite hall was empty. Only the Australian and the *croupier* were there. They smiled at one another. And then the crystal palace was full again.

"I'd better get going. Can't have him getting home before his Mum." The Australian kissed the *croupier* on each androgynous cheek. She was already on her way.

"Next time, Archivist!" called the *croupier*, laughing, and the brown-skinned girl was gone.

END

* *croupier*: the person in charge of a gaming table, gathering in and paying out money or tokens.

****The Mandelbrot set*: a mathematical set of points whose boundary is a distinctive and easily recognizable two-dimensional fractal shape. The set is named after the mathematician Benoît Mandelbrot, who studied and popularized it.

*****anahata: (Sanskrit.) The undefeated heart. The heart *chakra*. The fourth primary *chakra* according to the Hindu Yogic and Buddhist Tantric traditions.

TRUE TRUST TALES

*H*ere are four true-life stories that illustrate some of the principles expressed in this book. In each person's tale, it is easy to see the support of the conscious loving Universe as it guided them on their paths into the unknown. Some of the events may look like miracles, but in fact, these stories are demonstrations of everyday reality in the Trust Frequency.

A PASSPORT IN ONE DAY
Suzy Collins, New Harbor, Maine

A few years ago I was publishing an alternative newspaper. Another woman in town also started one, with a more spiritual angle. She told me she'd like to go to India and check out the ashrams there. I said I'd go too. She wrote to one master, Babaji, and got permission to visit his center in northern India and I sent my passport to get a visa stamp on it.

However, the day we were to go, my passport had not come back. I felt dejected, thinking, "Babaji doesn't want me to go." A friend who was staying with us told me, "Maybe he's testing your will." At this thought, I called a travel agent and asked where I could get a passport. He said, "In Washington, D.C., or at Rockefeller Center in New York."

I was familiar with Rockefeller Center as I used to work

there, so my friend and I got on the plane to New York, took a cab to Rockefeller Center and entered the passport center. There was a queue that filled the room. My friend prayed to Sai Baba, a powerful guru, and I to Babaji, and I went up to a counter that by-passed the line. A woman stuck her head out and I told her my problem. "Well," she said, "first you have to have your picture taken downstairs. Go on down."

I called my husband in Cincinnati and told him I would either be back Monday or see him in a month. I went down and had my picture taken, returning to the passport room, saw the same lady, filled out some papers and in a minute she handed me my passport. I still had to have a visa stamp on it from the Indian Embassy at 55th Street, so we ran out into the 5 o'clock Manhattan traffic and tried to flag down a cab. One pulled over with a rider in it and the man yelled out the window, "What are you doing, running around in the street?" I yelled back, "We've got to get to the Indian Embassy to get a visa stamp tonight!" He said, "Hop in, my wife went through the same thing!"

At this point I was high as a kite, but when we got to the Embassy there was a sign on the door, "Closed." I beat on the door and when someone answered I told him my problem and he let us in. I got my visa stamp and we ran out and got a cab to the main taxi stand. The one we were in did not go to the airport. There was another crowd and I yelled, "Does anyone want to share a cab to the airport?" Two women raised their hands and off we went. We boarded our 8 o'clock plane with great relief.

We had a fabulous stay in India, visiting the ashrams of several masters and learning from them, but as I look back, one of the greatest lessons I learned was from this experience before I left. If my friend hadn't encouraged me to try for it, if I had gotten caught in the queue or the midtown traffic, if the visa office hadn't let me in, it would have been a different story. The lesson was: If you want something badly enough, go for it full bore, but be ready to accept that the Universe may have an entirely different (and possibly better) plan for you. Be ready for it!

JOURNEY TO TEOTIHUACAN
Hinton Harrison II, planetary citizen

The Harmonic Convergence on August 16, 1987 was a worldwide activation for Oneness. It was a global coming together of souls with a purpose. People all around the world responded to this spiritual call to honor Nature. It was an awakening to the presence of abundant universal love. It was an expression of gratitude for our Earth Mother. At sunrise on the 16th, everyone was invited to join in this worldwide celebration of unity, wherever you may have been on the planet.

I was driving through Los Angeles a few days before the 16th and in the back of my mind I was aware that the place to be was Teotihuacan, an ancient pre-Columbian city in the Basin of Mexico established around 100 B.C. The name can be translated to "Where the Gods were Made." It contains massive pyramid structures, the largest in the Americas. Jose Arguelles, the visionary

who unraveled the harmonic code of the ancient Maya, suggested
that Teotihuacan would be the perfect place to participate in the
Harmonic Convergence. His research revealed valuable keys to
understanding the next twenty years of human evolution. His
book *The Mayan Factor: The Path Beyond Technology* inspired my quest
and put me on a path to connect with cosmic resonance.

Teotihuacan, located thirty miles northeast of modern-day
Mexico City, was where I focused my intention and set my goal.
The challenge was how to get there. I had no money. (Actually,
I had about $14.) Responding to my intuitive instinct, I called
my friend Howard Schwartz to check in and see what he was up
to. When I called, he said, "come on over to Century City." He
needed some help coordinating an aerobic competition, so my call
was perfectly timed.

Once there, I was at his service until the event was over.
He asked me what I wanted for helping out. I responded "a
plane ticket to Mexico City." He immediately called his secretary
and instructed her to book my flight. It was about 2:30 in the
afternoon and I wanted to catch a flight out of LAX that evening.
Howard hung up the phone, turned to me and said: "It's done."
My next challenge was to get to the Valley to meet his secretary
and pick up my ticket. By 3:00 p.m. I was on the freeway heading
to LAX. The traffic was heavy, but flowing in my favor, moving
quickly to my destination. I arrived at the airport about 3:45 p.m.
with only the clothes on my back, no luggage, and about $14.00 in
my pocket.

I ran up to the ticket counter to discover the plane was

leaving. The agents told me I was too late to catch the plane. I trusted my intuition again that I would make the flight, and asked them to call the gate to hold the flight just long enough for me to board. I made it! As I sat in my assigned seat, I took a deep breath of relief and smiled. With a satisfied sigh, I realized I was actually on my way to Mexico City.

Arriving late in Mexico City I walked to the curb. A taxi driver asked me: "Where you going?" I said, "Teotihuacan." He said "Let me take you to my brother's hotel for the night. You can catch a bus in the morning. I felt a high vibrational loving trust frequency pulsing through my whole body. The room and cab fare combined was less than $5. Now, I have $9 dollars in my pocket.

I couldn't sleep. The noise in Mexico City was intense, so I lay sweating in the heat of the night, excited about my adventure yet to come. Just as I finally fall asleep, the phone rings. It is now the morning of August 15th. The cabby was waiting for me in the lobby to take me to the bus station. He took me all the way to the ticket window, helping me purchase my bus ticket. It cost about a dollar.

I got on the bus to Teotihuacan so tired I started nodding out while I was standing up. A passenger seated about three quarters of the way back on the bus gestured for me to come and sit in his seat. I expressed gratitude, thanking the older man for the offer, but felt he should keep his seat. He insisted, so I sat down and promptly fell asleep.

The same gentlemen awakened me. He indicated this was my stop and it was time to get off the bus. Rising, I thanked him,

"Muchas gracias, Señor!" Looking in the faces of each passenger, I saw a twinkle of light in all of their precious eyes. It felt like they were blessing me, as they watched me exit. I was standing in front of Teotihuacan. I made it!

There was a concession stand where I saw blankets. I realized I might need something to keep warm at night. Proving the abundant universe would provide what I needed, a sweet lady offered me the blanket she was sitting on. I found a piece of rope on a fence that I used to wrap it up and carry it over my shoulder.

As I was walking along, I ran into two ladies who turned out to be nuns. We introduced ourselves. They invited me to lunch. We shared our delight and commitment for being at Teotihuacan. They were on their way to the Tule Tree, a 2000-year-old Montezuma cypress tree with a massive girth of 165 feet. They had rented a hotel room at the local Spa for a week and they offered it to me. I was humbled and gratefully stayed in the room. I would have gladly slept under a tree, but their offer was most appreciated. They also gave me 65 pesos. Again, a generous gift which enabled me to eat for the next few days.

I settled into my comfortable accommodations, then set out for the temple. When I arrived at the top of the pyramid, I met an interesting Mayan shaman doing a sunset ceremony. He was waving a condor feather over an abalone shell burning copal incense. I joined him, watching an incredible cloud formation, as the sun set. Before departing, he invited me to join him for a ceremony at the temple later that night.

I headed back to my room to rest. As I drifted into dreamtime, I had a vision. I saw a bowl filled with burning embers in the center and skulls around the top rim. Sensing it was time to go, I awakened suddenly. There was a snake-like line of torches illuminating the stairs to the Temple. Along the way, I met a young man who did not speak English. I gestured toward the temple. At that moment led me to a hole in the fence. I decided to trust him and followed him through a tunnel that led to the best stairs up to the temple. Guards were roaming the grounds and firing their rifles to scare people who were trying to get in through the gate to climb Teotihuacan that special night. It required courage for me to follow this stranger, the kind of courage that arises when you replace the vibration of fear or doubt with trust.

We made it to the top of Teotihuacan. As I arrived, I noticed a group of people sitting in a circle. In the middle of the circle, there was a bowl filled with burning copal. The bowl had skulls around the top of the rim. It was precisely what I had seen in my vision. I sat down in the circle, as I thanked spirit for guiding me to this moment, this place, this sacred ceremony. The group sat in reverence until dawn. As I turned to face the rising sun, I experienced another vision with my 'intuitive eye.' Quetzalcoatl flew directly into the portal of my soul. Quetzalcoatl is a significant deity of the MesoAmerican people. He is believed to have organized the cosmos and participated in the creation and destruction of previous world epochs. Quetzalcoatl is known as the Serpent Snake, the keeper of knowledge and wisdom.

The Feathered Serpent had initiated me. My kundalini energy was ignited, fully awakened. I felt the return of the Bird

Tribes. The Children of the Stars, the Seeded Ones had gathered. It was the Star Tribe. In Stardust We Be One. This journey was a profound lesson in trust. I was where spirit had guided me to be present, Teotihuacan the Sun Temple for the Harmonic Convergence, 1987.

For those who have been on the path, December 21, 2012 marks a great awakening and alignment with the Trust Frequency. Follow your heart, listen deeply to your intuition. Allow the Great Mystery to assist you. Be open to experience more balance, greater awareness and truth in life. It's a celebration in a harmonious inter-connective vibration with all life and the infinite possibilities of humanity to live in Harmony and Peace on this precious place we call Earth.

WALKING IN TRUST
Jean Owen, Carbondale, Colorado

My life experience has been one of learning to trust with a lack of evidence or prudent reassurance that I am placing my trust wisely. Rather I have had to learn to 'leap' into the unknown, believing that the action I was about to take would be for my betterment. I use the word trust as a verb rather than a noun, because I believe 'faith without works is dead'. Action is a key component to the activity that surrounds trusting someone or something. You may not have reason, or what others believe to be soundness of mind for the actions you have or are about to take but if it feels right, and your intuition and gut supports you in taking the action – do it!

Self-doubt & procrastination are the two biggest obstacles to trusting. Along with the misguided idea that having more information will make a better decision. In the end, trust is a matter of instinct over theory. The energy behind trusting propels you toward movement. Then once movement (action) begins to occur the force (frequency) of movement itself helps to carry you through the unknown. Sometimes this can occur with the blink of an eye. Sometimes the process unfolds over a longer period of time and in stages. I liken it to navigating your way down a cliff which you have never taken before. Each step is taken into an unknown space. Whether taken with trepidation or wholehearted steadiness the result may be the same. The experience however, is very different.

I have referred to this action as a frequency – because there is a certain heightened energy that accompanies the action taken. Trust, truly letting go, surrender of the need to know, or the acceptance that we are not in control, this is employing real trust – grace in the face of the unknown. This is why the experience of trusting can be frightening and exhilarating at the same time. Once the trust frequency is used to overcome some real fear or obstacle we learn that it can be used again to grow and thrive.

I am not an adrenaline junkie, nor do I propose that those not experienced in the dance of trust go out and take unneeded risks. On the contrary, I invite everyone to take small steps in trust every day – do something out of the ordinary for you; call the person you've wanted to make contact with out of the blue. Just try to employ and get a sense of what the trust frequency feels like. Once you've had success with the risk you've taken and trusted yourself through the 'black hole' of the unknown, you'll be surprised at your ability to take on the next challenge with less fear.

Recently, I've had to practice letting go of the idea that working for someone else would give me greater assurance of stability. I've learned the hard way that relying upon others for this security proved to be a false belief. So I am trying in every way possible to create a new way of viewing my security. I've taken on the task of building inner strength, believing more in my ability to re-invent myself, even at the age of 63. I challenge myself daily to learn new skills; new computer applications and new words in books I read. These are ways to expand myself and my thinking about who I am in light of my new found capabilities.

Most of all, I've had to practice trusting myself, especially since I have few in my life that I can depend upon to give me the assurances. I have had to prove to myself that I am trustworthy of greater and greater responsibilities and therefore think of myself as a very experienced, resourceful and capable person who can handle any situation or challenge which comes my way. As a result of this thinking (employing the Trust Frequency) and the actions I've taken to exercise and strengthen this belief in myself, I now have more people asking me to assist them in their lives. This is somewhat astounding to me, and sometimes I can feel overwhelmed at the prospect of actually conducting the work for others that I have set out to do.

All in all, I am profoundly grateful that I have agreed to continue to grow and seek new experiences. My choice to trust my life and myself and others in it has made for a more fulfilling journey. Happy trails to you...

NO MORE VICTIM
Jeannie Russell, Aspen, Colorado

Something about having everything growing up created in me a need for drama. By age fourteen I had become a tennis star. I was popular, cute, well-educated and had everything. What was lacking was a grounded, well-founded sense of self. My parents emphasized winning, being pretty, getting a man, and staying thin at all costs. It was this last value that really grabbed me. I started a fifty-year-long battle with food and body image. I always fell short in my attempts to "control" my life through "getting thin." Ultimately I was a constant failure.

I did get married, had three lovely children, lived in Aspen in a beautiful place, stayed with my husband for thirty six years, travelled, hung out with famous people - ostensibly had a dream life. But ultimately I judged myself every day by how well I had eaten. This kept me living a very narrow life, a life of lots of self-judgment and little true joy.

Luckily, my husband, despite his personally rigid view of faith, exposed me to many new spiritual ideas... and church every Sunday! It forced me to look at my own values around faith. We disagreed on everything - children, God, people, and sex. I now realize I allowed him to control me, just as I had my father, and virtually everyone else in my life. I did not know how to say "no" to anyone. Back then, however, I was passive aggressive in the way I expressed myself. I smoked pot, stayed out late with "my" friends, went dancing, learned about other spiritual perspectives that I knew he would think were "of the devil," and undermined him to other people every chance I got. It was a dishonest life. Underneath, I hated myself.

It was right around age fifty (fifteen years ago) when I was living full time with my husband and our last child was finishing high school that everything blew up. I had convinced myself that the failings of our relationship were his fault. He was the ogre, the villain, the culprit for my unhappiness. I wanted a divorce, but did not have the strength to just come out and ask for it directly. So I started acting out with other men. I needed attention, something I had not had at all from my husband, and I found it - in other places.

Four years later he found out. It was a very scary time. I thought he might lose his mind or kill me. I did not want to be with him, and I did not want to leave him alone.

In the course of the next five years, we both went to regular counseling. We learned that we each had individual problems that needed addressing, that we each blamed the other person for our own inability to be truly honest about who we were. I saw how I had chosen to stay stuck in a negative spiral.

The exciting news for me was that I had choices. I could choose to be positive, I could choose to be free from my self-destructive thinking, I could choose to be different. What freedom! I did not have to continue to be the person I had been.

Since then I have gotten divorced (our whole family is

happier,) I am living alone (something that had seemed way too scary,) I am learning to stand up for myself (which is a constant challenge,) and I am charting my own path (something I had always looked to others to do.) I believe so strongly in tuning in to the higher frequencies of this life, and I have experienced a different journey when I do this. It is exciting and real and joyful.

One of my missions now is to be a model for choosing love instead of fear, for choosing life instead of death, for choosing the higher road over the lower road. The more I do it, the more it is part of me.

I hope in my own quiet way, I can be a beacon to people who are still chained to their own negative thinking - and do not know it. The great news of this generation is that we CAN choose our response to the Universe - and our choice does affect the universe in a very big way every single day. What a sense of significance can come from moment-to-moment living in self-awareness and authenticity. Each of us does indeed have unlimited power to affect this world - if we so choose.

*V*OWS OF LOVE

I will faithfully reflect the light and beauty that is in your heart.
I will also mirror for you all of your wounds and insecurities
and will help you make friends with your shadow,
those parts of yourself that you do not yet love.
I will, as well, thank you and honor you for mirroring for me
the parts of myself that I cannot see.
Each time I try to blame you and judge you,
I will remind myself to look inside and articulate and
bring into the light my shadow side
that you have shown me.
I realize that by entering into a relationship with you
I have agreed to walk with you into deep unconscious levels
on the journey toward wholeness.
If at any time I decide to end this relationship
I recognize that it will be because we have served each other's
growth as best we can.
I look forward to the day
when the fruit of our time together will have ripened
through the many seasons of our relationship.

Connie Baxter Marlow
1992

CONNECTION EXERCISE

When you have absorbed the information in this book, sit quietly, eyes closed, and breathe softly. Connect your in-breath and your out-breath. Feel the air entering and leaving your body. Ponder. Think about how extraordinary this is. Air, one of the rarest substances in the entire Universe. Without air, a finely-balanced mixture of nitrogen, oxygen, carbon dioxide, and a few other trace elements, life as we know it is not possible. Air occurs only in a very thin film that encircles planet Earth, and nowhere else in the known Universe. Each time we breathe, we are intimately connecting with every living, breathing organism on the planet. It is the same air whether you are a diatom in the ocean, an Olympic athlete, a dolphin, a deer, a bacterium, or a tree. It is the very same air that was breathed by the dinosaurs, by Jesus, by your great-great grandmother. It is the very same air that will be breathed by your grandchildren and your great-grandchildren, in the fine new world that you are busy inventing for them. Know this, and be happy.

> *The challenge before us is to create a new civilization based on a cosmology - a story of the origin, nature, and purpose of creation - that reflects the fullness of our current human knowledge; a story to guide us to mature relationships with one another and with a living Earth.*
> David Korten, PhD. Author, *The Great Turning: From Empire to Earth Community*

RECOMMENDED READING

Here is a list of some of the thinkers and their visionary writings which have inspired us over the decades:

Andrews, Lynn V. *Medicine Woman.* HarperSanFrancisco, 1983.
    Jaguar Woman (Medicine Woman Trilogy.) Harper Collins, 1995.

Aurobindo, Sri. *The Life Divine.* Pondicherry. Sri Aurobindo Ashram.
    The Future Evolution of Man. Lotus Press, 2003.
    The Evolution of Consciousness. Essay. 1930 Found in Sri
Aurobindo's Major Works. Volume 10.
    Essays Divine and Human. Pondicherry. Sri Aurobindo Ashram.

Abraham, Ralph. *Chaos, Gaia, Eros: A Chaos Pioneer Uncovers the Three
    Great Streams of History.* New York. HarperSanFrancisco a
    division of HarperCollins. 1994. Republished 2011.

Bhaktivedanta, A.C. Swami. *The Bhagavad-Gita As It Is.*
    With Translation and Purports. Bhaktidevanta Book
    Trust, Los Angeles, 1975.

Beckwith, Michael Bernard. *Spiritual Liberation: Fulfilling your Soul's
    Potential.* Atria Books/Beyond Words, 2009.

Beyondananda, Swami, Bhaerman, Steve. *Driving your own Karma:
    Beyondananda's Tour Guide to Enlightenment.* Destiny Books,
    1989.

Bhaerman, Steve and Lipton, Bruce. *Spontaneous Evolution: Our Positive
    Future and a Way to Get There from Here.* Carlsbad, CA. Hay
    House, 2009.

Black Elk, Nicholas and John C. Neihardt. *Black Elk Speaks.*
    University of Nebraska Press. 1932, 1959, 1972.

Black Elk, Wallace and Lyon, William S. Black Elk. *The Sacred Ways of
    a Lakota.* HarperSanFrancisco, 1990.

Bohm, David. *Wholeness and Implicate Order*. New York. Routledge, 1995.

Browne, Mary, T. *Life after Death*. Ivy Books, 1995.

Campbell, Joseph. *The Hero With A Thousand Faces*. Princeton University Press, 1972.
with Bill Moyers. *The Power of Myth*. Doubleday, 1988.

Capra, Fritjof. *The Tao of Physics*. Boston. Shambhala Publications, 1991.

Carey, Ken. *Return of the Bird Tribes*. New York. HarperSanFrancisco, a division of HarperCollins, 1988.

Childre, Doc. *The HeartMath Solution: How to Unlock the Hidden Intelligence of your Heart*. Piatkus Books, 1999.
with Deborah Rozman, PhD. *Transforming Depression: The HeartMath Solution to Feeling Overwhelmed, Sad, and Stressed*. New Harbinger Publications, Inc., 2007.

Chopra, Deepak. *Quantum Healing: Exploring the Frontiers of Mind Body Medicine*. Bantam Dell Publishing Group, 1990.

de Chardin, Pierre Teilhard. *The Future of Man*. Harper & Row Publishers, Inc., 1964. Originally published 1950.
The Phenomenon of Man. 1955.

Elgin, Duane. *The Living Universe: Where are We? Who are We? Where are We Going?* Berrett-Koehler Publishers, 2009.

Emerson, Ralph Waldo. *The Best of Ralph Waldo Emerson: Essays – Poems – Addresses*. Roslyn, NY. Walter J. Black, Inc., 1941.

Einstein, Albert. *The World as I See It*. Secaucus, NJ: A Citadel Press Book, 1956/1984. Carroll Publishing Group Edition, 1999.

Erdoes, Richard. *Crying for a Dream: The World Through Native American Eyes.* Bear & Co., 1989.

Fenwick, Chris. *The 100th Human.* New Kingstown, PA. Sunbury Press. 2006-2007.

Fixico, Donald. *The American Indian Mind in a Linear World: American Indian Studies and Traditional Knowledge.* Taylor Francis Ltd, 2003. *Call for Native Genius and Indigenous Intellectualism.* Indigenous Nations Studies Journal, Vol. 1, No. 1, Spring ,2000.

Ghose, Sisirkumar. *Mystics as a Force for Change.* Wheaton, IL. Theosophical Publishing House, 1981.

Goldberg, Philip. *American Veda. From Emerson and the Beatles to Yoga and Meditation – How Indian Spirituality Changed the West.* New York. Harmony Books, 2010.

Goswami, Amit. *The Self-Aware Universe.* New York. Penguin Putnam, Inc., 1993.

Grof, Stanislav and Hal Zina Bennett. *The Holotropic Mind: The Three Levels of Human Consciousness and How They Shape our Lives.* HarperCollins, 1993.

Hagelin, John. *Manual for a Perfect Government: How to Harness the Laws of Nature to Bring Maximum Success to Governmental Administration.* Iowa. Maharishi University of Management Press, 1998.

Harrison, Hinton ll. *My Journey for Peace.* Bookstand Publishing, 2007.

Henderson, Hazel, PhD *Building a Win/Win World.* Berrett-Koehler Publishers, 1997. Co-author with Daisaku Ikeda *Planetary Citizenship: Your Values, Beliefs and Actions can Shape a Sustainable*

World. Middleway Press, 2004. *Beyond Globalization: Shaping a Sustainable Global Economy*, Kumarian Press, 1999. *Paradigms in Progress: Life Beyond Economics.* BerrettKoehler Publishers, 1995.

Hoff, Benjamin. *The Tao of Pooh.* Penguin Group USA, 1983.

Houston, Jean. *The Possible Human.* New York. Jeremy P. Tarcher/ Putnam-Penguin Putnam, Inc.,1982. *A Mythic Life: Learning to Live our Greater Story.* Harper Collins.1996. *The Power of Yin: Celebrating Female Consciousness* with Barbara Marx Hubbard, Hazel Henderson. Cosimo Books, 2007. *The Wizard of Us. Atria Books/Beyond Words. 2012.*

Hubbard, Barbara Marx. *Conscious Evolution: Awakening Our Social Potential.* New World Library, 1998.

Hughes-Calero, Heather. *Woman Between the Wind.* Higher Consciousness Books, 1991.

Huxley, Aldous. *Island.* New York: Harper and Row. 1962. *The Doors Of Perception.* thINKing Classics, 1954. *The Perennial Philosophy.* HarperCollins, 1990.

Illion, Theodor. *In Secret Tibet.* 1934. Reprinted. Kempton, IL. Adventures Unlimited Press.

Jung, Carl Gustav. *Man and His Symbols.* New York. Doubleday, 1964.

Keeney, Bradford. *Kalahari Bushmen Healers.* Sedona, AZ. Ringing Rocks Press, 1999.

Khan, Pir Vilayat Inayat. *Toward the One.* Harper & Row, 1974. *Thinking Like the Universe: The Sufi Path of Awakening.* London. Thorsons, 2000.

Korten, David. *The Great Turning: From Empire to Earth Community.* Kumarian Press, Berrett-Koehler Publishers, 2006. *When Corporations Rule The world.* Kumarian Press, Berrett-Koehler Publishers, 1995.

Krippner, Stanley & Jones, Sidian Morning Star. *The Voice of Rolling Thunder*. Rochester, VT. Bear & Co., 2012.

Laszlo, Ervin. *Science and the Akashic Field: An Integral Theory of Everything*. Rochester, VT: Inner Traditions, U.S.A., 2004. *Chaos Point: The World at the Crossroads*. Hampton Roads Publishing, 2006.

Leon-Portilla, Miguel. *Time and Reality in the Thought of the Maya*. Norman, OK. University of Oklahoma Press, 1988.

Lewis, C.S. *The Lion, the Witch, and the Wardrobe. (The Chronicles of Narnia. Book 1)* New York. HarperCollins, 1994.

Littlebird, Larry. *Hunting Sacred. Everything Listens*. Santa Fe, NM. Western Edge Press., 2001. *Hunter's Heart*. Audio Cassette.

Lipton, Bruce. *The Biology of Belief: Unleashing the Power of Consciousness, Magic and Miracles*. Carlsbad, CA. fundamental Hay House, 2008. With Bhaerman, Steve. *Spontaneous Evolution: Our Positive Future and a Way to Get There from Here*. Carlsbad, CA. Hay House 2009.

Luppi, Diana. *E.T. 101*. Santa Fe, NM. Intergalactic Council Publications, 1990.

Mountain Dreamer, Oriah. *The Invitation*. HarperOne, 1999.

Nurbakhsh, Javad. *In the Tavern of Ruin: Seven Essays on Sufism*. KN Publications, 1992.

O'Dell, Lucille & Arnold, Robin. *The Endless Song of Infinite Balance*. Self-published, 1974.

Peat, F. David. *Blackfoot Physics*. York Beach, ME. Weiser Books, 2002.

Rand, Ayn. *Atlas Shrugged*. Signet, 1992.

Radin, Dean. *The Conscious Universe.* New York: HarperEdge a
    division of HarperSanFrancisco and HarperCollins, 1997.
    Entangled Minds. New York. Paraview Pocket Books, 2006.

Ray, Paul H. *The Cultural Creatives: How Fifty Million People are Changing
    the World.* New York. Harmony Books, 2000.

Ray, James. *The Science of Success.* La Jolla, CA. SunArk Press, 1999.

Russell, Peter. *The Global Brain: Speculation on the Evolutionary Leap to
    Planetary Consciousness.* Tarcher, 1983.
    *Waking up in Time: Finding Inner Peace in Times of Accelerating
    Change.* Origin Press, 1998.

Sheldrake, Rupert. *A New Science of Life: The Hypothesis of Morphic
    Resonance.* Vermont. Park Street Press, 1995.

Scheinfeld, Robert. *Busting Loose from the Money Game: Mind-Blowing
    Strategies for Changing the Rules of the Game you Can't Win.* Wiley,
    2006.

Schlitz, Mandala Marilyn, with Vieten, Cassandra and Amorok, Tina.
    *Living Deeply: The Art and Science of Transformation in Everyday
    Life.* Noetic Books/New Harbinger Publications, 2008.

Steiger, Brad. *Indian Medicine Power.* Schiffer Publishing, Ltd., 1995.
    *Medicine Power: The American Indian's Revival of his Spiritual
    Heritage and its Relevance for Modern Man.* Doubleday, 1974.

Storm, Hymeyohsts. *Seven Arrows.* Ballantine Books, 1972.

Swimme, Brian. *The Hidden Heart of the Cosmos: Humanity and the New
    Story.* Orbis Books, 1999.

Talbot, Michael. *The Holographic Universe.* New York.
    HarperCollins, 1991.

Tolle, Eckhart. *The Power of Now.* Novato, CA.
    New World Library, 1999.

Thoreau, Henry David. *The Maine Woods*. New York: Penguin Books, 1988. *Walden and Other Writings,* Bantam Classics, 1983.

Tzu, Lao. *Tao Te Ching*. Penguin Classics.

Yogananda, Paramahansa. *Autobiography of a Yogi*. Self-Realization Fellowship, 1946.

Van der Post, Laurens. *A Far-off Place*. Morrow,1974. *The Heart of the Hunter: Customs and Myths of the African Bushman*. Penguin Books Ltd, 1971.

Waters, Frank. *The Book of the Hopi*. Penguin Books, 1977.

Watts, Allan. *This is It*. New York. Vintage Books, 1960.

Wilber, Ken. *A Brief History of Everything*. Shambhala Publications, 1996.

Wolf, Victor Vernon. *Holodynamics: How to Develop and Manage your Personal Power*. Harbinger House, 1990.

ADDITIONAL RESOURCES

The authors' books, films, websites, YouTube channels, etc.

BOOKS
Greatest Mountain: Katahdin's Wilderness
by Connie Baxter Marlow

FILMS
IN SEARCH OF THE FUTURE: What do the Wise Ones Know?
www.InSearchOfTheFutureMovie.com

THE AMERICAN EVOLUTION: Voices of America DVD Series
www.TheAmericanEvolution.com

WEBSITES
www.TheTrustFrequency.net
www.TheAmericanEvolution.com
www.TheBaxterProject.org

YOUTUBE CHANNELS
www.YouTube.com/TheTrustFrequency
www.YouTube.com/InSearchofTheFuture
www.YouTube.com/TheAmericanEvolution
www.YouTube.com/PeaceHealingAmericas
www.YouTube.com/Flyweagles
www.YouTube.com/TheINNstitute
www.YouTube.com/ForeclosureFree

CONNIE'S WRITINGS
www.Scribd.com/ConnieBaxterMarlow

ABOUT THE AUTHORS

Andrew Cameron Bailey and Connie Baxter Marlow
are original thinkers, filmmakers and social philosophers
whose films, books, workshops and public appearances
spread their optimistic vision of the future of humanity.
They have a home-base in Sedona, Arizona, but spend
most of their lives on the road in their custom TrustMobile.
They love every moment of it.

Join the conversation!
Blog: www.TheTrustFrequency.net
E-mail: TRUST@TheTrustFrequency.net